The United States Contested

Why is America contested by Europeans? This new book seeks to answer this question and contribute to a better understanding of contemporary transatlantic tensions.

Adopting different theoretical perspectives, the contributors to this volume assess the European discontent with America and relate this to the unilateral turn of US foreign policy in the 2000s. American unilateralism is interpreted by all the authors as the expression of a new conservative nationalism which has been growing in the country since the 1970s and became culturally hegemonic after 9/11.

While conservative nationalism is reaffirming the identity of America as a Westphalian state, Europe, through the European Union, is striving for a post-Westphalian global order. Bringing together leading American and European experts, this book explores:

- the rise of American conservative nationalism
- US foreign policy
- transatlantic relations
- anti-Americanism
- the Iraq war
- the future of American political and cultural hegemony.

This book will be vital reading for students of international relations, foreign policy analysis, American and European politics.

Sergio Fabbrini is Professor of Political Science and Director of the Ph.D. Programme in International Studies at the University of Trento, Italy. He is the editor of the "Rivista italiana di scienza politica".

The United States Contested

American unilateralism and
European discontent

Edited by Sergio Fabbrini

Routledge
Taylor & Francis Group

LONDON AND NEW YORK

First published 2006 by Routledge
2 Park Square, Milton Park, Abingdon, Oxon, OX14 4RN

Simultaneously published in the USA and Canada
by Routledge
711 Third Avenue, New York, NY 10017

Routledge is an imprint of the Taylor & Francis Group

© 2006 Sergio Fabbrini for selection and editorial matter; individual
contributors, their contributions.

Typeset by Keyword Group Ltd

British Library Cataloguing in Publication Data

A catalogue record for this book is available from the British Library

Library of Congress Cataloging in Publication Data

The United States contested : American unilateralism and
European discontent / edited by Sergio Fabbrini.– 1st ed.
      p. cm.
   Includes bibliographical references and index.
   ISBN 0-415-39090-7 (hardback : alk. paper) – ISBN 0-415-39091-5 (pbk. : alk. paper)
1. United States–Foreign relations–2001. 2. United States–Foreign relations–Europe.
3. Europe–Foreign relations–United States. 4. Anti-Americanism–Europe.
5. Conservatism–United States. 6. Unilateral acts (International law)
I. Fabbrini, Sergio. II. Title.
   E902.U55 2006
   327.7304–dc22

                                                              2005018535

ISBN13: 9-78-0-415-39090-3 (hbk)
ISBN13: 9-78-0-415-39091-0 (pbk)

Contents

Tables

Figures

Contributors

Emanuela Bozzini is a researcher in Political Sociology at the University of Essex (United Kingdom).

Bruce E. Cain is Robson Professor of Political Science and Director of the Institute of Governmental Studies at the University of California at Berkeley (USA).

Richard Crockatt is Professor of American History and Head of the School of American Studies at the University of East Anglia (United Kingdom).

Mario Del Pero is Assistant Professor of International History and United States Diplomatic History at the Faculty of Political Science 'Roberto Ruffilli' of Forlì, University of Bologna (Italy).

Sergio Fabbrini is Professor of Political Science and Director of the PhD Programme in International Studies at the University of Trento (Italy). He is the editor of the *Rivista italiana di scienza politica*.

Mark F. Gilbert is Associate Professor of Contemporary International History at the University of Trento (Italy).

Pierangelo Isernia is Professor of International Relations and Director of the PhD Programme in Comparative and European Politics at the University of Siena (Italy).

Rob Kroes is Professor and Chair of American Studies at the University of Amsterdam (The Netherlands). He is a past president of the European Association for American Studies.

Carlo Ruzza is Associate Professor of Sociology at the University of Trento (Italy).

Douglas Stuart is the first holder of the J. William and Helen D. Stuart Chair of International Studies at Dickinson College. He is also an Adjunct Professor at the US Army War College.

Roberto Tamborini is Professor of Political Economy and Director of the Department of Economics at the University of Trento (Italy).

Scott M. Thomas teaches in the Department of Economics and International Development at the University of Bath (United Kindom).

Preface

Why is America contested by Europeans? This book is an attempt to answer this question, thus contributing to a better understanding of contemporary transatlantic tensions. Although adopting different theoretical perspectives, the contributors to this volume tend to assess that the European discontent with America has to do with the unilateral turn of its foreign policy in the 2000s. American unilateralism is interpreted by all the authors as the expression of a new conservative nationalism which has been growing in the country since the 1970s and became culturally hegemonic after 9/11. This cultural hegemony found an institutional predominance with the elections of 2002 and 2004. The current conservative nationalism, with its unilateral foreign policy, has presented itself as a radical alternative to American liberal nationalism of the post-World War II era and its multilateral vision of the international system. Moreover, American conservative nationalism appears to be at loggerheads with the post-national evolution of the European states. The latter was largely supported by liberal America in the past and is in the final stages of providing a supra-national constitution for the future. Thus, while conservative nationalism is re-affirming the identity of America as a Westphalian state, Europe, through the European Union, is striving for a post-Westphalian global order. Here resides the rationale for the structural contrast between America and Europe.

Chapter 1 identifies the relationship between the unilateralism of American foreign policy and the new conservative (or neoconservative) nationalism. The rest of the book is divided into three parts. Part I reconstructs the rise and success of American conservative nationalism. Chapter 2 by Mario Del Pero examines the historical and ideological roots of the neoconservative persuasion; Douglas T. Stuart in Chapter 3 locates it in the context of the choice that America had to face between adaptation to, or transformation of, the international system; and Richard Crockatt in Chapter 4 defines the different scenarios of global order within which the new American nationalism has to operate. Part II is devoted to an analysis of the terms of the European reaction to the new American conservative nationalism. Rob Kroes in Chapter 5 discusses the fact that although anti-Americanism is an underlying sentiment in European culture, it took on an emotional basis with the US intervention in Iraq in Spring 2003. Carlo Ruzza and Emanuela Bozzini in Chapter 6 show how this sentiment was particularly felt by the politically active elite involved in the peace movement; and Pierangelo Isernia in Chapter 7 clarifies that the European mistrust towards America has significantly increased in coincidence with the US invasion of Iraq. Part III investigates whether the cultural and political hegemony of conservative America is going to last. Indeed, the chapters hypothesize that it will be an unlikely outcome. Bruce E. Cain in Chapter 8 shows how the neoconservative coalition is barely majoritarian in the country, which is culturally divided more than realigned around conservative politics. Roberto Tamborini shows in Chapter 9 how it is implausible for conservative America to continue to pursue its unilateral policies, given the country is a great debtor, and great debtors cannot be unilateralist for long because they depend on others. Scott Thomas argues in Chapter 10 that conservative America faces an effective cultural resistance in the Islamic world in its effort to spread American values because of the perception of America as a world model which simultaneously attracts and repels. In conclusion, Mark Gilbert in Chapter 11 discusses the relationship between American power and contestation of it in a historical perspective.

The book project emerged from two seminars, organized and sponsored by the School of International Studies of the University of Trento, held in Trento in June 2003 and November 2004. I wish particularly to thank my colleague Mark Gilbert for generously helping me in the organization of the seminars and in the design of the book project. He was a very constructive advisor for the project all along. I wish also to acknowledge the financial support of the School of International Studies of the University of Trento. The School, with its accomplished scholars and enthusiastic PhD students, is an extraordinary laboratory of ideas and discussion. Finally, I wish to thank my research assistant Alessia Donà for her support in the complex work of editing a book written by scholars living in different countries and continents. However, in a time of transatlantic discontent, this prolonged and critical cooperation across the ocean and within the European continent might represent a sign of hope for a better transatlantic future.

S.F.
Trento University
February–May 2005

Introduction

Why is America contested?

1 US unilateralism and American conservative nationalism

Sergio Fabbrini

Introduction

The military invasion of Iraq by the United States (US) in the spring of 2003 triggered a widespread movement of protest in Europe and elsewhere. Active protesters conquered public squares and dominated public debate, especially in Europe where, soon after, the movement against the war assumed an unequivocally anti-American tone. If the vast majority of European public opinion rallied around America immediately after the terrorist attacks of 9/11 2001 on New York's Twin Towers and Washington's Pentagon, in a few short years the cry *'Nous sommes tous Américains'* has been transformed into *'Nous sommes contre les Américains'*. With the US decision to invade Iraq, anti-American sentiment reappeared on the surface of public debate in many, mainly Western European countries (Fabbrini 2004a). This chapter will argue that such a contestation is due primarily to the unilateralist foreign policy that characterized the first presidential term of George W. Bush (2001–2004) and which has subsequently been confirmed by his re-election to a second term. Anti-Americanism is also an underlying sentiment in European culture, particularly among political active elites such as those involved in the peace movement. However, with the international crisis of the US unilateral invasion of Iraq, this time the European mistrust towards America has significantly increased in magnitude.

My argument is that the unilateralist turn-around in American foreign policy is due to the internal growth, followed by the electoral success, of an ideological and political coalition characterized as *neoconservative*. This coalition is the outcome of distinct cultural traditions which have successfully merged into an overriding vision – a vision based on the assertion of a new American nationalism. Thus, with the term 'neoconservative', I intend a family of different currents and streams of *conservative nationalism*, not only the self-identified group of ('Scoop' Jackson) Democrats which moved on the Republican side *because of their militant view of the global role of America*. This nationalism has deep roots in the democratic history of the country and has emerged whenever the country has had to face either domestic or external transformations, or both. This time the transformations were induced by the crisis of welfare liberalism that began in the 1960s and the end of the Cold War in the 1990s, and were dramatically deepened by the 9/11 2001 terrorist attack. Each time America has had to face radical transformations, a part of it has run back to its cultural roots, to its founding identity. To confront periods of turmoil, America (or a part of it) has tended to deploy its *conservative nationalism*, conservative because it based its political project of the future on the cultural values of the past. However, given the exceptionalism of American cultural identity (for its faith in liberty and democracy), this backward-looking perspective has been perceived as a celebration of universal rather than particularistic values. In America it is possible to be nationalist and universalist at the same time, because America is perceived by its citizens as the *universal nation*. It is against this conservative nationalism, which conflates the national interest of America with the interests of the world, that the European anti-American mood analysed here has developed.

The unilateral turn of American foreign policy since 2000 can be seen as the outcome of a complex process of cultural and political redefinition of the American national identity (McCartney 2004). Certainly, the unilateral turn has been imposed by the contingent factor of the terrorist attacks of 9/11, but it is also certain that it was initiated much before that (especially in 1994, with the Republican conquest of the Congress' majority). As Mauro Del Dero explains in Chapter 2, the unilateralism of the late 1990s is the outcome of a long-drawn critique of the influential currents of America foreign policy in the post-World War II era (such as realism, inter-independence and the liberal left's idealism), whose common trait was the idea (unacceptable to neoconservative critics) of the moral equivalence between America and the rest of the world. It is this idea of an American exceptionalism that neoconservatives have resurrected and counterposed to the trauma of the civil rights movements and the defeat of the Vietnam War. This conservative nationalism is a reaction to the *liberal nationalism* which, in the post-World War II era, oriented the country domestically towards multiculturalism and internationally towards multilateralism, in keeping with the pluralist tradition and the Madisonian logic of American democracy (Dahl 1956; 1976). A *liberal* nationalism because it was based on the political (or better constitutional) identity of the country (Walzer 1996; Shklar 1991), rather than on its cultural or religious or ethnic background.

This chapter will be organized in the following way. First, I will define the terms of European anti-Americanism. Second, I will attempt to describe American foreign policy from the end of the Cold War to the 2000s, in order to show how the unilateralist strategy fully asserted itself only with George W. Bush's victory in the November 2000 elections. In fact, for a good part of the 1990s, with the Democrats in charge of the presidency with Bill Clinton and a Republican Congress from the mid-term elections of 1994, America was torn by a battle between a neoconservative and a neo-liberal view, rather than unified around a unilateral perspective. This is why in the 1990s, although there was criticism of US foreign policy, that criticism did not develop into anti-Americanism as it did in the following decade. Third, I will try to uncover the domestic social and ideological changes that led to the victory of conservative nationalism in the elections of 2000 and 2002, and more fully in 2004. With those elections, at least at the institutional level, the battle between the two Americas has been institutionally settled in favour of the conservative one. Finally, I will ponder whether such internal changes and their external consequences are destined to push liberal American nationalism into an irreversible decline. This point is especially important for Europe because the integrated Europe of today (the European Union or EU) is one of the fruits of liberal America. Indeed, the influence that the latter exercised on international institutions and on the democratic processes within European countries following World War II created the conditions for the integrationist experiment.

The cultural and political hegemony of conservative America will continue to generate contestation by Europeans for two reasons. First, because if it is true that unilateralism is the result of deep changes within American society, then it is possible to claim that the conservative nationalism which supports it is not destined to disappear easily from the international scene. Second, and simultaneously, because if it is true that the process of European integration has reached a point of no-return, whether or not the constitutional treaty on the future of Europe will be finally approved by the EU member states, it is also possible to claim that the European project of supra-nationalism is not destined to disappear from the international scene easily either. Thus, America and Europe are likely to continue to be allies and partners in many aspects of the international system, but they are also destined to clash because one partner looks at the world from a nationalist point of view (charged, moreover, with missionary components) while the second views it from a post-nationalist perspective (which expresses itself primarily in juridical terms). The question which remains to be answered is: how will this tension evolve?

Anti-Americanism in a European perspective

Throughout history, all great powers have tended to be criticized by those who have resented their power. In the case of the US, this sentiment is particularly troubling since it targets a country which was largely admired for its capacity to confront and finally to defeat its post-war rival superpower, the Soviet Union. Additionally, anti-American sentiment has emerged against a country recently wounded by the most horrific terrorist attack of the modern era (Crockatt 2003). Furthermore, this anti-American mood became manifest at the turn of the century, in a context of the apparently undisputed success of liberal democracy and of the market economy, whose structural features and ideological values were traditionally represented by the US. A strong anti-American mood had been traditionally widespread in less developed countries of the world, such as those of Latin America, where American power was frequently exercised to control domestic political processes and to impose external economic interests. Widespread anti-Americanism is much more striking when it is seen to be emerging in the developed countries of Western Europe where American power was crucial in re-establishing democracy in several countries after the war, namely Italy and Germany. Moreover, the prolonged American military presence on the European continent has been a condition for its pacification and integration.

However, in politics as in economics, even substantial amounts of capital run the risk of dissipating, which is precisely what has happened to the US under the presidency of George W. Bush. The determination with which he pursued a unilateralist strategy in Iraq in his first term produced a widespread reaction in Europe, not to mention in Latin America and the Muslim world, because such a strategy applied in Iraq appeared unjustified. To the eyes of Europeans (Garton Ash 2004), in fact, a good part of the justifications given for the preventive military intervention proved unreliable: weapons of mass destruction were never found in Iraq; links between Saddam Hussein and Osama Bin Laden were never proven; American troops were not welcomed as liberators by the Iraqi people. As if that were not enough, the American concern with taking immediate control of the oil wells while neglecting to make arrangements for the complex problems of the country's civil reorganization further served to highlight European criticism of the unilateralist strategy. If one then considers how the military intervention soon turned into an occupation devoid of juridical rules, to the point of legitimating (through an official directive from the Department of Defence supported by the positive opinion of the Department of Justice) the torture of Iraqi prisoners at Abu Ghraib (carried out as well by English troops in another camp), then it is understandable why the re-election of George W. Bush as President in November 2004 has produced a widespread feeling of consternation throughout Europe and in a good part of the rest of the world, as Robert Kroes argues in Chapter 5.

According to a BBC News opinion poll on 19–20 January 2005, a wide majority of the European citizens interviewed believed that Bush's re-election constituted a negative factor 'for peace and security in the world'. More precisely, his re-election is viewed negatively by 77 per cent of Germans, 75 per cent of French, 64 per cent of English and 54 per cent of Italians (but only 27 per cent of Poles). When non-European countries are considered, an equally dramatic majority – 79 per cent of Argentines, 78 per cent of Brazilians, 68 per cent of Indonesians – view Bush's re-election negatively. Among the 21 countries considered (representative of the various geographic areas of the world), an average of 58 per cent of those interviewed believe that Bush's re-election is destined to make the world more dangerous. Nevertheless, in his inauguration speech of 26 January 2005 to launch his second presidential term, George W. Bush did not mitigate his unilateralist strategy. In fact, he rendered more explicit the reasoning that supports it: the US must intervene wherever there is tyranny in the world, not only where there are already ascertainable links between specific tyrannical regimes and terrorist cells such as those that organized the September 11 attacks. He said, in fact, that 'it is the policy of the United States to seek and support the growth of democratic movements and institutions in every nation and culture, *with the ultimate goal of ending tyranny in our world*' (italics added). In other words, the reasons originally advanced to justify the intervention in Iraq (and later revealed as unreliable) have now been definitively abandoned. The battle against terrorism has been replaced by a battle against tyranny. Of course, it is plausible to claim that only the diffusion of democracy can create the conditions for peace and global stability. However, *how* or by which means democracy has to be promoted is an open question. Moreover, *where* democracy must be diffused is also an open question. Indeed, George W. Bush's conception of tyranny led him to consider (justly) the Iranian regime as tyrannical, but not that of Pakistan, Saudi Arabia or Egypt – countries whose tyrannies are dismissed because they are allies of the US. Notwithstanding all this, George W. Bush suffered no doubts in reconfirming the missionary role of his country. As he said in his second inaugural address, 'America, in this young century, proclaims liberty throughout all the world and to all inhabitants thereof'.

With this state of affairs, it is clear why BBC News announced with concern that 'negative feelings about Bush are high and are being extended to the American people who re-elected him'. Obviously, anti-Americanism was not born with the war in Iraq; rather, it constitutes a deep current within European politics, however regionally differentiated (more emphasized in France than in Great Britain, more on the continent than on the islands). In other words, the contestation of America has a history in Europe (Fabbrini 2002), at least as long as European criticism of modernity (economic, political, cultural). In some sense, anti-Americanism is one of the founding discourses of European modernity in so far as the latter has tried to define its modernity as distinct from (if not opposed to) American modernity (Rubin and Rubin 2004). However, equally long-lasting, is the slippery and ambiguous use of anti-Americanism to de-legitimize *all* criticisms of the latter, both those *of principle* (related to its nature) and those *of fact* (related to its policies). The same thing has happened within America with the charge of un-Americanism levelled at critiques of what America *is* and what America *does*. The boundary between these critiques, of course, does not always appear clear in the arguments advanced by critics (Ross and Ross 2004). In fact, the terms in which they are expressed are often confused, for they originate from contradictory considerations, as has become clear during the war in Iraq. However, there is sufficient evidence, as Pierangelo Isernia shows in Chapter 7, to argue that, in the case of the Iraq war, the contestation of America concerned primarily what it did (in terms of foreign policy choices), rather than what it is.

Yet, it remains to be explained why the Europeans in particular reacted so strongly to US unilateralism. As the chapters of this book suggest, this is due to the fact that US unilateralism was perceived as the expression of a new American nationalism. New, however, relative to the post-World War II period, not to the long democratic history of the country. Thus, although it is true that anti-Americanism represents an underlying current in European politics, European criticism of America has nevertheless been fed by an unconstrained manifestation of American power as such. For the first time in the post-World War II period, Europeans have had to come to terms with an American nationalism which is not ashamed to assert American sovereignty over other national, international and supra-national institutions. As suggested above, it is a nationalism peculiar to itself and different from other nationalisms, in that it postulates a connection between the interest of America and that of the world. The defence of America coincides with the promotion of freedom in the world. It is a conservative nationalism because it bases the primacy of America on the cultural, religious and ethnic traits of its experience (Lieven 2004). This is a novel development since, from the end of the Second World War, the US has actively worked to build a system of international institutions which, through multilateral management, have effectively regulated its own nationalist ambitions or impulses (Ikenberry 2001), intermingling them with other national expectations.

Never before in history has a victorious power undertaken so strongly, as the US has, to constitutionalize its own hegemony (in the Western sphere), setting in motion relations of reciprocal recognition between the interest of the leading hegemon (namely, the US) and those of the hegemonized (countries of Western Europe, but also Japan). This has given life to an American hegemony defined by commentators as benign or reluctant. Still, this hegemony has never been translated into a nationalistic predominance, as happened between the Soviet Union and its satellites in Eastern Europe. Western Europeans, who had to pay appalling costs (in terms of human life and material destruction) for expansionistic and militaristic nationalism, ended up seeing in the US an example of aggregating separated units into a common project (*et pluribus unum*). After all, America was by definition a multinational melting-pot fed by a continuous flow of millions of immigrants coming from all parts of the world; was the country of constitutional patriotism rather than of identity or ethnic nationalism (King 2004); was a political nation which accommodated and tolerated different cultures and different interests (Walzer 1997). It is not so astonishing, then, that the dramatic shift in American foreign policy (seen first in Congress in the 1990s and then in the presidency beginning in 2000) generated such a widespread and deep reaction among Europeans.

American hyper-power in the 1990s

With the fall of the Berlin Wall in 1989 and the collapse of the Soviet Union in 1991, the United States remained the only superpower on the face of the Earth, which is why it has also been called a hyper-power. At the beginning of the 1990s, America seemed unwilling to take full advantage of this unprecedented situation, possibly because the country didn't have sufficient resources to support its new global role. This was due to the huge budget deficit that the Clinton administrations (1993–2000) inherited from the previous Republican administrations of Ronald Reagan (1981–1988) and George H.W. Bush (1989–1992). In fact, George H.W. Bush (the Republican 'foreign policy President', the proponent of a 'new world order', the victor of the Gulf war of 1991), was defeated in the presidential elections of 1992 by Bill Clinton, the Democratic candidate, precisely because he forgot that 'it's the economy, stupid' which decides electoral outcomes. Consequently, the first two years of the Clinton mandate were mainly devoted to domestic political issues, such as the reform of the public health system (which failed notwithstanding that Congress had a Democratic majority in both chambers between 1993–1994). Of course, significant decisions were also taken in foreign policy, such as the promotion of North American Federal Trade Agreement (or NAFTA) or the Partnership for Peace with Russia; but presidential attention was mainly focused on domestic issues. This concentration on domestic politics only increased after the mid-term election of 1994, which saw the spectacular success of a new Republican majority (led by the neoconservative Newt Gingrich, who became the Speaker of the House), both in the House of Representatives and in the Senate. Moreover, with the new Republican majority in Congress, the divided government of the previous decades was again re-established, although this time with a Democrat in the White House and a Republican Congress.

The return to the White House of the Democrats under Bill Clinton for the first time since Carter's defeat in 1980, with the Republican control of Congress (a longstanding bastion of New Deal and liberal politicians) was of great importance to the fate of US foreign policy. In fact, both congressional parties in the 1980s and 1990s (but especially the Republican caucuses of the House and Senate) attained a significant internal ideological cohesion, thus moving towards more centralized patterns of leadership and coordination. The era of cross-party coalitions (with the Southern Democrats frequently allied with the Republicans, and Northern Republicans frequently allied with the non-Southern Democrats) seemed to have ended. In particular, neoconservative congressional Republicans transformed the divided government into a formidable tool to weaken, or even to call into question, the legitimacy of the Clinton presidency. A tremendous assault on the presidency was initiated from Republican quarters, with the aim of impeachment. This assault deepened after Clinton's re-election in 1996. From 1994 to 1998, the new Republican majority in Congress acted as if it was the only legitimate governmental majority of the country. Eric Schickler (2002: 99) observes that the Speaker of the House of Representatives, Newt Gingrich, portrayed 'himself as a Prime Minister with more influence over policy than President Clinton'. The assault on Clinton appeared so constitutionally improper that it backfired in the mid-term elections of 1998, where the Republicans showed a very poor performance. For the first time since 1934 in a mid-term election, the President's party gained seats in the House. This unexpected outcome brought the resignation of Newt Gingrich from his congressional seat, officially for the mismanagement of financial contributions in the electoral campaign. Nevertheless, even with the less extremist Speaker Denny Hastert, the impeachment strategy of the Congressional Republican party continued until a formal vote of the Senate in 1999 failed to produce the necessary 2/3 majority to remove the President from office.

This dramatic conflict between the two governmental branches further weakened the only institution of the American governmental system capable of giving coherence and continuity to foreign policy, the presidency. Reagan and George H.W. Bush tried hard (between 1981 and 1992) to re-establish the power of the presidential institution after its dramatic fall following the Vietnam defeat and the Watergate scandal; Clinton's subsequent entanglements led to a serious undoing of the work previously done. David Calleo notes that:

> over the past three decades, the Congress, the courts and the states have frequently combined to cut the presidency down to size. Nothing illustrates this trend more than Clinton's ordeal. Despite the President's continuing popularity with the electorate and his impressive achievements in the economic field, his presidency has been subjected to the most savage constitutional attack since Nixon's time.
>
> (Calleo 2000: 72)

The Congress became more and more assertive on a growing number of foreign policy issues, but that meant also that foreign policy decisions were largely conditioned by private lobbies and interests, corporate groups, political action committees, and district or state constituencies. In the 1990s, according to Calleo (*ibid*: 73), the Congress 'pursued an incoherent aggregate of private agendas. In trade legislation, congressional unilateralism regularly defied not only presidential authority, but also the country's treaty obligations'. In a series of polemical positions, the Congress refused to ratify the Comprehensive Test Ban Treaty (CTBT); it opposed the extension of the Nuclear Non-Proliferation Treaty; it boycotted the Chemical Weapons Convention; it criticized the Convention on the Rights of the Child; and asked the President to renegotiate the ABM Treaty to favour crucial domestic economic and military groups. Moreover, the disdain for international institutions led Congress to hold back American dues to the United Nations (UN) and to impose unilateral conditions over the International Monetary Fund, the World Bank and the World Trade Organization or WTO.

President Clinton tried to answer this mounting congressional activism through an internationalist strategy, which became more and more pronounced after his re-election in 1996, a strategy inspired by the twin principles of democratic enlargement and economic engagement. James McCormick (2000: 61) has argued, in his appraisal of Clinton's foreign policy, that the strategy was basically the following: 'enlarge the number of democracies, since democracies don't fight one another, and expand the number of market economies and global prosperity, since prospering nations do not have time to fight one another. According to this design, global peace and security would be pursued indirectly.' Certainly, this strategy aimed to foster American hegemony in the global system. However, because this strategy of enlargement and engagement was pursued through multilateral institutions (such as NATO, WTO and the UN), it came to clash with the unilateralist impulses of the Republican Congress. Nevertheless, Clinton was able to advance through Congress important components of his foreign policy agenda. On the trade side, Clinton achieved the approval of NAFTA and the Fast Track, which brought significant policy gains. On the side of expanding democracy, Clinton successfully secured congressional support for the settlement of the Bosnian conflict through the Dayton Agreement (21 November 1995) and for the NATO military intervention in Kosovo in the spring of 1999, which prevented the ethnic cleansing of Muslims in that region.

More than acting as a unipolar power, America in the 1990s behaved as a schizophrenic hyper-power because of the ongoing battle between a neoconservative Congress and a. neo-liberal President. This schizophrenia reflected both the depth of the ideological division between the two parties and the difficulty in managing such a division within a political system based on a separation of powers. In fact, as Nye explains

> American foreign policy making is a messy process for reasons deeply rooted in our political culture and institutions. The Constitution is based on the eighteenth-century liberal view that power is best controlled by fragmentation and countervailing checks and balances. In foreign policy, the Constitution has always invited the President and Congress to struggle for control. That struggle is complicated when the Congress and presidency are controlled by different political parties.
>
> (Nye 2002: 112)

In the 1990s, this complex domestic institutional structure combined with the new global role of the US (due to the disappearance of the Soviet Union) made it nearly impossible to define something close to a national interest. To a certain extent, through the ascendancy of the Congress, important issues of foreign policy were *privatized* given the enormous role played by specific pressure or ideological groups within the legislature. For instance, as Robert Jervis (1999: 217) has remarked, 'American policy towards Cuba has been "captured" by the émigrés in Florida in a way that is very familiar to students of American regulatory politics'. Inevitably, this schizophrenic approach was resented by other countries who perceived that, in the post-Cold War climate of the 1990s, the United States enjoyed excessive global power and, correspondingly, an extremely incoherent domestic basis from which to exercise it.

The unilateralist majority post-September 11

Facing the dissipation of presidential leadership and the disappearance of the Soviet menace, the Republican winner of the presidential election in 2000, George W. Bush, chose to end the previous foreign policy schizophrenia, not only substituting the internationalist strategy of his predecessor with a selective engagement approach, but also expressing his support for the unilateralist perspective previously pursued by the Republican Congress. This foreign policy shift was facilitated because the Congress remained largely in Republican hands after the 2000 election, given that Republicans retained the majority in the House and lost the Senate majority by only one seat. Thus, before September 11, 2001, American foreign policy appeared less schizophrenic because it was more *unapologetically unilateral*. However, the events of September 11 pressed George W. Bush to abandon his selective engagement doctrine (erroneously regarded as an isolationist attitude by many) to embrace a more activist global perspective. To be sure, in order to create the conditions for the intervention in Afghanistan, the Bush administration engaged in a wide diplomatic campaign of coalition-building, successfully pulling together friends and prior foes in support of the American military operation. Moreover, to secure the necessary international legitimacy for the intervention, the Congress was finally persuaded to pay the outstanding American dues to the UN. A spirit favourable to more international cooperation seemed to emerge from the public statements of the President and his team, even encouraging some commentators to speak of an end to American unilateralism.

Such optimism, however, was premature. As Stanley Hoffmann (2001: 6) has remarked concerning the perceived end of American unilateralism, those commentators 'have announced its demise too soon'. Notwithstanding its diplomatic overtures, America has become even more unilateral since September 11. In June 2002, the *Economist* (Emmott 2002: 20) remarked that America, under George W. Bush, 'has shunned a new international criminal court, the treaty for which has been ratified by (now 76) other countries [...] has pulled out of efforts to agree on a verification protocol for the Biological Weapons Convention. It also rejected the 1997 Kyoto Protocol on climate change [...] Perhaps most alarming, however, has been its recent disregard for the Geneva conventions on prisoners of war in determining the legal status of people it has captured in Afghanistan and taken to Guantanamo Bay for questioning.' The *Economist* (*ibid*: 24) further called this approach a *parallel* unilateralism, a 'willingness to go along with international accords, but only so far as they suit America, which is prepared to conduct policy outside their constraints'. Thus, September 11 represented a definite turning point in US foreign policy, but the seeds of this change were already in the Republican Congress of the post-1994 period and in the presidency emerging from the election of 2000. Facing a formidable terrorist challenge, the Republican President and the new Republican majority in Congress (thus finally controlling both chambers after the mid-term elections of November 2002), decided to break with the multilateral tradition of US post-war foreign policy and to steer the country towards a unilateral affirmation of American national interests.

The US military invasion of Iraq in Spring 2003 was the foremost expression of this unilateral approach; it was pursued notwithstanding its unequivocal opposition by a majority of the members of the UN Security Council (and particularly by two strategic European allies, France and Germany, both members of the UN Security Council in 2003, although only the first has a permanent seat). The US was unable to make a case for the war, failing to convince the UN Security Council of the existence of weapons of mass destruction in Iraq and of a connection between the terrorists of September 11 and Saddam Hussein's regime. Notwithstanding the opposition to the war by the majority of UN Security Council members, the US decided to proceed anyway in invading Iraq with only the support of Great Britain and a few other countries. The invasion testifies to the seriousness of the new, grand strategy that President Bush made public on September 20, 2002, a new strategy based on four main principles (Ikenberry 2002).

First, America has the moral duty to keep its military superiority over all great powers in the world (including, implicitly, the European countries). The international system is militarily unipolar and so it must remain. Second, America has to free itself from the multilateral constraints of the previous era. Its power needs to be free to pursue and guarantee its national interests, and the interests of its allies and partners, according to its own determination. Third, in facing the new borderless challenge of international terrorism, America claims the right to intervene anywhere in the world to anticipate a plausible threat to its own security. As Bush (*ibid*: 15) argues 'to forestall or prevent ... hostile acts by our adversaries, the United States will, if necessary, act preemptively [...] The United States cannot remain idle while dangers gather.' According to this new world order, Washington, DC gets to decide whether or not a country is an international threat, thus giving its own national sovereignty more weight than that of all other countries in the world. Furthermore, America alone will decide who are its legitimate partners or allies. As Defense Secretary Rumsfeld specified: 'The mission must determine the coalition; the coalition must not determine the mission. If it does, the mission will be dumbed down to the lowest common denominator, and we can't afford that' (reported by Ikenberry 2003: 54). Fourth, America should not work for the promotion of the stability of the international status quo because that stability does not prevent apocalyptic violence. That is, America will have to be more militant and less respectful of existing global alliances and balances, as neoconservative thinkers were suggesting long before September 11 (Kaplan 2001). A unilateral militancy devoted to diffusing freedom in the world, or better, to exporting democracy, because democracies do not fight each other is evidence that a neo-Wilsonian rhetoric has been put at the service of a Jacksonian strategy (Mead 2002). However, while Woodrow Wilson tried to make the world safe for democracy through multilateral institutions like the League of Nations (Smith 1994), George W. Bush is trying to export democracy in the world through the unilateral exercise of American power.

Furthermore, the President and the Congress agreed to radically reform the internal structure of the national security apparatus, claiming that 'our best defense is a good offense, we are also strengthening America's homeland security to protect against and deter attack' (Bush 2002: 6). Through a Federal Act signed in November 2002, the Bush administration instituted a new Department of Homeland Security, something unprecedented in American history. Justified by the terrorist attacks of September 11, the Bush administration triggered a formidable process of centralizing decision-making within the White House, which has no equivalent even in the Cold War administrations. Moreover, this centralization has been accompanied by an unprecedented restriction of the rights of individuals suspected (by public officials) of 'complicity with the enemy'. The approval by Congress of the Patriot Act in 2002, and immediately signed by the President, epitomizes the transformation of state and society relations induced by the war on terrorism. Of course, the President (and the Republican Congress) presented this historic change in US foreign policy as a need to defend the American nation.

In sum, although the new doctrine was inspired by different groups, such as the assertive nationalists and the democratic imperialists (Daalder and Lindsay 2003), it delivers a clear message: following September 11, the US must affirm the primacy of its national interest vis-à-vis all other national interests or international jurisdictions (Halper and Clarke 2004). The confusion of the previous decade over the meaning of national interest has been cleared up. It is the national interest of America to guarantee its security, but because its security depends on the diffusion of democracy, the defensive approach is married to an expansionist one. The new national sovereignty theory (Dumbrell 2002; Spiro 2000) was and is also used to re-order the domestic policy-making process, in accordance with the priorities of the war on terrorism. Important areas of foreign policy are still privatized, but this reality seems to be functional with the new strategy. For instance, with the invasion of Iraq, the Bush administration has assigned to powerful, private corporations and business groups important contracts for rebuilding crucial economic sectors (such as the oil sector) of that country. In conclusion, the new American approach to foreign policy is certainly an expression of the formidable threat posed by international terrorism, a threat which is, most likely, not fully perceived in Europe. It is also certainly the outcome of the role played within the first George W. Bush administration by a neoconservative foreign policy elite. But it seems plausible to assert that the new approach is also the expression of the culture of a new *nationalistic* coalition, institutionally represented by the Republican party, and finalized to reaffirm the moral exceptionalism of the country. America is different – and this is why it has been attacked. America is the land of liberty – and this is why it is different. It is now time to deal with the domestic roots of this coalition.

The domestic ascent of American neoconservatism

A number of vast internal and international transformations of the twentieth century led to the affirmation of New Deal liberalism in the US. In particular, the economic crisis of 1929 and the projection of the country onto the international stage following the Second World War did not allow for a weak or minimal state, nor was it possible to face the problems of mass unemployment as well as racial and social discrimination without public policies of social and economic intervention. Thus, reinterpreting liberalism in the context of an advanced society, beginning in the 1930s, the Democratic party succeeded in transforming itself into the new government party. Even if to a more limited extent than Western Europe, America in the post-World War II period transformed itself into a welfare state in order to favour the integration, as never before in the past, of ethnic and racial minorities and marginal social groups. Between the end of the Second World War and the 1970s, liberal America defined itself as a country open to external multilateral coalitions (obviously in the Western sphere) and to internal multiracial and multicultural integration (following the long winter of civil rights' denial to Afro-Americans). In sum, those years represented the confirmation of the American liberal thesis.

And yet, the very triumph of democratic liberalism contained the seeds for the rebirth of its conservative antithesis. The growth of public intervention had increased the fiscal burden of the white middle classes. The policies of racial integration had emphasized the sense of frustration of the white majority, particularly in the Southern states. The policies of civil rights had thrown into question the centrality and legitimacy of the country's traditional Anglo-Saxon and Protestant identity. And, obviously, the US military defeat in Vietnam had mortally wounded the nationalistic sentiment. In this way, already by the 1960s and then more fully in the 1970s, a strong conservative movement aiming to react to the self-criticism of the liberal thesis (that is to the tendency of liberalism to criticize America for its unfulfilling promises) was already taking shape. After the failure of the presidential campaign of the outsider Barry Goldwater in 1964, this conservative movement grew increasingly closer to the Republican party, with the aim of transforming it into the American nationalistic party. This plan began to bear fruit with the victory of Ronald Reagan in the presidential elections of 1980, following which the Republican party became an umbrella party for all the conservative elements of the country, including those (particularly in the Southern states) that for a long time (since the end of the Civil War) had acted within the Democratic party. Consequently, there took place the progressive marginalization of the more moderate (if not liberal) elements within the Republican party. By the 1980s, the two parties became more antagonistic towards one another because they were more culturally homogeneous within their respective constituencies. Ever since, these two parties have represented the ideological fracture of the country between conservatives and liberals, a fracture without precedent in its clarity and intensity in the long history of the federal Republic.

The conservatism which emerged as a reaction to New Deal democracy is the result of an extraordinary operation led by political entrepreneurs and by intellectuals gifted with an undoubted ideological ability and organizational capacity (Micklethwait and Wooldridge 2004). So much was this so that it was defined as a new conservatism (or neoconservatism) because of its ability in combining its traditional properties, and especially in adapting them to the new context (Nash 1998). Neoconservatism came to be defined as a move-ment that was simultaneously nationalist and anti-statist, as well as populist and communitarian while simultaneously individualist and capitalist. It could also be defined as an anti-political movement, in the sense of being irre-ducibly against the use of the federal state to promote social integration, something the Democratic party had practised since the 1930s. In other words, neoconservatism succeeded in transforming big government into the root of all social problems, thus addressing and expressing that populist feel-ing which, in the past (one thinks of the period at the turn of the twentieth century), had been directed towards big business (Kazin 1995). In other words, if for liberalism the state was the solution, for neoconservatives it had become the problem.

Such neoconservatism has always had, and continues to have, its social and electoral roots in the Southern states as well as those of the Midwest and in ethnic-religious communities which were constituted through two phases of emigration. The emigration of Afro-Americans who left the South to head North as an effect of civil rights' legislation in the mid-1960s, although a consistent migration to factory jobs in the North already started during and after the Second World War (consider that they constituted 41 per cent of the population in Southern states in 1860, and only 19 per cent in 2002), and the white middle class emigration which moved in the opposite direction, south-ward, as technological advances made the Southern states climatically and economically desirable, to such an extent that by 2002, Southern whites rep-resented a full fifth of the country's whole population. In the words of Nelson Polsby (2004), the revolution of air-conditioning enabled the South to become more homogeneously white, well-off, elderly and religious, thus giv-ing life to an ethnic-religious America much more similar, for the intensity and diffusion of its religious convictions, to developing societies than to those developed ones in Western Europe (even if the former are economically com-parable to the latter and not to the societies of developing countries). In a February 2005 Pew Global Attitudes survey, the percentage of those who completely agreed with the statement 'Religion is a Personal Matter and Should be Kept Separate from Government' was 55 per cent for America but 73 for France, 70 for Great Britain, 68 for Germany and 67 for Italy. One has to consider such countries as Russia, Lebanon, Uzbekistan or Bangladesh to find the same percentage as in America. As Lieven (2004) has shown, the meeting between *this* America and the forces of cultural, social and economic change has produced a kind of hurricane, a wind so powerful that it has swept away a good part of the New Deal policy of the Democratic party.

If the Clinton presidency had succeeded in slowing down the ascent of the neoconservatism, it was, nevertheless, unable to stop its course. As witnessed in the 2004 elections, America has become a conservative country to such an extent as never before in the post-World War II period. George W. Bush obtained 59,459,765 votes (against 55,949,407 for his opponent John Kerry), to which correspond 286 electoral college votes (against 252 for his democratic opponent). The Republican party increased its majority in the House of Representatives (from 229 to 231 seats) and in the Senate (from 51 to 55 seats). Furthermore, Republicans maintained their majority among state governors (28 Republican, 21 Democrat, 1 Independent), as well as dominating the legislative branches of the states. These successes were obtained, of course, by a narrow margin, since more than 48 per cent of Americans voted for the Democrat John F. Kerry and, in more than a few electoral districts and colleges, the Republican candidates' success was by a very narrow margin. Bruce Cain is right when he writes in Chapter 8 that the country is politically divided, rather than firmly re-aligned around the Republican party. However, indisputably, the election results confirmed that the political epicentre of the country moved to the right, the geographic epicentre to the South, and the social one to the religious middle classes.

In fact, Bush won in the Southern and Midwestern states where the majority of the country's population resides, leaving his opponent the coastal states of the Atlantic and Pacific. In particular, he won in the big Southern states (including the old confederate states and Oklahoma, Missouri, Kentucky and West Virginia), in which reside (according to the 2000 Census) more than one-third of the national population. Above all, he was elected by a net majority of white voters (57 per cent); elderly voters (53 per cent); well-off and rich voters, that is, those with an annual income of $50,000–$75,000 dollars or more (55 per cent); strongly religious voters (58 per cent of Protestants and 51 per cent of Catholics); voters who go to church more than once per week (63 per cent); and those who go at least once per week (58 per cent). These last figures are telling, especially when one considers, as the *Economist* (2004: 30) reported, that '80 per cent of Americans (say) they believe in God and 60 per cent (agree) that "religion plays an important part in my life"': not to mention that almost 40 per cent of Americans identify themselves as born-again Christians (Lieven 2004: ch. 4).

American conservative nationalism

Thus, behind the ascent of neoconservatism lie complex domestic social and cultural factors, which generate in turn two large political currents. In the first place, the tide of white nationalism, fed by the insecurities of those broad middle classes which identify themselves with the very roots of white, Anglo-Saxon and Protestant America. (These gradually adjusted to the presence of white Catholics coming from central and southern Europe, if for no other reason than to oppose greater resistance to non-whites or to those whites that did not want to recognize themselves in the traditional roots (Swain 2002).) This first political current describes an America wounded by multiculturalism (Lind 1996), which it perceives as a threat to the legitimacy of the values that made possible the American experiment with democracy and rule of law. This threat is represented by new groups of immigrants (coming from Latin America and, in particular, from Mexico) who apparently refuse to identify with the American creed, to which they counterpose their own linguistic and religious identity. This is more easily preserved thanks to the geographic proximity of the places of origin of these immigrants to those where they have settled in the States, which allows them to maintain their ties to their national communities much more easily than had been possible for other groups of immigrants originating from Europe or, more recently, from Asia (Huntington 2004). This America is more nationalistic than patriotic, in the sense it acknowledges itself in ethnic-cultural phenomena instead of constitutional or political ones. This reflects its basic distinction from American liberal nationalism: whereas conservative nationalism is based on the specific cultural traits of white Anglo-Saxon protestants, liberal nationalism is based on the universal political values of the constitution. This is why conservative America is fearful of being invaded or occupied by national groups (like the Mexicans) which it has already defeated in the past, groups which are gaining control culturally over the same territories (Texas, New Mexico, Arizona and California) that long-ago they controlled politically (Huntington 2004).

The second current is that of popular Protestantism, and towards it converge several cultural and religious experiences, foremost the cultural tradition of the Frontier, more than ever alive in the big Southern states (Lieven 2004). This tradition, generally defined as Jacksonian for its markedly populist and nationalist character (Mead 2002), is the tradition of the Scottish and Irish Protestants that dominated the frontier era and promoted (by force) continued expansion; for this reason, it acquired a decidedly militaristic and expansionistic character. However, towards this pole also gravitated the religious tradition of evangelical Protestantism (Morone 2003) which was crucial in giving to the Frontier its communitarian nature (a community, however, in which Indians and Afro-Americans were excluded), thus aggregating (and civilizing) those acting in a context lacking a juridical and political infrastructure. The roots of this tradition go back to the English and Scottish Puritanism of the seventeenth century, characterized by hostility toward the Anglican church (and the Catholic church), as well as toward professional and religious elites. The encounter between Scottish–Irish Puritanism and the experience of the Frontier produced a populist feeling which periodically emerged in the Southern and agrarian states. In the 1970s, this populism converged with evangelical Protestantism, rendering even more radical its critique of modernity and of its intellectual justifications (one thinks, for example, of its rejection of the Darwinian theory of evolution).

It is useful to note that such a tradition is very similar to that of Protestant Ulster from which it derives, and which has been also characterized by an explosive mix of religion and nationalism (explosive at least for Catholics who long bore its consequences). As Lieven (2004) has noted, now that the South African Boers have surrendered to the black majority, the only populace that, in the developed world, resembles (in mentality and culture) Protestant Ulster is evangelical America of the South. The Old Testament has given to these Irish, South African and American settlers the theological justification for the right to take away land from others (that is, from the native inhabitants). Even today, the Old Testament is the source of inspiration for evangelical populism and its criticism of a secularized America (as well as of 'godless' Europe). Moreover, this explains the peculiar theological *entente* developed between the evangelical Protestants and the Jewish settlers in Palestinian territories: both acknowledge themselves as people chosen by God, a new and old Israel that has a divine mission to perform on Earth (which no one, obviously, has the right to obstruct). Thus, within the US, the most modern society in the world lives alongside a traditional one characterized by its religious fundamentalism (one needs only think of the theological defence for capital punishment) and its egalitarian militarism (one needs only think of the fervent firearms culture). The evangelical Protestant movement became more radicalized starting in the 1970s with the opposition to legalized abortion and continues today with its opposition to gay marriage. This radicalization marked the ascent of Baptists at the expense of Methodists and, above all, of the more moderate Episcopalians.

The encounter between white nationalism and religious populism produced a political movement that first gained ground within the Republican party and, through this, within the main government institutions of the country. September 11 only served to emphasize the strength of this movement, for religious nationalism seemed to provide a bulwark to terrorist aggression. Scott Thomas is right in Chapter 10 when he cautions against making direct connections between the religious right and US foreign policy. However, fundamentalist religious Protestantism undoubtedly provided the frame (cognitive and linguistic) within which the answer to Islamic terrorism was elaborated; for example, expressions such as 'fighting the devil' or 'battling evil' were widely used by puritanical ministers during the English Civil War in the mid-seventeenth century (Lieven 2004).

Today, Texas is one of the principal political and financial bases of this religious nationalism and George W. Bush represents it as no one else can. Religious nationalism was propagated in the South of the country then spread throughout traditionally liberal states such as California. It can be said that in his language and his vision, Bush epitomizes this religious nationalism in its purest form. Texas, in fact, was the testing ground for a veritable neoconservative political experiment (Lind 2003). It is the state of Protestant populism that is both individualist and communitarian. It is the state of possessive individualism, with its emphasis on the capacity of man (more than woman) to conquer the environment and bend it to his will. This has produced a buccaneering capitalism (Micklethwait and Wooldridge 2004) especially in sectors such as oil, agriculture, high-tech and finance, that is closer to a game of chance than to the Weberian ethic. It is a capitalism that likes risk, but not rules; in particular, those rules which protect the environment from excessive exploitation. Texas is a vast state (bigger than Great Britain and France together), but deserted and hostile, where it is difficult to develop a sensitivity to the natural world. Texas is also a state with a widespread evangelical Protestant community, which has been charged with many of the tasks of social policy (such as the integration of immigrant Latinos through school programmes) that were traditionally in the public sector.

Texas can be seen as the ideal-type of the minimal state. The Texas legislature meets only once every two years for a session that lasts only 140 days. The legislators' salary is among the lowest in the country, around $7,200 dollars in 2000. Moreover, the governor does not have the power to appoint his/her own cabinet. It is a minimal state that has entrusted the tasks of governing to the local economic oligarchy, such as the Bush family, which certainly does not need public funds or resources to exercise power. Texas is also the state by definition of militant nationalism, partly because it is one of the most important sites of the military industrial complex (housing military bases and strategically important arms industries) and also because it is a state with an entrenched firearms culture, the outcome of a frontier experience which was one of the most violent in the country. This is a culture with clearly masculinist propensities. Not surprisingly, Texas is also a state where the death penalty is very popular. For instance, George W. Bush, in the last year of his mandate as governor, authorized 40 executions. At the same time, precisely because of its origins, Texas is one of the most expansionist states, constantly searching for new frontiers and, today, new markets. Thus, the domestic minimal state came to be accommodated with an external expansionist one. In synthesizing the Southern and Western political traditions, Texas has become the new epicentre of national politics, as once was New York or Massachusetts.

The transatlantic implications of American conservative nationalism

This religious and militant nationalism is the engine which powered the unilateralist turn in foreign policy since the 1990s (in the Congress) and since 2000 (in the presidency). It is the core of the new conservative nationalism, which of course comprises other conservative currents. This conservative nationalism has tried successfully to appeal to the tradition of American exceptionalism, interpreted however in cultural rather than political terms. To conservative nationalists, America is exceptional because of its cultural past more than for its political future. This past confirms that America is exceptional for its enduring faith in democracy and freedom. But if America is *exceptionally* good, then it also can be *exceptionally* powerful, because its power will be only used in the pursuit of good. To neoconservatives, America is necessarily good whatever she does internally and externally. Thus, the new conservative exceptionalism has recovered America from the contrition of liberal nationalism of the 1960s. It has rehabilitated the myth itself of American exceptionalism, which had been seriously brought into question (externally) by the defeat in Vietnam and (internally) by the criticism of the civil rights movement. For conservative nationalism, America has to rely on itself, domestically and internationally. It has the moral quality and the military power to shape itself and the world in accordance with its founding (cultural and religious) values.

It is not surprising that American conservative nationalism has provoked resistance in a good part of the world, and in Europe in particular (Peterson and Pollack 2003). Not only because nationalism in a hyper-power constitutes, in and of itself, a threat, but also because Europe, largely prodded by liberal America, has put in motion a process of supra-national integration that is leading it in the opposite direction from where America now stands. As happened in America with the War of Independence of 1776, albeit in a more complex context, independent European nation states have decided to pool together significant parts of their national sovereignty and to realize a project of supra-nationalism (Kupchan 2002). While it is true that the national interests of the EU member states still play a role in constraining EU foreign policies, those national interests, nevertheless, have never asserted themselves against the decisions of international multilateral institutions. In Europe, particularly on the continent (to a lesser degree on the islands), nationalism continues to be considered (by both elites and public opinion) as a demon which needs to be tamed or kept in check; a demon responsible for three civil wars on the continent and, above all, for the political, economic and moral decline of Europe. This is why European nation states have moved in the direction of a multilateral post-nationalism, giving birth to the most advanced experiment in a post-Westphalian state (Caporaso 1996). A post-national experiment which, oddly enough, had been historically foreshadowed by the American experience of confederating separate territorial units (Fabbrini 2005).

This suggests that the contrast between the US and the principal continental countries of the EU during the Iraq war was anything but accidental. This contrast, in fact, was not the expression of national rivalries, such as one between France and the US in the 1960s; rather, this time the contrast reflected a much deeper difference. In opposition to the nationalist unilateralism of the Republican majority in the presidency and the Congress, the continental countries of the EU presented a post-nationalist multilateral vision. These conflicting positions were not in the least occasional, for there continue to be significant differences between the US and the EU (this time including Great Britain) on crucial issues of international politics. The EU, in opposition to the US, favours strengthening the role of the UN as the sole structure equipped with international legitimacy, enforcing international arms control treaties or promoting new multilateral institutions of international law such as the International Criminal Court or the International Environmental Protection Agency. In addition, the EU has a different interpretation to the US on the crisis in the Middle East and its solution, as Rob Kroes argues in Chapter 5. For the EU, any solution is impractical which does not involve the active participation of international institutions such as the UN (which is abhorred by Israeli political authorities and regarded with suspicion by the George W. Bush administration).

America and Europe, then, look at the world from different points of view – nationalistic in the first case, supra-national or post-national in the second (Cooper 2003); or Westphalian in the first case and post-Westphalian in the second case, as Richard Crockatt argues in Chapter 4. This difference has led the two sides of the Atlantic to different evaluations of the causes of global disorder and its possible solutions, although both recognize global terrorism as the main international threat. For unilateralist America, global terrorism constitutes a challenge to liberty and democracy, and particularly to the ways in which these are represented in America (Kagan 2003). For this reason, faced with a terrorist threat, America must recover its freedom to act, that is to say its decisional autonomy, if it does not want to surrender to anti-Western fundamentalism. Ultimately, the democratic nature of its domestic political process is a sufficient guarantee that its discretionary decisions do not become arbitrary. As such, the US can pursue power politics in the international system on the grounds that power will be at the service of democracy. Military and economic power is considered, by unilateralist America, the necessary resource to promote democracy globally.

The unilateralist interpretation is certainly right to recognize that the current international system is not adequate to quickly and effectively respond to new terrorist threats (Newhouse 2003). The organization of that system, in fact, reflects the necessity of regulating Cold War relations between two super-powers, a condition which no longer exists. There are, however, weaknesses with this interpretation, because it entrusts only the military means of the hyper-power (and its willing allies) with the task of neutralizing terrorism (Nye 2003). Unilateralist America resembles one who, having a hammer in hand, sees problems only as nails (Garton Ash 2004). Yet, terrorism is not a traditional territorial state, which one can defend against using only military strength. While it is not directly motivated by poverty or ignorance (Bin Laden is rich and educated), terrorism cannot be circumscribed and weakened without a complex series of structural policies that confront the diffusion of these problems in the world. As Scott Thomas argues in Chapter 10, using only a problem-solving approach is ineffective in the case of terrorism; indeed, using only a hammer aggravates the problem instead of solving it. Without interventions that are legitimated by multilateral international organizations (such as the UN or NATO), it is unrealistic to think that the hearts and minds of others can be won over in countries with sympathies for anti-Western terrorism. In sum, legitimacy does not coincide with the use of force;

and legitimacy continues to be monopolized by multilateral institutions (including the EU), as even unilateralist America is forced to recognize (Kagan 2004).

For multilateralist Europe, on the contrary, global terrorism has to be considered as the outcome of a global context crippled by injustice and resentment. Terrorism cannot be defeated militarily but only through a concerted and complex array of international policies carried out by a plurality of nations within the frame of the UN. Acting outside that frame could make things worse rather than better. For the 2004 Pew Global Project Attitudes, in Britain, France and Germany, contrary to the US, a majority of people say 'the war in Iraq has hurt the fight against terrorism more than it has helped'. The European interpretation is certainly convincing when it acknowledges the complexity of the social, economic and cultural factors which feed anti-Western terrorism (including unresolved international crises, such as the one between Israel and Palestine). The European strategy of promoting an international system based on norms, rules, agreements and formalized procedures represents an important counter-weight to the militaristic tendencies present in the international system (Kupchan 2002). However, it too has its weaknesses (Fabbrini 2004b). This is not only because positing an EU civil power in contrast to US military power is destabilizing, but also because it seems to underestimate the fact that law without power can become mere rhetoric. Legal power is necessary but may not be sufficient to stabilize the world after September 11. This is also due to the fact that existing international law, based on the principle of non-interference in the internal affairs of a country, can preserve the status quo favourable to existing non-democratic regimes.

In conclusion, the transatlantic differences are not based on contingent factors; rather, they reflect the projection onto the international scene of radically divergent visions – nationalist, in the American case, and post- or supra-national in the European case. This also explains why a growing number of Europeans want the EU to develop into a superpower that can act independently of the US in world affairs. In the Transatlantic Trends 2004 (which consider, on the European side, countries as diverse as Great Britain, Italy, Poland, Germany, France, Netherlands, Portugal, Slovakia and Spain), '71 per cent of Europeans believe the EU should become a superpower like the US'. Although, 'when those Europeans who favour an EU superpower were asked if they would favour it even if it required higher levels of military spending, nearly half – 47 per cent – withdrew their support' (*ibid*: 6). This view of the EU as a countercheck to the US has also been largely shared by the European peace activists, as Carlo Ruzza and Emanuela Bozzini show in Chapter 6. That difference notwithstanding, the two sides of the Atlantic are linked by historical ties and friendship (Wallace 2001), by highly interdependent economic systems (Risse 2002), and by a political culture that is liberal and democratic. Moreover, the difference is not only between the two sides of the Atlantic, but also within each of them. And that makes the transatlantic tension more complex – and less frightening. For the Transatlantic

Trends 2004, 'Americans ... are divided as Europeans on a range of issues' (*ibid*: 24). Or better,

> Democrats appear to share a number of the same views toward legiti-
> macy, the use of force, the future of the EU, and US policies as many
> Europeans. Republican and Independents support the deployment of
> American forces in Iraq, while Democrats oppose it.
>
> (ibid: 29)

One might say that, in a transatlantic perspective, it is Republican America which is at the far right of the mainstream centre constituted by Europeans and Democratic America.

Conclusion

For a long time America was interpreted as a country that was *naturally* lib-eral (Hartz 1955). It was the first new nation of the modern era (Lipset 1979), the very first historical experiment in practising liberal nationalism (Tamir 1993). Born of an anti-colonial revolution, with solid roots in the British notion of self-government and the rule of law, and sustained by highly-favourable natural conditions, America was gradually consolidated as a con-stitutional Republic that aimed to guarantee and promote the individual liberty of its citizens, that is, the millions of individuals who emigrated to its shores from all parts of the world. This gave life to a multinational America held together primarily by a constitutional pact that became the civil religion of the country (Greenfeld 1992). Indeed, the theory of liberal exceptionalism, originally elaborated by Tocqueville in the 1830s, was based on the follow-ing assumption: America was exceptional with respect to Europe because its liberalism had prevented both conservatism and socialism within the country (Lipset 1996). These latter two visions were strongly related in that they were expressions of hierarchical and communitarian tendencies that had pre-liberal roots. There emerged, particularly in the twentieth century, a consensus amongst scholars on both sides of the Atlantic that America was different because both citizens and elites shared a belief in liberalism (Shafer 1991), rather than in ancestry or traditional identity. And because it was precisely supported by this belief, in the post-World War II era America went on building a multilateral structure of the international institutions which constrained its own nationalism in exchange for the adherence to the new international rules by its Western allies. This was the institutional bargain (Ikenberry 2001) between the hegemon and the hegemonized which struc-tured the Western world during the Cold War period. As American liberal nationalism adapted domestically to accommodate within the constitution the plurality of interests and cultures which constituted the domestic polity, internationally it worked towards constitutionalizing, through a complex set of multilateral institutions, the multiplicity of national interests which constituted the international community.

Of course, this interpretation has a solid historical basis. But things were not so simple. In fact, historically, the American political experience was far more contradictory (Rodgers 1998; Smith 1993) than the argument about liberal exceptionalism allowed (Lipset and Marks 2000). Right from the beginning of the Republic, the liberal creed was challenged, sometimes successfully, at other times not, by an opposing vision that can be defined as conservative, because it has interpreted America as a cultural rather than a political nation: a cultural nation consistent with the religious and ethnic values of its founding *settlers* and not its immigrants (Huntington 2004). It was a different conservatism (at least partially) with respect to the European one in that it had absorbed some elements of the liberal creed, thus protecting it from the authoritarian and anti-democratic temptations to which European conservatism fell prey in its celebration of cultural and racial differences. Nevertheless, those liberal elements did not prevent it from interpreting democracy (when and where – in some states and some phases for example – it was influential) in terms compatible with slavery, racism, xenophobia, exclusion, thus giving life to cycles of paranoid politics that clearly weakened the liberal creed of the country (Hofstadter 1965). This domestic paranoia traditionally reflected or caused a unilateral attitude towards the world, be it imperialist or isolationist. Thus, the American experiment with democracy appears to have been much more complex and ambivalent than is generally supposed. After all, America is the country of contradictions and not coherence (Fabbrini 1999), and its strength has resided in its capacity to progress despite those contradictions.

In spite of the formidable success of conservative nationalism, it cannot be assumed that liberal nationalism has been rejected. Rather, the latter has been challenged by the former as never before in the past 40 years. To be sure, conservative nationalism has been favoured by exceptional conditions, such as those created by the end of the Cold War and the terrorist attacks of September 11. However, the roots of its success have to be found in the profound historical, social and cultural changes in America since the 1960s, as well as in the response to the dramatic issues raised by the terrorist challenge. This conservative nationalism has combined different elements but at its core there lies the conjunction of the religious and anti-statist populism of the evangelical Protestantism with the militant nationalism of the Jacksonian frontier tradition. It is not the first time that America has seen this type of nationalism; it is certainly the first time, however, that it has become a majority position in public opinion and, with the 2004 elections, in all the governing institutions, Presidency, House and Senate (and, probably, also in the Supreme Court). Will this conservative nationalism take the place of the liberal creed as the hegemonic culture of the country in the future? Will its persistence make unilateralism the foreign policy strategy of the future?

It is too early to answer these queries, and I will limit myself to two considerations. First, America after September 11 is certainly a more conservative country than it has ever been in the past. It expresses a conservative nationalism that has mobilized its illiberal tendencies, as evidenced by the approval of the Patriot Act of 2002, by the detention of Taliban Afghans at Guantanamo beyond the protection of national and international law, and by the use of torture on prisoners in the Iraq war (Brown 2003). Second, these illiberal tendencies, when they have appeared in US history, have traditionally met effective constraints which tamed their impact. The religious and ethnic nationalism was effectively tamed by the constitutional structure of the country. The America of ethnic-religious identity, of cultural nationalism, has always found a check in pluralist America, in liberal nationalism, and in constitutional patriotism (Wiebe 2002). Moreover, American democracy has shown that it possesses the institutional and cultural mechanisms to correct itself in moments of hysteria (from the Alien and Sedition Act of the 1790s to the McCarthyism of the 1950s). The American constitution has clear defects, as Robert Dahl (2001) courageously argues, but it is nevertheless effective in safeguarding the democratic development of the country. In fact, also in the dramatic climate of post-September 11, the Supreme Court, with a sentence rendered on 28 June 2004, dismantled as unconstitutional the administration policy on the Guantanamo detention. George W. Bush's unusual concept of *enemy combatants* has been further refuted by a sentence of the US District Court of Colombia of 31 January 2005.

How will the tension between the liberal creed (and its institutional basis) and the absolutist impulses of conservative nationalism be resolved? It is plausible that conservative nationalism can be moderated by pressure from the system of the separation of powers (as argued by Bruce Cain in Chapter 8), or by domestic economic difficulties (as argued by Roberto Tamborini in Chapter 9), or by external cultural resistance (as argued by Scott Thomas in Chapter 10). It is also plausible to assert that even Europeans, if they are able to avoid contesting America in principle and to propose viable alternatives to its unilateralism, can help in moderating that nationalism. And in fact, in the State of the Union address delivered by George W. Bush on 2 February 2005, one might perceive a more sober approach to the world, when he affirmed that 'The United States has no right, no desire, and no intention to impose our form of government on anyone else'. Whatever happens, it is easy to hypothesize that as long as conservative nationalism continues to have a majority presence in America, contestation of America will go on in a large part of the world, notably in Europe. However, that contestation will not become anti-Americanism *in principle* if conservative nationalism continues to be challenged within the US by a liberal alternative.

Note

1   I wish to thank Vincent Della Sala, Gianfranco Poggi and Larry Rosenthal for their very challenging comments to a previous draft of the chapter.

References

BBC News (2005) 'Global poll slams Bush leadership' at http://news.bbc.co.uk

Brown, C. (ed.) (2003) *Lost Liberties. Ashcroft and the Assault on Personal Freedom*, New York: New York Books.

Bush, G.W. (2002) *The National Security Strategy of the United States*, Washington DC, 20 September 2002.

Calleo, D.P. (2000) 'The US Post-Imperial Presidency and Transatlantic Relations', *The International Spectator*, 35 (3): 69–80.

Caporaso, J.A. (1996) 'The European Community and Forms of State: Westphalian, Regulatory or Post-modern', *Journal of Common Market Studies*, 34: 29–52.

Cooper, R. (2003) *The Breaking of Nations. Order and Chaos in the Twenty-First Century*, London: Atlantic Books.

Crockatt, R. (2003) *America Embattled. September 11, Anti-Americanism and the Global Order*, London: Routledge.

Daalder, I.H. and Lindsay, J.M. (2003) *America Unbound. The Bush Revolution in Foreign Policy*, Washington DC: Brookings Institution Press.

Dahl, R.A. (1956) *A Preface to Democratic Theory*, Chicago, IL: Chicago University Press.

Dahl, R.A. (1976) *Democracy in the United States. Promise and Performance*, Chicago, IL: Rand McNally, 3rd edn.

Dahl, R.A. (2001) *How Democratic is the American Constitution?* New Haven, CT: Yale University Press.

Dumbrell, John (2002) 'Unilateralism and "America First"? President George W. Bush's Foreign Policy', *The Political Quarterly*, 73 (3): 279–87.

Economist (2004) 'The Triumph of the Religious Right', *The Economist*, 13 November 2004.

Emmott, B. (2002) 'Present at the Creation', *The Economist*, 27 June 2002.

Fabbrini, S. (1999) 'American Democracy from a European Perspective', *Annual Review of Political Science,* 2: 465–91.

Fabbrini, S. (2002) 'The Domestic Sources of European Anti-Americanism', *Government and Opposition*, 37 (1): 3–14.

Fabbrini, S. (2004a) 'Layers of Anti-Americanism: Americanization, American Unilateralism and Anti-Americanism in a European Perspective', *European Journal of American Culture*, 23 (2): 79–94.

Fabbrini, S. (2004b) 'America and Europe in the Post-Cold War Era', in R. Janssens and R. Kroes (eds), *Post-Cold War Europe, Post-Cold War America*, Amsterdam: VU University Press, pp. 87–100.

Fabbrini, S. (ed.) (2005) *Democracy and Federalism in the European Union and the United States. Exploring Post-National Democracy*, London: Routledge.

Garton Ash, T. (2004) *Free World. America, Europe, and the Surprising Future of the West*, New York: Random House.

Greenfeld, L. (1992) *Nationalism: Five Roads To Modernity*, Cambridge, MA: Harvard University Press.

Halper, S. and Clarke, J. (2004) *America Alone. The Neo-Conservatives and the Global Order*, Cambridge: Cambridge University Press.

Hartz, L.B. (1955) *The Liberal Tradition in America*, New York: Harcourt Brace Jovanovich.

Hoffmann, S. (2001) 'On the War', *The New York Review of Books*, 48 (17): 7.

Hofstadter, R. (1965) *The Paranoid Style in American Politics. And Other Essays*, Cambridge, MA: Harvard University Press.

Huntington, S.P. (2004) *Who Are We? The Challenge to America's National Identity*, New York: Simon and Schuster.

Ikenberry, J. (2001) *After Victory. Institutions, Strategic Restraint and the Rebuilding of the Order After Major Wars*, Princeton, NJ: Princeton University Press.

Ikenberry, J. (2002) 'America's Imperial Ambition', *Foreign Affairs*, 81 (5): 44–60.

Ikenberry, J. (2003) 'Is American Multilateralism in Decline?', *Perspectives on Politics*, 1 (3): 533–50.

Jervis, R. (1999) 'Mission Impossible: Creating a Grand Strategy', in D.J. Caraley (ed.) *The New American Interventionism: Lessons from Successes and Failures*, New York, Columbia University Press, pp. 205–18.

Kaplan, R.D. (2001) *Warrior Politics. Why Leadership Demands a Pagan Ethos*, New York: Random House.

Kagan, R. (2003) *Of Paradise and Power. America and Europe in the New World Order*, New York: Alfred A. Knopf.

Kagan, R. (2004) *American Power and the Crisis of Legitimacy*, New York: Alfred A. Knopf.

Kazin, M. (1995) *The Populist Persuasion. An American History*, New York: Basic Books.

King, D. (2004) *The Liberty of Strangers: Making the American Nation*, Oxford: Oxford University Press.

Kupchan, C.A. (2002) *The End of the American Era. U.S. Foreign Policy and the Geopolitics of the Twenty-First Century*, New York: Alfred A. Knopf.

Lieven, A. (2004) *America Right or Wrong. An Anatomy of American Nationalism*, Oxford: Oxford University Press.

Lind, M. (1996) *The Next American Nation. The New Nationalism and the Fourth American Revolution*, New York: The Free Press.

Lind, M. (2003) *Made in Texas. George Bush and the Southern Takeover of American Politics*, New York: Basic Books.

Lipset, S.M. (1979) *The First New Nation. The United States in Historical and Comparative Perspective*, New York: Norton, 2nd edn.

Lipset, S.M. (1996) *American Exceptionalism; A Double-Edged Sword*, New York: Norton.

Lipset, S.M. and Marks, G. (2000) *It Didn't Happen Here. Why Socialism Failed in the United States*, New York: W.W. Norton.

McCartney, P.T. (2004) 'American Nationalism and U.S. Foreign Policy from September 11 to the Iraq War', *Political Science Quarterly*, 119 (3): 399–423.

McCormick, J.M. (2000) 'Clinton and Foreign Policy. Some Legacies for a New Century', in S.E. Schier (ed.) *The Postmodern Presidency: Bill Clinton's Legacy in US Politics*, Pittsburgh, PA: University of Pittsburgh Press, pp. 68–83.

Mead, W.R (2002) *Special Providence. American Foreign Policy and How It Changed the World*, London: Routledge.

Micklethwait, J. and Wooldridge, A. (2004) *The Right Nation. Conservative Power in America*, New York: Penguin Press.

Morone, J.A. (2003), *Hellfire Nation. The Politics of Sin in American History*, New Haven, CT: Yale University Press.

Nash, G.H. (1998) *The Conservative Intellectual Movement in America Since 1945*, Wilmington: Intercollegiate Studies Institute.

Newhouse, J. (2003) *Imperial America. The Bush Assault on the World Order*, New York: Alfred A. Knopf.

Nye, J. (2002) *The Paradox of American Power. Why the World's Superpower Can't Go Alone*, Oxford: Oxford University Press.

Nye, J. (2003) 'U.S. Power and Strategy After Iraq', *Foreign Affairs*, 82 (4): 60–73.

Peterson, J. and Pollack, M.A. (eds) (2003) *Europe, America, and Bush. Transatlantic Relations in the Twenty-First Century*, London: Routledge.

Polsby, N.W. (2004) *How Congress Evolves. Social Bases of Institutional Change*, Oxford: Oxford University Press.

Risse, T. (2002) *Democratic Global Governance in the 21ˢᵗ Century*, Working Paper of the European University Institute.

Rodgers, D.T. (1998) 'Exceptionalism', in A. Molho and G.S. Wood (eds), *Imagined Histories. American Historians Interpret the Past*, Princeton, NJ: Princeton University Press, pp. 21–40.

Ross, A. and Ross, K. (eds) (2004) *Anti-Americanism*, New York: New York University Press.

Rubin, B. and Rubin, J.C. (2004) *Hating America. A History*, Oxford: Oxford University Press.

Schickler, E. (2002) 'Congress', in G. Peele, C.J. Bailey, B. Cain and B.G. Peters (eds) *Developments in American Politics*, New York: Palgrave, pp. 97–114.

Shafer, B.E. (ed.) (1991) *Is America Different? A New Look at American Exceptionalism*, Oxford: Clarendon Press.

Shklar, J. (1991) *American Citizenship. The Quest for Inclusion*, Cambridge, MA: Harvard University Press.

Smith, R.M. (1993) 'Beyond Tocqueville, Myrdal, and Hartz: The Multiple Traditions in America', *American Political Science Review*, 87 (3): 549–66.

Smith, T. (1994) *America's Mission. The United States and the Worldwide Struggle for Democracy in the Twentieth Century*, Princeton, NJ: Princeton University Press.

Spiro, Peter (2000) 'The New Sovereigntists', *Foreign Affairs*, 79 (6): 9–15.

Swain, C. (2002) *The New White Nationalism in America*. Cambridge: Cambridge University Press.

Tamir, Y. (1993) *Liberal Nationalism*, Princeton, NJ: Princeton University Press.

Transatlantic Trends 2004, A project of the German Marshall Fund of the United States and the Compagnia di San Paolo of Turin, Italy.

Wallace, W. (2001) 'Europe, the Necessary Partner', *Foreign Affairs*, 80 (3): 16–34.

Walzer, M. (1996) *What It Means to Be an American. Essays on the American Experience*, New York: Marsilio.

Walzer, M. (1997) *On Toleration*, New Haven, CT: Yale University Press.

Wiebe, R.H. (2002) *Who We Are. A History of Popular Nationalism*, Princeton, NJ: Princeton University Press.

Part I

The rise and success of American conservative nationalism

2 The historical and ideological roots of the neoconservative persuasion

Mario Del Pero

Introduction

'A balance of power that favors freedom.' This phrase, indicating the alleged primary aim of post-9/11/2001 United States (or US) foreign policy, is repeated five times in the September 2002 *National Security Strategy of the United States of America* (hereinafter NSS). Since then, many important officials of the first Bush administration (2001–2004) have also used it frequently. Among them, the now Secretary of State and former National Security Adviser Condoleeza Rice, a scholar who prior to this had impeccable realist credentials, and often criticized America's missionary zeal and US tendency to misuse the military as an instrument of nation and democracy-building (NSS 2002; Rice 2000; Rice 2002).

Much less dissected than other rhetorical virtuosities of the NSS 2002, this sentence encapsulates, in its simplicity, the basic intellectual and political tenets of neoconservatism. It helps us to understand its ideological foundations, its powerful rhetoric, its strong appeal to different sectors of the American electorate; but also its intrinsic, and ultimately inescapable, contradictions.

In the first part of this chapter I will identify the genealogy of neoconservatism. I will therefore concentrate on its formative period: the 1970s. At the time, neoconservatism aspired to be a response (and a solution) to the crisis the US had undergone in the late 1960s and early 1970s. A solution, however, whose main intellectual and political traits had been defined in opposition to the other political and intellectual responses to that crisis. In the second part, I will concentrate on recent events and explain why neoconservatives were able to exert a relevant influence on the foreign policy of the first George W. Bush administration, particularly after the terrorist attacks of 9/11. By concentrating primarily on its historical and ideological foundations, I will try to illustrate why neoconservatism, as a visionary and utopian form of 'crisis internationalism', was ideally fit to dominate post-9/11 US foreign policy discourse.[1]

At the origin of neoconservatism

The critique of realism

Returning to the US after a long trip abroad, which included a stopover in what was then called Leningrad, American realist diplomat and historian George Kennan decided to call National Security Adviser Henry Kissinger. It was September 1973. Kissinger, almost at the height of his fame, was about to be appointed Secretary of State. The Watergate drama was unfolding with unexpected rapidity. Détente with the Soviet Union, the keystone of Nixon's and Kissinger's grand strategy, was beginning to be excoriated domestically, by an unlikely coalition of conservative republicans and disaffected liberal democrats. The latter were led by senator Henry Jackson (from Washington state) and were soon to be labelled as 'neoconservatives' (Brinkley 1994; Ehrman 1995; Kaufman 2000).

One of the main problems Kissinger had to face at the time was an amendment to the 1973 Trade Reform Act, sponsored by Jackson and by senator Charles Vanik (a Democrat from Ohio). The Jackson–Vanik amendment tied the granting to the Soviet Union of Most-Favored Nation Status – a crucial element of the set of agreements achieved by Washington and Moscow – to the lifting of restrictions on the emigration of Soviet Jews. The amendment represented an obvious interference in Soviet domestic affairs. Political variables (Jackson's presidential ambitions and Nixon's difficulties), traditional anti-Communism, emotional attachment to the state of Israel and genuine concern for the violations of human rights in the USSR and the rest of the Soviet bloc were the main factors behind Jackson's initiative. Furthermore, the Jackson–Vanik initiative was soon complemented by the neoconservatives' embracing of the cause of Soviet dissidents, which opened another front of tension with Kissinger (Garthoff 1994: 453-63; Hanhimäki 2004: 340–42; Kaufmann 2000: 242–60).

In his conversation with Kissinger, Kennan thundered against this attempt to influence US foreign policy. According to the verbatim reconstruction left by a stenographer not very well versed in Soviet names, Kennan stressed that 'nothing as yet has actually happened to either Sofarov [sic] or Soldzamechen [sic]'; on the contrary, the dissidents were troublemakers and 'many of the issues that they' had with the Soviet government were 'simply ones they themselves had provoked', to the point of splitting 'the whole Russian intellectual and esthetic [sic] community'. This, according to Kennan, had induced 'a lot of the most important other Russian intellectuals' to 'turn against them' ('then' – added Kissinger caustically – 'you know what would have happened to them under Stalin'). Kennan's bitter conclusion was quintessential realism: 'I don't think in any case that it's right for a great government such as ours to try to adjust its foreign policy in order to work internal changes in another country'.[2]

Non-interference, the separation of domestic politics from foreign policy, national interest: some of the basic elements of a general realist creed were all contained in a simple phone call. This creed fitted well, although only for a short period, within post-Vietnam US foreign policy. Much appreciated by a majority of Americans, it was an answer to the failure in Vietnam and to the crisis – political, diplomatic, economic, cultural and, in some ways, also of identity – that the country was undergoing. However, the creed and its implicit promise to teach Americans the hard and immutable laws of international politics were about to be severely challenged, and ultimately defeated. The challenge to the alleged realist turn Kissinger had imposed on American foreign policy was led by Cold War liberals, like Jackson and future ambassador at the United Nations (UN), Daniel Patrick Moynihan, and by the new right about to launch the presidential candidacy of Ronald Reagan.

What was imputed to Kissinger's realism? And how did this critique contribute to the moulding of a new conservative approach to foreign policy and national security? As American Enterprise Institute scholars Tom Donnelly and Vance Serchuk recently put it, for neoconservatives 'realism' has always been 'deeply at odds with both American political principles and American national interests'; it reflects 'a dogmatic, inflexible, even reactionary ideology' that 'stand[s] opposed to the great liberal tradition of American strategic culture'. Such tradition, oddly enough, would include 'Abraham Lincoln, Theodore Roosevelt, John F. Kennedy, Ronald Reagan, Bill Clinton, and George W. Bush' (Donnelly and Serchuk 2004a; Donnelly and Serchuk 2004b).[3]

In the 1970s, the target of the attack was obviously détente, the historical anomaly to which Donnelly and Serchuk implicitly refer. Collaboration with the Soviet Union was condemned from a strategic and moral perspective. Strategically, Jackson and others strongly denounced the Salt agreements on the limitation of nuclear weapons. Many of these criticisms concentrated on the various technical flaws of the first Salt treaty. The limits the treaty imposed on the amount of US offensive weapons were denounced as conferring on the Soviets a *de facto* condition of nuclear advantage. It was claimed that the negotiations were exploited by the Soviet Union to achieve a condition of superiority that would pay a high political dividend. From this perspective, as historian Dana Allin has pointed out, neoconservatism offered from the beginning 'a distinct world view, in particular, a pronounced pessimism about the Soviet threat' (Allin 1995: 54).

More important, nuclear equivalence with the Soviet Union was unacceptable because its corollary could be (and should be, in strict realist terms) that the two superpowers were also morally equivalent. It was in these years – Donnelly and Serchuck maintain – that '"moral equivalence" between East and West slipped into the mainstream of US strategic thought, and so a critique advanced by left-wing dissenters during the Vietnam years was adopted by a right-wing administration in the White House' (Donnelly and Serchuk, 2004a). Simply negotiating with the Soviet Union meant granting the communist superpower a *de facto* recognition of legitimacy. At the same time, not supporting Soviet dissidents represented a moral abdication on the part of the US: the only country to date capable of standing up to the Soviet ideological and civilizational challenge. Détente was, in the end, a form of self-defeating neo-appeasement, which placed the US in grave danger, just as it did with Britain in the 1930s: as sympathetic biographer Robert Kaufman (2000: 243) wrote, 'Jackson's admirers and the senator himself saw a parallel between his relentless campaign against détente during the 1970s and Winston Churchill's campaign against appeasement during the 1930s'.

This explains the longing of many neoconservatives for the relaunching of the dichotomies of Cold War discourse, and for the clarity they provided. And, along with these, for the reaffirmation of the faith in the moral potential of US power. The first objective thus became to dismantle the idea there could be any form of equivalence between the US and the Soviet Union (and, indeed, between the US and the rest of the world). To achieve this goal it was necessary to tackle what was considered the basic precondition of the Faustian deal that the US was imprudently accepting: the belief that strategic interdependence was inescapable and perennial, and that America's 'quest for absolute security' had entered an impenetrable labyrinth (Chace and Carr 1988).

The critique of interdependence and new left

Interdependence became a fashionable, as well as useful concept, in the 1970s. It expressed the belief that a trend was set in modern and contemporary international relations towards a greater, albeit not linear and progressive, interconnectedness among its various parts. As such, it was not a new idea. During the twentieth century, interdependence had developed in different forms and thanks to various transformations which involved, at one stage or another, trade and commerce, communications, mass tourism, cultural diplomacy and financial transactions. But it was war, and the destructive capacity it acquired, that gave interdependence a frightening face and made it necessary, indeed vital, to regulate it. Collective security, arms agreements, international institutions embodying (and projecting) the community of power that Woodrow Wilson and others wanted to create, all aimed at preventing a war which, thanks to huge technological breakthroughs, could become uncontrollable. Attempts at regulation and juridification followed suit: a process that, with stops (like those witnessed after 9/11) and starts, has lasted until today (Knock 1992; Ninkovich 1998).

Nuclear arms took strategic interdependence to yet another dimension. Mutual Assured Destruction (MAD) illustrated clearly the post-Clausewitzian (and, indeed, postmodern) nature of atomic arms. The genie of war has simply evaded the bottle provided by politics. During the Cold War, then, both powers rapidly learned to abide by the rules of nuclear deterrence. Nuclear arms radically constrained states' military sovereignty. For some scholars, this proved that nuclear proliferation could be a positive force for the overall stability of the system. Others identified in the absolute weapon and the fear of Armageddon one of the crucial factors on which a supposedly post-World War II long peace had been based (Gaddis 1987).

The two sides accumulated huge nuclear stockpiles, although the US maintained a steady lead till the late 1960s/early1970s. When rough parity was finally achieved, it became obvious that negotiations had to be undertaken. An arms reduction, or at least the disciplining of a potentially uncontrollable arms race, was needed for economic reasons and – according to many, but not to all strategists – to reduce the risk of a war that could annihilate the planet. However, parity and MAD were difficult to swallow for many Americans, including the soon-to-be neoconservatives. For these, they amounted to a form of appeasement. Security based upon deterrence was security based primarily, if not exclusively, upon fear; and fear could paralyse will, inhibit courage, blind judgement and lead to inevitable defeat.

Furthermore, deterrence seemed to put the safety of the US into the hands of others. Or, better, into the hands of the very 'other': the Cold War absolute and, up to a few years earlier, illegitimate enemy of the US (Stephanson 1998). Again, moral and strategic imperatives were combined in the denunciation of those who were making America vulnerable and weak, by abandoning the traditional objective of strategic primacy. For neoconservatives, 'the United States had succumbed to the evasion and alibis of appeasement. This appeasement was embodied in an intellectual and moral error – the concept of "nuclear sufficiency"' (Allin 1995: 59).

This argument was played over and over again: against the Nixon (1969–1974) and Ford (1974–1976) administrations; against the alleged leftist bias of the American scientific community; against the liberal tendencies of CIA analysts. Strategic interdependence was thus presented as unacceptable: because it undermined US credibility vis-à-vis allies and enemies; because it tied American hands and constrained its freedom of action; because it was immoral to build peace upon the certainty of global destruction in case of war; because, as Paul Nitze put it in 1979, superiority still mattered, since 'to have an advantage at the utmost level of violence helps play at every lesser level' (Allin 1995: 65).

The attack on interdependence, however, was not limited to its strategic dimension. Also coming under assault were those post-World War II international organizations, whose goal was to regulate and manage interdependence, and whose promotion had been a basic tenet of American liberal internationalism. The UN General Assembly, in particular, was dominated at the time by anti-US views. Many new African and Asian states formed a voting bloc whose positions now found some support also in the US, in a vociferous as well as multicoloured new left, who became – after realists and liberal interdependentists – the third target of neoconservative arrows.

Providing a coherent description of the new left is impossible, for the simple reason that new left was often nothing more than a convenient catch-all formula, describing a multifaceted movement, whose common denominator – the search for an agenda for a generation – was from the beginning far too loose and vague. Student activists, intellectuals, artists and the many other new leftists were influenced by different, and not always complementary, sources: from C. Wright Mills's critical sociology to theories of participatory democracy, from French existentialists to Frantz Fanon and anticolonialism (Gitlin 1987; Isserman 1987).

Impossible to define, the new left was, however, very clearly profiled by its liberal and conservative opponents. In a way, the sudden emergence of a radical critique of everything Americans stood for during the Cold War catalysed the emergence of neoconservatism. In its first, embryonic stages, neoconservatism was, in fact, primarily a reaction to the political, cultural, moral, revisionism of the mid/late 1960s.

Such revisionism was hardly monolithic and consistent. Its sources of inspiration were multiple and often contradictory. However, to its enemies (and not just to them) it was based upon a premise that was very difficult to accept: the outright rejection of the moral certainties and the unchallengeable values of Cold War liberalism, and of the vision and political project that stemmed from them (Buhle and McMillian 2003). The 'conservation of liberalism', and the reaffirmation of its intrinsic 'expansionist' character thus defined, *ab origine*, neoconservatism and what it stood for (Lindberg 2004).

In particular, the cultural relativism of new left and its defiance of the basic universalistic tenets of liberalism were unacceptable to many liberals. It was no coincidence that a classic primer of Cold War liberalism – Arthur Schlesinger's *Vital Center* – was exhumed in this period. As historian John Ehrman has stressed, in the late 1960s Schlesinger's *Vital Center* was frequently brandished against the new left's radical criticism of American foreign policy: 'the leading neoconservatives – Irving Kristol, Norman Podhoretz, Daniel Patrick Moynihan, Nathan Glazer, to name a few were veterans of the vital center' (Ehrman 1995: 34; Mariano 1999).

More or less concurrently there was a progressive rediscovery among disaffected liberals of the intellectual anchor of the Cold War: the politically and intellectually 'ubiquitous category of totalitarianism' (Pal Singh 2003: 173). This concept, an analytical tool and a rhetorical device that had been widely employed during the early post-World War II years, had faded progressively from the Cold War discourse, particularly after the season of détente had begun. Totalitarianism – 'the great mobilizing and unifying concept of the Cold War', which 'provide[d] a plausible and frightening vision of a Manichean, radically bifurcated world' (Gleason 1995: 1) – had originally offered a politically convenient instrument, which complemented both theoretically and rhetorically the political dichotomies of the early Cold War (Adler and Paterson 1970). Its rediscovery, particularly during the 1970s, had not been limited to the US and to the Anglo-Saxon world: many Western European leftist intellectuals adopted it. However, this second youth of totalitarianism as the primary analytical tool to decrypt the script of international politics bloomed mainly in the US. It culminated in a famous article published in 1979 by neoconservative political scientist Jeane Kirkpatrick, which distinguished right-wing/transformable authoritarianisms from left-wing/unredeemable totalitarianisms (Kirkpatrick 1979; Kirkpatrick 1982).[4]

As such, totalitarianism could also be used against the intolerable moral and cultural relativism that qualified the new left. A relativism that expressed itself in the strong fascination with Third World alternatives to the East–West divide, such as Maoism, Castroism, Portuguese variants of Nasserism or new, mainly African, versions of anti-imperialism.

Such third-worldism found a warm reception in the UN General Assembly, whose internal equilibria had been drastically altered by the admission of new states emerging from the ruins of the last European colonies. In the general assembly, an organ that the US had once been able to dominate, Washington suddenly found itself in a condition of minority, excoriated for its alleged imperialist and colonial policies. These anti-American attacks were often stereotyped and ideological. However, geopolitical considerations had indeed led the US (and the Nixon administration in particular) to frequently embrace putrescent European empires, thus further alienating many recently decolonized countries (as was the case with the Portuguese colonies: before the 1974 revolution, Washington had staunchly supported Lisbon, vetoing the admission to the UN of Guinea-Bissau, which had been widely supported in the general assembly).

This anti-American and anti-Western attitude of the general assembly reached its climax with the famous UN resolution no. 3379, which stated that Zionism was 'a Form of Racism and Racial Discrimination'. The resolution, approved in November 1975, had been sponsored by 25 states, including some notorious dictatorships (such as Idi Amin's Uganda). To many future neoconservatives this event signalled the moral bankruptcy of the UN and the substantial unreformability of what had once been a primary tool of US hegemony. The resolution, and the philosophy it expressed, were scathingly denounced by the US ambassador at the United Nations, neoconservative Daniel Patrick Moynihan. On that occasion, Moynihan used words that had often been reserved to the relativism of the domestic new left: 'the damage we now do to the idea of human rights and the language of human rights could well be irreversible' – Moynihan claimed

> most of the world believes in newer methods of political thought, in philosophies that do not accept the individual as distinct from and prior to the State; in philosophies that therefore do not provide any justification for the idea of human rights and philosophies that have no words by which to explain their value. If we destroy the words that were given to us by past centuries, we will not have words to replace them, for philosophy today has no such words. But there are those of us who have not forsaken these older works, still so new to much of the world. Not forsaken them now, not here, not anywhere, not ever.
>
> (Gerson 1997: 172–73)

A few months later, Moynihan would call the UN vote 'a doubly ominous event' which suggested 'a moral callousness in the West, or moral weakness'.

> Israel has become a metaphor for democracy in the world. If the Israeli democracy, which persists in the face of the uttermost peril and difficulty, can be discredited, then it can clearly be established that democracy is not a political and cultural system that can survive in a perilous and difficult world. The dustbin of history is for us.
>
> (Moynihan 1976)[5]

Un-Americaness and exceptionalist nationalism

The universalistic and neo-liberal attack on third-worldism and philosophical relativism was integrated by the denunciation of the lack of patriotism of those who embraced these ideas in the US. New left intellectuals, and the many liberal fellow travellers, were therefore targeted for their alleged unpatriotic betrayal of America's historical, timeless and universal values. The new left was first and foremost un-American. It was a culturally, politically, intellectually and morally alien phenomenon. Under attack, Jeane Kirkpatrick (1973) claimed, was the belief that the US, in spite of everything, was a decent and successful – though imperfect – society. Irving Kristol asserted that American young radicals were

> far less dismayed at America's failure to become what it ought to be than they [were] contemptuous of what it thinks it ought to be. For them as for Oscar Wilde, it [was] not the average American who [was] disgusting; it [was] the ideal American.
>
> (I. Kristol 1970: 4)

What was considered a vituperation of America generated a cultural and political backlash, which would contribute to the shaping of a distinct neoconservative identity and to the rise, in the second half of the 1970s, of the new right. As one disgruntled US political scientist would later recall, neoconservatism arose

> in reaction to what was perceived as an American political establishment that had come to see the US as the major problem in the world, both in the East–West Cold War and in the Third World. Neoconservatives, on the other hand, saw the US as the major solution in the world, especially with a Cold War still on in both East–West and North–South terms.
>
> (MacDonald 2003)

Third-worldism and the new left were therefore presented as extraneous to real America, to its way of life, its values, and its beliefs; most of all, to its faith in the role that the US should play in the world, and in the moral and transformative potential of its power. What is relevant for our analysis is that the same kind of criticism was directed towards the other two products of (and responses to) the crisis of the late 1960s/early 1970s: realism (in its Kissingeresque or continental variation) and interdependence (primarily in its liberal-institutionalist academic variant). Kissingerism, interdependence and the new left shared a common element in the eyes of their neoconservative critics: their un-Americaness and their extraneousness to American political and even philosophical traditions.

Realism, as we have seen, was presented as a typically un-American way of conceiving international relations and the conduct of US foreign policy. The Vietnam War and the discredit it brought upon idealist crusades and modernization strategies had made amoral *realpolitik* attractive and appealing to the American public. The idea that America could finally move out of perennial adolescence and be initiated into the harsh realities of world politics was indeed very popular in the early 1970s. Kissinger, the American Metternich, conveniently (and opportunistically) played the role of the statesman that could teach the US how to behave in the international arena. On this, the German émigré turned American statesman was able to build for a short span of time his fame and his political fortunes, both of which reached their apogee in 1973–74. Continental realism, in its Kissingerian variant, thus seemed to offer a way out of the tunnel that the US had entered (Hanhimäki, 2004; Isaacson 1992; Gaddis 1994).

However, Kissinger's fame faded rapidly. The crusade for a new morality in US foreign policy, launched by the neoconservatives and by Reagan's new right, hit Kissingerism hard. The supposedly un-American nature of Kissinger's approach to international affairs, indeed its initially mesmerizing Europeaness, began to be harshly rebuked. One *National Review* commentator went as far as to describe Kissinger as an 'unassimilated outsider … a European by heritage and cultural choice, a cosmopolitan by circumstance, an American by deliberate (and hazardous) calculation' who 'revealed the derivative nature of his national identity in almost pathetic fashion' (Laqueur 1973: 46).

Kissinger ended up being attacked within the Ford administration. In 1975 he lost his position as National Security Adviser and saw détente with the Soviet Union denounced by new members of the administration, such as the young Ford's chief of staff and then Secretary of Defense, Donald Rumsfeld. As ambassador at the UN, Daniel Patrick Moynihan systematically challenged Kissinger's approach during his tenure. The principal of non-interference was rejected outright by Moynihan. Freedom, he believed, could not survive in one country alone. Instead of retreating into his shell, the US should re-embrace its security tradition, based upon the spread of democracy and free-markets, the defence of human rights and the rejection of any form of amoral power politics. In a talk called *Was Woodrow Wilson right?*, Moynihan, claimed that the US had to accept the 'duty to defend and, where possible, advance democratic principles in the world at large' for democracy in one country was not enough simply because it would not last ... There will be no struggle for personal liberty (or national independence or national survival) anywhere in Europe, in Asia, in Africa, in Latin America which will not affect American politics. In that circumstance, I would argue that there is only one course likely to make the internal strains of consequent conflicts endurable, and that is for the United States deliberately and consistently to bring its influence to bear on behalf of those regimes which promise the largest degree of personal and national liberty.

(Moynihan, 1974: 26–28).

Thus, a moralized version of Wilsonian idealism was juxtaposed to the alleged realist turn of the early 1970s. Its popularity showed that the mood in the country had changed. In fact, Reagan's calls for a return of morality in foreign policy during the Republican nomination process of 1976 reached many ears. Although Reagan did not gain the nomination, the banner of the morality issue became crucial to the democratic candidate Jimmy Carter for defeating Ford and bringing to an end Kissinger's experience in Washington DC. Kissinger – Carter proclaimed critically a few days before the elections – had promoted a foreign policy 'obsessed with power blocs' and 'spheres of influence'; 'a foreign policy based on secrecy' that by definition 'has had to be closely guarded and amoral' (Hanhimäki 2004: 435–36 and 450–51).

At the same time interdependentists were also condemned as a manifestation of an un-American (and very European) virus that was spreading, unchecked, through a once healthy America. In sum, America's traditional claims to moral superiority did not easily fit also into the interdependence vision. While realism stressed independence as much as moral equivalence, interdependence emphasized mutual dependence and interconnectedness: the inexorable loss, or significant reduction, of national sovereignty. All countries being interconnected, and mutually dependent, they claimed that even the US, once unique and exceptional nation, found itself constrained by an objective situation and by a set of rules, norms and practices that it had itself crucially contributed to create. Interdependence thus seemed to put the fate of America also, when not primarily, into the hands of others.

In particular, it was strategic interdependence that proved impossible for neoconservatives to accept. As in the past, their stress on nuclear power preponderance was justified in psychological terms. In a total symbolic war, as the Cold War was, America's unchallengeable superiority would strengthen Washington's credibility vis-à-vis its friends and enemies. And credibility was an invaluable asset in the perennial post-1945 struggle for the hearts and minds of the people (Leffler 1992; Ninkovich 1998). On the contrary, the stress on the realist principle of nuclear sufficiency was considered to be just a one-way ride towards inferiority. This explains the loud request by the neoconservatives for a return to the safer and more acceptable principle of superiority. Even more, it explains the developing of a dream that is still very much with us: the creation of a defensive shield, capable of defending the country and of making it, once more, unassailable. A shield that would allow the country to regain its lost sovereignty and, with it, its freedom of action. This reacquired independence would permit the US to remain an exceptional nation, exempted from those laws of history that the other nations had instead to abide by.[6]

Thus, the exceptionalism idea, that has accompanied the US from its inception and which had undergone a deep crisis in the turbulent 1960s and 1970s, was relaunched in the following years by the neoconservatives. American exceptionalism, as Australian historian Ian Tyrrel (1991: 1031) brilliantly illustrated some years ago, is based upon the 'pre-historicist idea of the United States as a special case "outside" the normal patterns and laws of history'. More than an idea, it is an ideology that conveniently overlooks the many interactions that have always existed between the US and the rest of the world, Europe in particular[7] (Bonazzi 2004; Rodgers 1998: 24).

Neoconservatism's vision of the world, and its idea of America's role and mission in the international arena, stemmed from this current of exceptionalist nationalism: an ideology of national greatness, based upon the premise that the US will not fall, whatever might happen. Cold War liberalism had adhered to such belief, and had contributed to a *de facto* globalization of American nationalism (Fousek 2000; Stephanson 1995). But this nationalist/universalist creed had been radically shaken by the Vietnam defeat, internal turmoil and, obviously, détente. Those years saw the disintegration of the consensus on which the universalist assumptions of Cold War liberalism had rested (Suri 2003).

Neoconservatism was therefore the last remake of US exceptionalist nationalism. It affirmed the intrinsic uniqueness of America. It asserted the superior quality of the American nation and the benign nature of the overwhelming power that the US had come over time to possess (Lieven 2004). However, exceptionalist nationalism could not, by itself, provide a sufficient and exclusive political and cultural platform.[8] Neoconservatism offered an intellectual and political exit strategy from the crisis, real or perceived, that the US underwent in the 1960s and early 1970s. An exit strategy from the abrupt disappearance of those moral and political certainties that had provided the pillars of US Cold War policies and discourse.

This strategy, however, was constructed in negative and oppositional terms. A neoconservative was originally defined as a liberal mugged by reality. Reality and realism were therefore brandished against the many political and philosophical utopias to which Americans had fallen prey. Utopias which had contributed to generate totalitarian projects or, as in the case of naïve liberals, had made them blind to the perils that the existential threat of Communism was still posing to the US.

There was (or there was supposed to be) a philosophical underpinning to this anti-utopian and anti-totalitarian new realism and it was distinctively anti-European. Anglo-American pragmatic liberalism, heir to the Anglo-Scottish

Enlightenment, was in fact contrasted to what Irving Kristol (1993) called the French-Continental enlightenment. According to Kristol, American liberalism had fallen under the influence of the 'insidious French continental tradition' (Gleason 1995: 193–94) pushing it *de facto* toward totalitarianism.

Mugged by a reality that many liberals had now chosen not to see, neoconservatives appeared nonetheless to have been also persistently mugged by the powerful and unavoidable legacy of traditional US missionary idealism. If realism was brandished against naïve utopianism of any kind, idealism was invoked against the cynical, amoral, value-free *realpolitik* then infecting US attitudes towards world affairs. Even from this perspective, Europe was the chief villain. It was again no coincidence that the realism under attack was frequently adjectived and qualified as continental (i.e. European) realism, much different from its Anglo-Saxon or American version. Continental realism was therefore presented as a self-defeating version of the realist creed; its primary trait – its critics maintained – was a deeply-embedded historical pessimism: in the future of the world and, most of all, in America's willingness and capacity to mould it accordingly to its values, needs and desires.

What qualified the neoconservative project was thus its belief in America's uniqueness and its optimistic faith that such uniqueness could be used as a force for good in the international arena. Neoconservatism was unmistakably American and optimist: 'the first variant of American conservatism in the past century that is in the American grain', according to Irving Kristol (2003), and therefore

> hopeful, not lugubrious; forward-looking, not nostalgic, whose general tone is cheerful, not grim or dyspeptic. Its twentieth century heroes were Theodore Roosevelt, Franklin D. Roosevelt, and Ronald Reagan. Such Republican and conservative worthies as Calvin Coolidge, Herbert Hoover, Dwight Eisenhower, and Barry Goldwater were politely overlooked.
>
> (Kristol 2003; see also Romero 2003; Ikenberry 2004)

In sum, optimism and anti-Europeanism were the twin keystones on which neoconservatism builted its strategy. However, they were complemented by an almost schizophrenic attempt on the part of neoconservatives to simultaneously play and reconcile realist anti-utopianism and utopian anti-realism; balances of power and universal freedoms. Neoconservatism, as its oxymoronic name implies, offered from the beginning a syncretic and ultimately incoherent message. This structural inconsistency contributed towards increasing its appeal, but undermined the coherence of its proposal from the start.

Out of the 1970s and into the new millennium

Reagan's success in the presidential elections of 1980 had a dual effect on neoconservatives. First, it catalysed a diaspora within the democratic camp that, with some notable exceptions (Moynihan among them), led most neoconservatives to join the Republican Party. Second, it granted to some neoconservatives – such as Jeane Kirkpatrick and Henry Jackson's *aide-de-campe*, Richard Perle – the possibility to play an important role in the new Republican administration.[9]

Reagan's nationalist posture, his morally bombastic rhetoric and, most of all, his support to missile defence elicited neoconservatives' enthusiasm. This enthusiasm, however, cooled rapidly. Reagan's Middle East policy, in particular, did not satisfy neoconservatives' requests for a radical change in the course undertaken the previous decade. Reagan's decision to sell the AWACS planes to Saudi Arabia, signalled his intention to follow Kissinger's strategy in the region. The goal remained to preserve an advantageous geopolitical configuration of power, and to maximize stability (and consequent access to resources), to the detriment of political transformation, democratization and extension of Western and US cultural hegemony.

Reagan's opening to Gorbachev was seen by many (although not all) neoconservatives as détente *redux*. The leading neoconservative magazine, *Commentary*, continued to emphasize the Soviet expansionist design, now camouflaged behind Gorbachev's bid to give a human face to Soviet Socialism. All in all, the business of governing a country, within the constraints that the Cold War still imposed, proved difficult to conciliate with the radicalism of the neoconservative vision.

The presidency of George H.W. Bush (1989–1992) saw a further decline in the neoconservatives' influence. US foreign policy became even more cautious and, for many neoconservatives, far too pro-Arab (Secretary of State, James Baker, in particular, was accused of being insensitive to Israel's security needs). Much to neoconservatives' disapproval, Kissinger's acolytes (Brent Scowcroft and Lawrence Eagleburger) and moderate conservatives, like Baker himself, took control of American foreign policy. Some neoconservatives – Joshua Muravchik among them – went as far as to endorse Bill Clinton in 1992 (Muravchik 1993; Ehrman 1995).

The 1990s were seen and interpreted very ambiguously by neoconservatives. The end of the Cold War was seen as a vindication of the policies they had supported in the 1970s. The Soviet Union – they claimed – had finally been trounced by Reagan's confrontational stance and by his relaunching of the arms competition, not by the appeasers' attempts to co-opt and integrate Moscow into the liberal and interdependent world order. Similarly, the impressive boom of the US economy in the 1990s, and the rapid waning of the much feared Japanese challenge, proved that talk of America's decline, which had inundated libraries and bookshops in the previous decade, was mostly unfounded. Declinism, the trendy and dominant paradigm in the 1980s, had simply been proved wrong. The gloomy post-Vietnam pessimism was finally overcome.

At the same time, however, the neoconservatives' marginalization continued unabated, in the country and in American conservatism at large. Many commentators, and some neoconservatives themselves, proclaimed the final and complete amalgamation of neoconservatives within American mainstream conservatism, in spite of their dissatisfaction with Bob Dole in 1996 and with the same George W. Bush in 2000 (some neoconservatives, including *Weekly Standard*'s editors, William Kristol and David Brooks, endorsed Arizona senator John McCain during the Republican primaries).

The very popular 'ends of history', in whatever form they were presented, left little room for the idealistic missions and the global crusades that neoconservatives had always been fond of. The 'clashes of civilizations', on the other hand, were simultaneously a manifesto (albeit very ambiguous) of a cultural relativism that was completely at odds with the neocons' universalism and of a surreptitious realism, in which civilizations replaced states as the ultimately impenetrable and antagonistic units of the international system (Fukuyama, 1991; Huntington, 1996).

Moreover, during the 1990s, the moral issue came again to the forefront of neoconservatives' preoccupations. Under the neoconservatives' critical gaze came the inherent philosophy of Clinton's foreign policy and his attempt to promote globalization and enlarge the area of free markets, without tackling the very political problems that were obstructing the full unfolding of US and Western hegemony. To neoconservatives this appeared not just as internationalism on the cheap, but as a fundamentally apolitical and amoral project, reflecting a sort of economic determinism that greatly overestimated the imminent transformative strength of economic mechanisms. It was – according to William Kristol and Robert Kagan – a situation reminiscent of the mid-1970s. To preserve and possibly expand US hegemony a neo-Reaganite foreign policy of military supremacy and moral confidence was needed. American foreign policy – Kristol and Kagan (1996) proclaimed – had to 'be informed with a clear moral purpose, based on the understanding that its moral goals and its fundamental national interests [were] always in harmony' (*ibid.*: 27). A (*ibid.*: 31) 'remoralization of America at home [required] remoralization of American foreign policy. For both follow from Americans' belief that the principles of the Declaration of Independence [were] not merely the choices of a particular culture, [but] universal, enduring, "self-evident" truths'. This was, after all,

> the main point of the conservatives' war against a relativistic multiculturalism. For conservatives to preach the importance of upholding the core elements of the Western tradition at home, but to profess indifference to the fate of American principles abroad [was] an inconsistency that cannot help but gnaw at the heart of conservatism.
>
> (Kristol and Kagan 1996: 31)

Similar concerns were expressed by Irving Kristol. The world – Kristol claimed in a 1997 op-ed for the *Wall Street Journal* – had

> never seen an imperium of this kind, and it is hard to know what to make of it. In its favor, it lack[ed] the brute coercion that characterized

European imperialism. But it also lack[ed] the authentic missionary spirit of that older imperialism, which aimed to establish the rule of law while spreading Christianity.

(I. Kristol 1997)

What it did offer the world was 'a growth economy, a "consumerist" society, popular elections and a dominant secular-hedonistic ethos ... a combination that [was] hard to resist – and equally hard to respect in its populist vulgarity ... an imperium with a minimum of moral substance' (I. Kristol 1997).

The liberal empire then taking form was very different to the one that neoconservatives had long dreamed of. This was despite the fact that some of the military interventions the neoconservatives had invoked were finally undertaken during the last decade of the twentieth century. Either defended as humanitarian wars or harshly denounced as expression of a new military humanism, these interventions were certainly coherent with neoconservatives' requests to exercise US overwhelming power for the defence of human rights and the global spread of democracy. Nonetheless, some neoconservative commentators, such as Charles Krauthammer (1999), denounced them from a realist perspective, presenting them as futile exercises, wasting American resources in areas (such as Kosovo) that were substantially irrelevant for the US national interest.

Neoconservatives were given an important role in the first George W. Bush administration. This was due to the new President's political ideas, which were more radical than those of his father or of the 1996 Republican candidate, Bob Dole. For the first time since the Reagan presidency, neoconservatives came to occupy important positions in the administration. John Bolton was appointed undersecretary of State for arms control; I. Lewis Libby became vice-President Cheney's chief of staff; Richard Perle headed the non-governmental, very influential Defense Policy Board; Stephen Hadley was named deputy National Security Adviser; many other neoconservatives were appointed to less important posts. But the most important prize was certainly won by Johns Hopkins University political scientist Paul Wolfowitz, who became Rumsfeld's deputy at Defense (Woodward 2002; Drew 2003; Mann 2004).

However, and despite later conspiratorial claims to the contrary, a neoconservative cabal did not take control of the US and of its foreign policy in January 2001. From its inception, the first Bush administration was a sort of coalition of different conservative breeds: hard-nosed nationalists (Cheney and Rumsfeld); self-proclaimed intellectual realists (Rice); traditional republican internationalists (Powell and Armitage); religious right supporters (Ashcroft); and, finally the neoconservatives themselves.[10] With the advent of George W. Bush, neoconservatives became very influential, but were not at all hegemonic, in the administration and within the American political and intellectual conservatism movement.

Then came 9/11 and the overall balance of power within the administration changed drastically. The neoconservatives' radical, and until then minority, vision was adopted as the Administration's policy. The neoconservatives' denunciation of the dis-functionality of the Middle East suddenly appeared prophetic. Their traditional condemnation of the Faustian deal accepted by the US in the region (i.e. stability and access to resources in exchange for lack of hegemony and cultural impermeability) were vindicated.

But why was this so? Why did neoconservatism seem to offer a viable political (and geo-political) response to the new challenge? Many critical commentators have claimed that 9/11 triggered into action the long-dormant projects of the new American right. Namely: to return to America's dominance in the Atlantic Alliance; to relaunch a vast programme of high-tech military investments, further consolidating and expanding the US's uncontested strategic primacy; to free intelligence agencies of the residual restraints imposed on them in the mid- and late 1970s; to finally get rid of Saddam Hussein and start the political and cultural transformation of the Middle East. There is more than a grain of truth in all of this. Neoconservatives certainly saw the proof that they had been right all along in the dramatic events of 9/11, and that their criticism of US foreign policy and its approach to external threats had been correct. And they seized this opportunity to convince Bush to adopt policies and implement actions they had long advocated.

But there was more to it than this. Once Bush declared a war against terrorism, a new surge of nationalism followed suit, and neoconservatism was principally, as we have seen, a manifestation of it. Once Islamic terrorism was declared a new totalitarian menace, by liberals and conservatives alike, the response could only be couched in moral absolutes.[11] Finally, and most importantly, the terrorist attacks on the Twin Towers and the Pentagon catalysed a request for bold visions and radical projects. Only the neoconservatives seemed to offer one, in the Republican world and, probably, in the entire country. Therefore, neoconservatism was (or seemed to be) at the time the only real 'crisis internationalism' available in the market of political ideas in the US. A 'crisis internationalism' is, in historian Frank Ninkovich's (1998: 10–12) apt definition, an attempt 'to develop new rules for navigating through a turbulent and unpredictable modern international environment', when relevant crises render 'the old rules of the game and foreign policy traditions out of date'. Such an attempt has a deeply embedded American grain, and reflects America's response to modernity and its dark face, of which Islamic radicalism appeared to be the new and latest expression: a response that is 'extraordinarily optimistic and progressive on the one hand, yet afflicted by a sense of extraordinary, perhaps unmanageable crisis, on the other' (Ninkovich, 1998: 10–12).

Conclusion

For many Americans, post-9/11 was not a time for cautious realism, because cautiousness is not appropriate in dramatic and emotional times. Nor was it a time for weak idealism or, even worse, irenic escapisms, because when survival is at stake, hesitations must be overcome and scruples must be abandoned. It was, in the final analysis, a time when power and ideas, strength and principles, force and mission had to be reconciled; when circumstances forced the US to be both utopian and implacable: because an alternative to what the world had become (and to the intolerable situation in the Middle East) was needed, and the will and determination to pursue that goal to the end, with whatever means, were necessary.

The syncretic neoconservative message was there to satisfy such a request. This was also due to the fact that what was really required was a persuasion, more than a policy. Americans asked for optimistic and sanguine responses, and not for fatalistic (as much as realistic) clichés, according to which terrorism could not be defeated and eradicated, but only contained and limited. And neoconservatism was indeed an optimistic persuasion, as Irving Kristol recently reminded us (I. Kristol 2003).

This explains the return of that very combination of utopianism and *realpolitik*, of morality and power that qualified, *ab origine*, the neoconservative message. And this explains also the reaffirmation of the traditional conviction that it is only the global expansion of US-style democracy that can ultimately guarantee the security of America itself; that the US, as asserted during World War II, cannot live in a world which is half free and half slave (Foner 1998: 219–47; Stephanson 2000).

Hence, the 'balance of power that favors freedom' of the NSS 2002: a 'confused' and 'even meaningless concept', according to US diplomatic historian Melvin Leffler (Leffler 2003: 10). Meaningless because it tries to associate a realist quintessential model – a situation in which overwhelming power cannot last, because power balancing is the inevitable (and intrinsic) fate of the international system – with a typically messianic and idealistic goal – spreading a preponderant and universal freedom, that by itself cannot be balanced. The former envisions equilibrium, the latter aspires instead to hegemony.[12] Nevertheless, through that concept, neoconservatism has tried to reconcile this duality. To promote, in Charles Krauthammer's words, a new and realistic 'democratic globalism': 'beyond power. Beyond interest ... expansive and utopian' yet sharing 'realism's insights about the centrality of power' and 'having appropriate contempt for the fictional legalisms of liberal internationalism' (Krauthammer 2004).

However, the war in Iraq proved that that contrast is problematic. The difficulties of the post-war period have shown that a persuasion is not sufficient. And they have shown, once more, that power – unchallengeable, unbalanceable and unprecedented as the one the US can currently deploy – is unlikely, on its own, to generate and spread liberty and democracy. Although undertaken to defeat international terrorism and change the Middle East, the military intervention in Iraq ended up in transforming the emergency and the crisis into normalcy and rule. The struggle against terrorism is ceasing to be a transient and transitory stage – a crisis indeed – to become the norm and the long-term perspective of the new international system. All in all, neoconservatism as a quintessentially crisis internationalism has contributed not towards solving the crisis, but towards both escalating and normalizing it.

Notes

1 On this second aspect I have been influenced by many analyses, the most important of which were Ikenberry (2004), Leffler (2003; 2004) and Robin (2002).

2 Telephone call between George Kennan and Henry Kissinger, 14 September 1973, 8.55 p.m., National Archives and Records Administration (hereinafter NARA), Nixon Presidential Material Project (hereinafter NPMP), Henry A. Kissinger Telephone Conversations Transcripts (hereinafter Telcons), Chronological File, Box 22.

3 A surprising omission from the pantheon of pre-neoconservatives suggested by the two authors is Harry Truman, whom many neocons continue to revere. The absence of the militarily, fiscally and socially conservative such as Dwight Eisenhower, and of the traditional conservative such as George H. W. Bush, is instead emblematic.

4 Despite claims to the contrary, the distinction was not new: it had been suggested, for instance, by US officials and diplomats supporting the immediate inclusion of Salazarist Portugal in the developing Atlantic *communitas*.

5 Daniel Patrick Moynihan, 'We are Sakharov', 5 July 1976, commencement address of Daniel Patrick Moynihan at the convocation of Hebrew University, Henry M. Jackson Papers, University of Washington Libraries, Manuscripts Collections, Seattle, WA (hereinafter, HMJP, UWLMC), Accession No. 3560-6 (Foreign Policy and Defense Issues), Subject Files, Box 37.

6 Vivid nationalist and exceptionalist *topoi* permeated, for instance, most of Reagan's speeches on the Strategic Defense Initiative (Fitzgerald 2000).

7 In Tiziano Bonazzi's (2003: 383) apt definition, exceptionalism expresses 'an acute need of Europe ... that cannot be explained only in psychological and cultural terms, but with the fact that, as much as it denied it, the United States belonged to Europe'. In America's exceptionalist self-representation, Europe would thus become a '*persona ficta*', an '*alter ego*' in which the United States could (and can) mirror and represent itself (Bonazzi 2004). By doing so, America's exceptionalism originates a 'rhetoric of absences', where the absences are, however, 'the ills and defects of a universalized external world' (Rodgers 1998: 24).

8 This was also because the other three responses to the crisis – Kissinger's realism, interdependence and the new left – all expressed in different ways a distinctive, some could say exceptional, American élan.

9 Kirkpatrick was appointed ambassador at the UN. Perle was named Assistant Secretary of Defense for international security policy.

10 These partitions are quite arbitrary. Many of these conservatisms do obviously overlap. However, they are useful to comprehend the multiform diversity of US conservatism and of the Bush administration itself. See Daalder and Lindsay (2003); Halper and Clarke (2004); Berman (1994).

11 According to the editor of the *Weekly's Standard*, David Gelernter, a terrorist is 'a totalitarian out of office' (Gelernter 2004). Similarly, liberal commentator Paul Berman presented the war against terrorism as a struggle against a new totalitarianism. The war in Iraq was therefore needed to discourage and defeat the mass

totalitarian movement of the Muslim world. Defeating totalitarianism – Berman claimed – was (and is) a necessary step to promote the global cause of 'liberalism' (Roundtable, Slate 2004; Berman 2003).

12 A different view from the one presented here can be found in Gaddis (2004).

References

Adler L. and Paterson T. (1970) 'Red Fascism. The Merger of Nazi Germany and Soviet Russia in the American Image of Totalitarianism, 1930s–1950s', *American Historical Review*, 75: 1046–64.

Allin, D. (1995) *Cold War Illusions. America, Europe, and Soviet Power, 1969–1989*, New York: St. Martin's Press.

Anderson, P. (2003) 'Casuistries of Peace and War', *London Review of Books*, 25, 6 March 2003, Online. Available HTTP: http://www.lrb.co.uk/v25/n05/ande01_.html

Berman, P. (2003) *Terror and Liberalism*, New York: Norton.

Berman, W.C. (1994) *America's Right Turn. From Nixon to Bush*, Baltimore, MD: Johns Hopkins University Press.

Bonazzi, T. (2003) 'L'antieuropeismo degli americani', *Il Mulino*, 52: 381–9.

Bonazzi, T. (2004) 'Europa, Zeus e Minosse, ovvero il labirinto dei rapporti euro-americani', *Ricerche di Storia Politica*, 7: 3–24.

Brinkley, A. (1994) 'The Problem of American Conservatism', *American Historical Review*, 99 (2): 409–29.

Buhle, P. and McMillian, J. (eds) (2003) *The New Left Revisited*, Philadelphia, PA: Temple University Press.

Chace, J. and Carr C. (1988) *America Invulnerable: the Quest for Absolute Security from 1812 to Star Wars*, New York: Summit Books.

Daalder, I.H. and Lindsay, J. (2003) *America Unbound. The Bush Revolution in Foreign Policy*, Washington DC: Brookings Institution Press.

Donnelly, T. and Serchuk, V. (2004a) 'John Kerry, Reactionary', *The Weekly Standard on-line*, 19 July 2004. Online. Available HTTP: http://www.weeklystandard.com/Content/Public/Articles/000/000/004/306spzzf.asp

Donnelly, T. and Serchuk, V. (2004b) 'Unrealistic Realism', *AEI online*, 9 July 2004. Online. Available HTTP: http://www.aei.org/publications/pubID.20875/pub_detail.asp

Drew, E. (2003) 'The Neocons in Power', *The New York Review of Books*, 50, 12 June 2003.

Ehrman, J. (1995) *The Rise of Neoconservatism. Intellectual and Foreign Affairs*, New Haven, CT/London: Yale University Press.

Fitzgerald, F. (2000) *Way Out there in the Blue. Reagan, Star Wars and the End of the Cold War*, New York: Simon & Schuster.

Foner, E. (1998) *The Story of American Freedom*, New York: Norton.

Fousek, J. (2000) *To Lead the Free World. American Nationalism and the Cultural Roots of the Cold War*, Chapel Hill, NC/Londra: University of North Carolina Press.

Fukuyama, F. (1991) *The End of History and the Last Man*, New York: Free Press.

Gaddis, J.L. (1987) *The Long Peace. Inquiries into the History of the Cold War*, Oxford/New York: Oxford University Press.

Gaddis, J.L. (1994) 'Rescuing choice from circumstances: the statecraft of Henry Kissinger', in Craig G.A. and Loewenheim F. (eds), *The Diplomats, 1939–1979*, Princeton, NJ: Princeton University Press.

Gaddis, J.L. (2004) *Surprise, Security and the American Experience*, Cambridge/London: Harvard University Press.

Garthoff, R.L. (1985; 2nd edn 1994) *Detente and Confrontation: American-Soviet relations from Nixon to Reagan*, Washington DC: Brookings Institution Press.

Gelernter, D. (2004) 'What Ronald Reagan Understood', *The Weekly Standard on-line*, 21 June 2004. Online. Available HTTP: http://www.weeklystandard.com/Content/Public/Articles/000/000/004/217kkfas.asp?pg=2

Gerson, M. (1997) *The Neoconservative Vision. From the Cold War to Culture Wars*, Lanham, MD: Madison Books.

Gitlin, T. (1987) *The Sixties: Years of Hope; Days of Rage*, New York: Bantam Books.

Gleason, A. (1995) *Totalitarianism. The Inner History of the Cold War*, Oxford: Oxford University Press.

Halper, S. and Clarke J. (2004) *America Alone: the Neo-Conservatives and the Global Order*, Cambridge: Cambridge University Press.

Hanhimäki, J.M. (2004) *The Flawed Architect. Henry Kissinger and American Foreign Policy*, Oxford: Oxford University Press.

Huntington, S. (1996) *The Clash of Civilizations and the Remaking of World Order*, New York: Simon & Schuster.

Ikenberry, J.G. (2004) 'The End of the Neoconservative Moment', *Survival*, 46: 7–22.

Isaacson, W. (1992) *Kissinger*, New York: Simon & Schuster.

Isserman, M. (1987) *'If I had a Hammer …': the Death of the Old Left and the Birth of the New Left*, New York: Basic Books.

Kaufman, R.G. (2000) *Henry Jackson. A Life in Politics*, Seattle, WA: Washington University Press.

Kirkpatrick, J. (1973) 'The Revolt of the Masses', *Commentary*, 55: 58–62.

Kirkpatrick, J. (1979) 'Dictatorship and Double Standards', *Commentary*, 68: 34–45.

Kirkpatrick, J. (1982) *Dictatorship and Double Standards*, Washington DC: American Enterprise Institute.

Knock, T. (1992) *To End all Wars. Woodrow Wilson and the Quest for a New World Order*, Princeton, NJ: Princeton University Press.

Krauthammer, C. (1999) 'The Short, Unhappy Life of Humanitarian War', *The National Interest*, 57: 5–8.

Krauthammer, C. (2004) *Democratic Realism*, Washington DC: The AEI Press. Available at: http//www.aei.org/doclib/20040227_book755text.pdf

Kristol, I. (1970) 'When Virtue Loses All Her Loveliness – Some Reflections on Capitalism and the Free Society', *The Public Interest*, 21: 3–16.

Kristol, I. (1993) *Reflections of a Neoconservative*, New York: Basic Books.

Kristol, I. (1997) 'The Emerging American Imperium', *The Wall Street Journal*, 18 August 1997.

Kristol, I. (2003) 'The Neoconservative Persuasion', *The Weekly Standard*, 47 (http://www.weeklystandard.com/content/public/articles/000/000/003/000tzmlw.asp).

Kristol, W. and Kagan, R. (1996) 'Toward a Neo-Reaganite Foreign Policy', *Foreign Affairs*, 75: 18–32.

Laqueur, W. (1973) 'Kissinger and the Politics of Détente', *Commentary*, 56: 46–52.

Leffler, M. (1992) *A Preponderance of Power: National Security, the Truman Administration, and the Cold War*, Stanford: Stanford University Press.

Leffler, M. (2003) '9/11 and the Past and Future of American Foreign Policy', *International Affairs*, 79: 1045–63.

Leffler, M. (2004) 'Think Again: Bush Foreign Policy', *Foreign Policy*. Online. Available HTTP: http://www.foreignpolicy.com/story/files/story2671.php

Lieven, A. (2004) *America Right or Wrong. An Anatomy of American Nationalism*, Oxford: Oxford University Press.

Lindberg, T. (2004) 'Neoconservatism's Liberal Legacy', *Policy Review*, 127. Online. Available HTTP: http://www.policyreview.org/oct04/lindberg.html

MacDonald, D. (2003) 'Straussian vs. Evangelical Influences', H-DIPLO. Online posting. Available e-mail: H-DIPLO@H-NET.MSU.EDU (18 June 2003).

Mann, J. (2004) *The Rise of the Vulcans. The History of Bush's War Cabinet*, New York: Viking.

Mariano, M. (1999) *Lo storico nel suo labirinto. Arthur Schlesinger Jr. tra ricerca storica, impegno civile e politica*, Milano: Franco Angeli.

Moynihan, D. P. (1974) 'Was Woodrow Wilson Right?', *Commentary*, 57: 25–31.

Muravchik, J. (1993) 'Why the Democrats Finally Won', *Commentary*, 95: 17–20.

Ninkovich, F. (1998) *The Wilsonian Century. U.S. Foreign Policy since 1900*, Chicago, IL: Chicago University Press.

NSS (2002) *The National Security Strategy of the United States of America*, September 2002. Online. Available HTTP: http://www.whitehouse.gov

Pal Singh, N. (2003) 'Cold War Redux: on the "New Totalitarianism"', *Radical History Review*, 85: 171–81.

Rice, C. (2000) 'Campaign 2000: Promoting the National Interest', *Foreign Affairs*, 79: 45–62.

Rice, C. (2002) *A Balance of Power that Favors Freedom*. Online. Available HTTP: http://www.manhattan-institute.org/html/wl2002.htm

Robin, C. (2002) 'Remembrance of the Empires Past: 9/11 and the End of the Cold War', International Center for Advanced Studies (ICAS), *Working Paper*, Online. Available HTTP: http://www.nyu.edu/gsas/dept/icas

Rodgers, D. (1998) 'Exceptionalism', in Anthony Molho and Gordon Woods (eds), *Imagined Histories. American Historians Interpret the Past*, Princeton, NJ: Princeton University Press.

Romero, F. (2003) 'America e Islam' in Romero F. and Guolo R., *America/Islam*, Roma: Donzelli, 2003, pp. 3–52.

Roundtable, Slate (2004) 'Liberal Hawks Reconsider the Iraq War. Paul Berman, Thomas Friedman, Christopher Hitchens, Fred Kaplan, George Packer, Kenneth M. Pollack, Jacob Weisberg, and Fareed Zakaria', *Slate*, January 13. Online. Available HTTP: http://www.slate.msn.com

Stephanson, A. (1995) Stephanson, *Manifest Destiny. American Expansion and the Empire of Right*, New York: Hill & Wang.

Stephanson, A. (1998) 'Fourteen Notes on the Very Concept of the Cold War', in G.Ó. Tuathail and S. Dalby (eds), *Rethinking Geopolitics*, London: Routledge.

Stephanson, A. (2000) 'Liberty or Death: The Cold War as US Ideology', in Odd Arne Westad (ed.), *Reviewing the Cold War: Approaches, Interpretations, Theory*, London: Frank Cass.

Suri, J. (2003) *Power and Protest. Global Revolution and the Rise of Detente*, Cambridge, MA: Harvard University Press.

Tyrrel, I. (1991) 'American Exceptionalism in the Age of International History', *American Historical Review*, 96: 1031–55.

Woodward, B. (2002) *Bush at War*, New York: Simon & Schuster.

3 The neoconservatives as a continuation and an aberration in American foreign policy

Douglas T. Stuart

> The neo-conservative moment is over.
>
> (Ikenberry 2004: 7)

> The unipolar moment has become the unipolar era.
>
> (Krauthammer, in Fukuyama 2004: 57)

Introduction

Two realities define the United States (or US) situation since the terrorist attacks of 11 September 2001: unprecedented power and an infinity of vulnerabilities. America is the first nation in history that commands so much power, in so many different forms, that it can realistically consider the option of ruling the world. At the same time, Americans have become acutely aware of their susceptibility to attack from both traditional and non-traditional enemies. The challenge for Washington has been to fashion a new strategy which both builds upon America's strengths and copes with its weaknesses in order to advance and protect US national interests. For over three years, that challenge has been taken up by a small coterie of individuals who, despite the fact that none of them were members of George W. Bush's first cabinet, have exercised an extraordinary amount of influence on American foreign policy. Most commentators refer to this group as the neoconservatives, but other titles have been offered as well. Ivo Daalder and I.M. Destler prefer the term 'democratic imperialists', while Charles Krauthammer (who contends that '...the use of the word "empire" in the American context is ridiculous') opts for 'democratic realists' (Daalder and Destler 2003: 46, Krauthammer 2004). This chapter will attempt to analyse the goals and values of the contemporary neoconservative movement, but in accordance with American democratic traditions it will assume that America's 'hard-right turn' in foreign policy is ultimately the responsibility of George W. Bush (Ikenberry 2004: 7). The almost complete domination of the Washington policy community by a few ideologically-driven individuals for a relatively long period of time is a rare occurrence in modern American history. But these are not normal times. The question on the minds of many commentators and policy-makers is: have the neoconservatives already set the United States on a path that will be irreversible for many years to come?

As Mario Del Pero argues in Chapter 2, the term neoconservative has been around for over 30 years, and has been used to describe a very diverse group of policy intellectuals. One important study, published by Peter Steinfels in 1979, described neoconservatism as 'a distinct and powerful political outlook' but also admitted that '[i]t has not even been easy to settle upon a label for this outlook, in itself a sign of the unfamiliar constellation of attitudes it displays' (Steinfels 1979: 1, 2). He describes the founding members of the neoconservative community (including Irving Kristol, Daniel Patrick Moynihan, Daniel Bell and Seymour Martin Lipset – a very mixed bag of thinkers) as liberals who became outraged by the anti-Vietnam and anti-establishment radicalism of the 1960s in the US. Steinfels commends this 'antibody on the left' for its tough-minded criticisms of the excesses of the 1960s and for its concern to preserve a moral core in contemporary political debate, but he ultimately condemns the neoconservatives for allowing themselves to become co-opted by the forces of oligarchy and corporatism which he views as a direct threat to American democracy (Steinfels 1979: 292–4).

There is much that is situation-specific about the values and goals of this first generation of neoconservative thinkers. First and foremost, their world views were shaped by fine distinctions between communists, socialists and 'fifty-seven varieties of Trotskyites' (Steinfels 1979: 29). They calibrated and recalibrated their own identities, and their views on friends, enemies and neutrals, by recourse to these ideological referents. During the 1970s they were especially preoccupied with identifying, and rooting out, Fabian socialists and Eurocommunists within the western alliance. Second, their domestic agendas were deeply influenced by conflicts over civil disobedience which reached a high-water mark during the Vietnam era. Indeed, concern over a 'crisis of authority' within American society was the *sine qua non* of the neoconservative movement during this period (Steinfels 1979: 53–4). Third, they were writing at a time when American power was circumscribed by the Soviet empire. Global unilateralism was not an option for the US during this period, and debates about the use of military power were always conditioned by the threat of mutual assured destruction. For these reasons, it is problematic to establish a clear genealogical link between the Cold War generation of neoconservatives and the community that is currently advising and influencing President Bush.

The most well-known neoconservative advisers to the first President Bush were Deputy Secretary of Defense Paul Wolfowitz, Under Secretary of Defense for Policy Douglas Feith and US Ambassador to Afghanistan Zalmai Khalilzad. Their primary patrons within the Administration were Secretary of Defense Donald Rumsfeld and Vice President Dick Cheney. As President Bush begins his second term, although not all of the above-listed individuals have retained their positions – there is no reason to expect significant policy changes for the next four years. Indeed, President Bush's decision to replace Colin Powell with Condoleeza Rice as Secretary of State, and his appointment of Porter Goss as Director of Central Intelligence, send a clear message that this administration intends not only to continue the foreign and defence policies of the past four years, but to fiercely defend them.

The neoconservatives within the Bush administration are backed by an impressive team of policy experts associated with various Washington think tanks (including the American Enterprise Institute, The Project for a New American Century and the Heritage Foundation) and publications (including the *Weekly Standard*, *Commentary* and *The National Interest*). This group includes Irving Kristol, Charles Krauthammer, Max Boot and Robert Kagan. Citizens who are looking for one book which presents the neoconservative agenda and also provides a good (if very disturbing) example of neocon rhetoric should obtain a copy of *An End of Evil: How to Win the War on Terror*, written by the former Chair of the Bush Administration's Defense Policy Board, Richard Perle, and former Bush speechwiter David Frum (Frum and Perle 2003).

Many commentators share the opinion of Michael Lind, who has described the neoconservatives as 'weird men' (Lind 2003). Some of these individuals do invite caricature by their occasional lapses into Strangelovian rhetoric. But they are far too influential, articulate and resilient to be dismissed. There are aspects of both the international and the domestic American situation at the start of the twenty-first century which have facilitated the rise of the neocon-servatives and will continue for the foreseeable future to bolster their influence in the Washington policy community. More importantly, as this chapter will attempt to demonstrate, their arguments touch enduring themes in US foreign policy and resonate with some key elements of American culture. Specifically, the chapter will discuss the goals and values of the neoconserva-tives by reference to one fundamental policy choice which has been central to American foreign policy since the founding of the republic: the choice between a *transformative* and an *adaptive* role in the international system. Every president since George Washington has been faced with this choice. But this chapter will also argue that there are aspects of the neoconservative response to this traditional policy choice which are both unique and problematic.

Choosing between transformation and adaptation in American foreign policy (I)

For nearly four decades – from the mid 1950s till the end of the 1980s – US experts on foreign policy focused almost exclusively on the Cold War. Students in a basic American Foreign Policy course during this period could be forgiven for believing that the world was created by the nuclear blasts in Hiroshima and Nagasaki. This curiously ahistorical approach to under-standing America's place in the world left most US experts (including US policy-makers) unprepared for life after the Soviet threat. It is only in the past couple of years that scholars have begun to place the Cold War in historical context and develop historically-based lessons for US policy-makers. Two particularly interesting and provocative examples of this new movement are John Gaddis' long essay on *Surprise, Security, and the American Experience* and Walter Russell Mead's book *Special Providence: American Foreign Policy and How It Changed the World* (Gaddis 2004, Mead 2001). These historically-based studies demonstrate that American leaders since the founding of the republic have grappled with a basic strategic choice between a transformative and an adaptive posture in international affairs. The defining characteristic of a transformative foreign policy is the quest for fundamental change in some key aspect(s) of the existing international order. Transformation is usually difficult and sometimes dangerous. US leaders have been attracted to this strategy for three reasons: because some characteristics of the existing situation were considered to be intolerable or untenable; because of perceived opportunity; or because of an overriding ideological imperative. By contrast, an adaptive foreign policy is generally indicative of either US contentment with the existing situation (status quo orientation) or a belief that the costs and risks of challenging the existing order outweigh the benefits of transformative change.

As both Gaddis and Mead make clear in their studies of the history of US foreign policy, the realities of power have had a significant influence on the choices that US leaders have made between transformative and adaptive foreign policies. But Gaddis argues that fear – triggered by a direct attack on American soil – has also played a key role in determining the direction of US policy. Gaddis contends that limited capabilities and intense insecurity combined to convince John Quincy Adams to pursue a selective transformation strategy following the British burning of the US Capital and White House in 1814. Adams reacted to this crisis by committing the US to a campaign of *continental domination* which would, to the extent possible, establish American control over the residual European holdings in the western hemisphere and eliminate those pockets of 'native Americans, pirates, marauders, and other free agents' (Gaddis's phrase) which threatened the security of an expanding American nation (Gaddis 2004: 16).

This transformational strategy also had a missionary element to it, as reflected in the well-known rhetoric of manifest destiny. This ideology made it easier for Americans to support a radical form of transformation with regard to the scattered and vulnerable Native American populations. In its most brutal manifestation this campaign involved conquest and mass deportations. In its more benign form, this campaign involved policies designed to educate Native Americans at government-sponsored institutions like the Carlisle Indian School in Pennsylvania. Richard Henry Pratt, the founder of the School, explained his mission as follows: 'In Indian civilization I am a Baptist, because I believe in immersing the Indians in our civilization and when we get them under holding them there until they are thoroughly soaked' (Dickinson College 2004: 8).

Gaddis claims that the strategy of continental domination continued to guide US foreign policy throughout the nineteenth century, and was not completely overturned until the Second World War. But transformation was always conditioned by capability, and each president during the nineteenth century recognized that a more cautious and adjustive approach was required in US relations with the European powers. Walter Russell Mead notes that American commentators had been arguing since the time of the French Revolution that the US had a responsibility to support

> every great European revolutionary movement of the nineteenth century. What we would now call Wilsonian voices called for intervention in the Latin American, Greek, Polish, Hungarian, and Cuban wars of indepen- dence. In 1848–49 the navy went so far as to pick up republican refugees after the collapse of the Roman republic. Wilsonians supported American interventions in Hawaiian politics as that kingdom slowly died, but Wilsonians were unable to trigger American armed intervention in a foreign war for independence until the intervention in Cuba in 1898.
>
> (Meade 2001: 164)

The important point is that successive nineteenth-century administrations resisted the temptation to meddle very directly in European affairs at a time when they were not yet strong enough to back up such actions.

To the extent that the campaign of continental domination and democra- tic transformation encouraged US leaders to focus on North America, it is often confused with isolationism. But successive nineteenth-century presi- dents recognized that their nation's interests required a proactive foreign policy which frequently played off one European nation against another in order to keep European governments from challenging US control over the continent. The US also used this tactic to extend its influence into Latin America by means of the Monroe Doctrine, which relied upon British naval power to help keep continental European governments at bay.

Gaddis notes that a 'central premise of the Adams strategy had been that distance itself was a means of defense' (Gaddis 2004: 40). It is a measure of the success of America's policies that by the end of the nineteenth century US leaders could be fairly confident that America was relatively secure, both from the vagaries of European power politics and from the various Native American tribes. As a result of its campaign of 'insular imperialism' the US had achieved uncontested control over the North American mainland from Canada to Mexico, established itself as an industrial great power, and begun to develop a tradition of military professionalism (Merk 1963: 228–60). This combination of relative security and growing power provided the US with the option of playing a more ambitious, and perhaps a transformative, role in world affairs, but Washington was not under any immediate pressure to do so. The stage was set for a lively political debate about the degree to which the US should involve itself in world affairs. William McKinley responded positively, albeit selectively and cautiously, to the proponents of a more assertive foreign policy. Following the US victory in the Spanish–American War, however, the United States government began to behave in a sustained manner as a great power on the world stage. After McKinley's assassination in 1901, Theodore Roosevelt threw his considerable energies into the game of great power competition. His success as a practitioner of 'old world power politics' made an enormous impression on Henry Kissinger:

> Unlike his predecessors, and most of his successors, Roosevelt did not think of the United States as a messianic cause but as a great power – potentially the greatest. Viewing its mission as that of guardian of the global equilibrium in much the same way Britain was protector of the balance of power in Europe, he was impatient with many of the traditional pieties of American thinking on foreign policy. Roosevelt rejected the supposed efficacy of international law ... [and] scorned the concept of disarmament'.
>
> (Kissinger 2001: 240)

Kissinger's depiction of Roosevelt as a practitioner of *realpolitik* fails to account for the President's ambitious ideological agenda. In fact, as John Judis argues in *The Folly of Empire*, Roosevelt harboured an intensely messianic vision of America's ultimate mission which had its roots in both religious and racialist theories of Teutonic supremacy (Judis 2004: 51–62). In a representative statement, which would warm the heart of any contemporary neoconservative, Roosevelt asserted that the US had a 'duty toward the people living in barbarism to see that they are freed from their chains, and we can free them only by destroying barbarism itself' (Williams 1962: 57).

It is worth emphasizing, however, that once he entered the White House, Roosevelt adjusted his goals to the logic of power. The President still yearned for the establishment of an American empire, but he recognized that there were very clear limits to what the US could accomplish on its own in the international system. Consequently, like his nineteenth-century predecessors, Theodore Roosevelt pursued a strategy which combined transformative and adaptive elements. His management of the Panama Canal issue and his promulgation in 1904 of the Roosevelt Corollary to the Monroe Doctrine are clearly illustrative of the first approach, while his mediation of the Russo–Japanese War in 1905 reflects the second approach to foreign policy. He also undertook largely symbolic actions, such as his deployment to the Pacific of the Great White Fleet of 16 American battleships in 1907, as low-cost and low-risk assertions of American greatness. The fact that the fleet was almost forced to turn back because the US did not have an adequate network of fueling stations was a nice reminder of the limits of such *gestes*. Roosevelt was frustrated at times by the fact that he could not do more to establish the 'empire of liberty' overseas, but as Kissinger has argued, he was still able to accomplish a great deal. In particular, by tacking between transformation and adaptation, Roosevelt succeeded in establishing the US as a permanent diplomatic and economic actor in the Pacific Rim.

Choosing between transformation and adaptation in American foreign policy (II)

The limitations of US power became increasingly apparent over the next 12 years, as the US, under Taft and Wilson, sought first to divert the European powers from war by means of diplomacy and then to establish completely new rules for international behaviour in the wake of World War I. Ex-President Theodore Roosevelt was especially critical of Wilson's policies during both the pre-war and post-war period, which he described as an attempt to 'supplant nationalism by internationalism' as a guide to US policy. Roosevelt warned one journalist 'never to allude to Wilson as an idealist. He is a doctrinaire' (Pringle 1931: 423). Not surprisingly, Henry Kissinger shares Roosevelt's negative views of Wilson's attempt to introduce 'a new and more wholesome diplomacy' in a world that was still governed by calculations of power and interest. Kissinger nonetheless admits that it is Wilson, rather than Roosevelt, who has had the most enduring and pervasive influence on American foreign policy.

> As early as 1915, Wilson put forward the unprecedented doctrine that the security of America was inseparable from the security of *all* the rest of mankind. This implied that henceforth it was America's duty to oppose aggression *everywhere* … . Every American president since Wilson has advanced variations of Wilson's theme.
>
> (Kissinger 1994: 47–53)

Kissinger attributes this influence to a powerful strain of naivety in American culture. Many realist writers and policy-makers (Kennan, Acheson, Nixon, Mearsheimer) have made similar claims. But other writers have interpreted the goals and motivations of President Wilson very differently. Arthur Link opted for the phrase 'higher realism' to describe Wilson's foreign policy. According to this argument, the President recognized that the failure of the great powers to prevent World War I confirmed the absolute unreliability of traditional approaches to international relations. Under these circumstances, radical transformative change in the rules of inter-nation behaviour was considered to be essential.

Wilson recognized that key elements of the evolving international situation were converging to create an intolerable threat to American security. According to Frank Ninkovich:

> The Wilsonian assumptions that later became axiomatic for American statesmen were fairly simple … Wilson believed that he could discern a number of prominent features in the emerging profile of international

relations. First, the advent of 'total war' made clear that war itself was no longer a useful or reliable instrument of diplomacy ... . Second, it created a new kind of danger that was distinctly different from old threats of physical conquest: the possibility of a poisoning of the world political environment by powers hostile to liberal democracy. Third, it suggested that the European balance of power ... had been permanently unhinged, beyond possibility of restoration. Fourth ... modern politics and warfare were global in scope. Finally, Wilson assumed that, given the obsolescence of the balance of power and the interconnections of the modern world, *any* conflict anywhere, unless nipped in the bud, threatened to escalate into another world war more calamitous than the first ... .

There is nothing utopian about all this. On the contrary, the key to understanding the Wilsonian century is that it was continually haunted by the fear of terrible failure.

(Ninkovich 1999: 13)

For Ninkovich, it is the fear-driven aspect of Wilson's world view that is least appreciated and most significant. He calls this approach to foreign policy 'crisis internationalism'.

Public frustration with the costs and benefits of World War I, and with America's failure to transform the post-war international system, provided the context for a neo-isolationist backlash. Throughout the 1920s and 1930s activist, internationalist leaders like Franklin D. Roosevelt (FDR) recognized that they could not get elected unless they paid homage to the rejectionist mood in American public opinion. Gaddis contends that 'the nation came closer during the late 1930s to *hiding* in the face of threats than it had done at any point since the years preceding the War of 1812' (Gaddis 2004: 45). FDR became increasingly concerned about this situation during the pre-war years. He worried that the US might not be able to compete with the seemingly more dynamic totalitarian regimes. Indeed, shortly before his inauguration in 1933, Walter Lippmann had warned him that 'The situation is critical, Franklin. You may have no alternative but to assume dictatorial power' (Kennedy 1999: 111). By the early 1930s, FDR was also acutely concerned about another evolving source of danger – new technologies for war fighting, including the development of airplanes capable of crossing oceans to bomb American cities. Roosevelt did what he could to prepare the US for war with the totalitarian powers, but he was not willing to jeopardize his presidency over this issue. Consequently, the US followed a pre-war strategy of adaptation in the face of transformative changes in Europe and Asia.

Pearl Harbor, and America's subsequent experience in World War II, permanently ended America's nostalgia for insularity. From this point on, American leaders would accept as gospel that the US could only be safe if it remained globally involved, with the military capability to back up its global mandate. The bipolar nature of the Cold War nonetheless placed limits on what the US could do, and where it could go, in the world. It also convinced US policy-makers that they could only achieve their transformative goal of containing, and ultimately overthrowing, the Soviet empire by means of multilateral cooperation.

In his classic study of international politics, *Discord and Collaboration*, Arnold Wolfers argues that America has historically preferred going it alone to going it with others. He notes, however, that this tradition was abandoned at the end of World War II in the face of a worldwide communist threat. An unsentimental realist, Wolfers reminded his readers that 'solidarity, even among close allies, has usually proved a perishable asset'. He goes on to describe numerous specific problems which confounded US attempts at alliance management during the Cold War, including '[t]he personalities and idiosyncrasies of leading statesmen, the preconceptions and biases of influential groups, and the emotions, resentments, fixed ideas, or peculiar anxieties of whole peoples'. He concludes, however, that the fact that alliance coordination is difficult 'does not mean that [US policy-makers] are relieved of the responsibility for success or failure. Stormy weather and treacherous currents are no excuse for shipwrecks that able navigation could have avoided' (Wolfers 1962: 205–16). It is one of the under-appreciated aspects of US foreign policy during the Cold War that Washington constructed and then maintained its worldwide network of allies for over four decades without falling prey to the temptation to mirror Moscow's management of its own alliance subordinates.

With the disappearance of the Soviet Union in 1991, Washington was faced with the challenge of establishing new strategic guidelines for global involvement. The advisers to George H.W. Bush echoed debates that had taken place in Washington during the period from 1945–47 (before the doctrine of containment was established as the lodestar of US foreign policy). While Bush's advisers accepted that the US had a unique global role to play as the sole remaining superpower, they were acutely concerned (as their post-World War II predecessors had been) about the risks of overextension, and they attempted (as their post-World War II predecessors had done) to make it clear to friends and allies abroad that the US would not allow itself to be drawn into every conflict (Stuart and Tow 1990: 24–46). This approach to foreign policy was tested from within in 1992, when some members of the Bush team attempted to introduce an ambitious new strategy of global *preponderance* into the Pentagon's Defense Planning Guidance. The President was quick to reject this radical plan for worldwide transformation, with its associated themes of preemption and unilateralism, and to recommit his administration to an adjustive foreign policy. By the end of his tenure, however, George H.W. Bush was facing problems on several fronts (Iraq, Somalia, Yugoslavia) which were making it difficult for his administration to maintain its standards of selectivity and caution in foreign affairs.

Bill Clinton came to office with no experience and very limited interest in world affairs. He nonetheless accepted the fact that America had a unique power position in the international system. Encouraged by a belief in the pacifying effects of democratization and free markets, he attempted to resolve this problem by policies of enlargement and engagement (the so-called 'en-en' doctrine). This doctrine of support for institutionalized globalization was designed to make the world less threatening and more manageable, while preserving America's dominant position in the international system at very low cost. These assumptions gradually eroded in the face of events during Clinton's first term, and by the time that he was re-elected he had accepted the fact that America was the world's only indispensable actor. He had also become increasingly frustrated with the problems of managing multilateral coalitions, for example, the Clinton team's criticisms of Kosovo mission led Britain's International Institute for Strategic Studies to predict that this would be 'the last war fought by the US under NATO rules' (IISS 2002: 133).

The frustrations of the Clinton administration provided the context for a much more assertive and unilateralist foreign policy under George W. Bush. The new President was comfortable with the fact of US indispensability and resolved not to favour multilateralism for its own sake. Following the attacks of 11 September, however, the Bush administration temporarily reassessed the value of multilateralism. For a few months it appeared that the President had concluded that the threat of catastrophic terrorism constituted a new kind of challenge to collective security, which could only be resolved by common effort. By the end of 2001, however, the Bush team had become convinced that international collaboration was more trouble than it was worth, and that America had the resources to manage the global war on terrorism on its own terms.

By the time that the World Trade Center and the Pentagon were attacked, the US had achieved a position of global pre-eminence which made it possible for the neocon advisers to President Bush to convince the President that a transformative foreign policy that was global in its scope, unilateral and militaristic in its procedures, and messianic in its ultimate goals was both necessary and achievable. The relatively calm and deferential reactions of Congress, the media and the Washington policy community to the neoconservative strategy is at least partly attributable to a form of post-traumatic stress, which made it hard for critics to frame their arguments without appearing to be soft on terrorism. A pervasive sense of victimization after 9/11 also made it difficult for anyone to criticize the Bush administration's domestic or international actions by recourse to traditional moral or juridical principles.

But as this chapter makes clear, the ultimate success of the neoconservative arguments in the post-9/11 environment was also due to the fact that their vision of fundamental transformation of the existing international situation resonated with a theme which had become very familiar during the twentieth century. Frank Ninkovich's emphasis upon the fear-based aspects of Wilsonianism is especially important for our understanding of the current situation. Wilson believed that key political and military developments would place the United States in an intolerable strategic situation in the near future. During the 1930s, Franklin Roosevelt became concerned about similar trends. Following World War II, the US found new sources of threat in Soviet communism, Third World instability and the development of nuclear and missile technologies. Under these circumstances, the US continued to follow the logic of 'crisis internationalism' until the collapse of the Soviet system.

Writing during the 1990s, Ninkovich concluded that, with the end of the Cold War, the US could finally turn away from its threat-based world view and return to 'normal internationalism' based upon 'traditional definitions of national interest – not simply American conceptions, but interest and power-based ideas that had dominated thinking about international relations for thousands of years' (Ninkovich 1999: 291). Both George H.W. Bush and Bill Clinton attempted to develop their foreign policies according to the logic of national interest. But Ninkovich (and Bush and Clinton) failed to account for the enduring effects of decades of fear-based thinking and planning upon the Washington policy community. They also could not foresee the degree to which the US would become vulnerable to the new threat of transnational terrorism. The US has responded to this new threat by once again loosening its controls on the messianic impulse, and committing itself to a new form of transformative foreign policy. In the concluding section of this chapter, I will argue that while the motivations for this campaign are understandable, and its goals are commendable, the way in which the neoconservative advisers have managed US foreign policy is deeply flawed.

An end to evil?

This chapter has drawn upon American history for insights about the neoconservative agenda. History can also help us to critique key aspects of this agenda.

The first point that is worth making is that George W. Bush is by no means the first US president to be attracted to an ambitious foreign policy designed to transform key elements of the existing international situation. Transformation has usually been a response to a calculation that some aspects of the existing or evolving international system constituted a direct strategic threat to the United States. This was the driving force in John Quincy Adams' decision to set his nation on a path of continental domination. It was also central to Woodrow Wilson's decision to sponsor a new and more wholesome international order after the First World War and the Truman administration's decision to pursue a global campaign of anti-Communist containment after the Second World War.

I have argued that there has also been an ideological element at the core of each American campaign to transform international relations. Indeed, every US leader since George Washington has been guided by a vision of America's ultimate purpose in the world which transcended the nation's existing boundaries. As early as 1630, when John Winthrop assured the members of the Massachusetts Bay Colony that they were part of a divine plan – a 'city on a hill' – Americans have assumed that they hold a unique place in history and in the international system. John Adams had made this very clear during the negotiations for the Paris Peace Treaty which established the US as an independent nation in 1789. America, he asserted, was destined to 'form the greatest empire in the world' (McCullough 2001: 395). His successors would develop the theme of an empire unlike any other in history – more benign, more generous, more welcoming – which would bring both the blessings of liberty and the benefits of the free market to all nations.

While every president since Washington has had both circumstantial and ideological reasons to be attracted to a transformative foreign policy, the central policy choice for each president was whether to actively press for fundamental change or to use the more indirect and cautious tactics associated with an adaptive agenda.

Most US presidents have been guided by a clear understanding of the costs and risks of an ambitious transformative strategy. In some cases, US leaders have concluded that they had no choice but to seek to alter key aspects of the existing international order in order to protect the national security, but they have also recognized the natural limits of this campaign. This was the case during the nineteenth century, when J.Q. Adams committed his nation to a continental domination strategy. Adams' campaign was successful precisely because it was limited to the Western hemisphere at a time when the leading European powers were either unwilling or unable to accord a high priority to this part of the world, and because it only required small-scale military operations against scattered Native American populations. Theodore Roosevelt also adapted his very great ambitions to the realities of power at the beginning of the twentieth century, pursuing a very selective, and in some cases a symbolic, transformation strategy designed to establish a place for the US among the great imperial powers without placing America on a collision course with these nations. At the end of World War II, Harry Truman set in motion a policy of 'long term, patient but firm and vigilant containment of Russian expansive tendencies', which transformed the international system into a bipolar stalemate. After an extensive debate about the nature and extent of America's post-war capabilities, Truman and his advisers concluded that they needed to overturn a 150-year tradition of eschewing peacetime alliance relations and 'go it with others' in order to sustain this containment strategy. Over time, US policy-makers also accepted severe constraints on the policies that they could pursue in order to achieve their Cold War goals, in accordance with the logic of mutual assured destruction.

Woodrow Wilson's support for a new international order based on collective security, global democracy and self-determination stands out as an anomaly in this survey of American foreign policy. Wilson's extremely ambitious campaign failed precisely because it was based upon an ideological agenda that did not correspond to the realities of power in the early part of the twentieth century. At the time, the US was the most powerful economic actor in the world. But its diplomatic and military capabilities were still quite limited by comparison to the other great powers. Furthermore, Wilson did not have a strong domestic power base upon which he could build his foreign policy.

Here, then, is the first important lesson for the advisers to George W. Bush: *Don't allow your ideological agenda to blind you to strategic realities.* Anyone who has read Richard Perle and David Frum's neoconservative tract will be astounded by the scope of their ideologically-determined ambitions. They commend President Bush for 'clutching Saddam Hussein's regime by the throat and throwing it against the wall', but they recognize that this is only the opening salvo in a campaign to root out the ultimate threat to American security – evil in its many incarnations. To accomplish this, they propose that the US: actively intervene in Iran to encourage the opposition to the regime in Tehran; develop a 'stern and uncompromising' policy toward Syria; and force the Saudis to 'act like the friend they say they are'. They also speculate that 'Independence for the Eastern Province [of Saudi Arabia] would obviously be a catastrophic outcome for the Saudi state. But it might be a very good outcome for the US'. The cornerstone of the neoconservatives' new Middle East strategy, according to Perle and Frum, is closer ties to Israel and a recognition that '[t]he distinction between Islamic terrorism against Israel, on the one hand, and Islamic terrorism against the United States and Europe, cannot be sustained'. Beyond the Middle East, they call for a 'comprehensive air and naval blockade of North Korea' backed by 'detailed plans for a preemptive strike'. They also assert that the US should 'acknowledge that a more closely integrated Europe is no longer an unqualified American interest' and accept that '[o]ur words and deeds must be aligned, and the United Nations as now constituted makes it impossible to align them'. Finally, they conclude that '[t]here is no middle way for Americans. It is victory or holocaust' (Frum and Perle 2003: 9, 103, 111, 115, 124, 137–40, 268).

When measured against this agenda, George W. Bush's actual policies look extremely tentative, and even timid. But when measured against America's 200-year tradition of foreign policy, Bush's decisions appear extraordinarily irresponsible and incautious. Indeed, the only comparable example of overstretch is Woodrow Wilson's campaign to fundamentally transform world politics, and Wilson recognized from the outset that he could not accomplish his goals without the active support of the world's leading nations.

This comment on Wilson's commitment to multilateralism leads us to the second historical lesson for neoconservatives: *US cooperation with other governments is not an exercise in American largess – it is a reflection of a sophisticated understanding of basic principles of power politics.* As illustrated in particular by US foreign policy during the Cold War, multilateralism can be an indispensable source of power in the face of complex and long-term security threats. During the nineteenth century, the United States frequently acted unilaterally and pre-emptively, but as the US became increasingly more integrated into the global community, it adjusted its foreign policies to take advantage of the benefits of going it with others. America's flirtation with isolationism in the inter-war period is an exception in this regard, and also one of the low points in the history of US foreign affairs.

The terrorist attacks of 11 September 2001 confirmed for all Americans that their security situation had become intolerable. Under these circumstances, George W. Bush was right to commit his nation to a transformative foreign policy. But the devil is in the details, and there is ample evidence to support the claim that details were in very short supply within the Bush administration as it began to plan for the Global War On Terror (GWOT) (Fallows 2004: 68–84). Under the guidance of neoconservative advisers, President Bush committed his nation to an open-ended military engagement in Iraq, as the cornerstone of his GWOT campaign. Rather than struggle with the demands of multilateral coalition politics, the President settled for a relatively small 'coalition of the willing' to support his actions. As a result, the United States is overextended and relatively isolated in the world community. In both Iraq and Afghanistan, the US may yet confront Teddy Roosevelt's warning that '[i]f we drove out a medieval tyranny only to make room for savage anarchy, we had better not have begun the task at all' (Judis 2004: 62).

Conclusion

The issues that the first Bush administration has addressed will endure also in the second. America will still need to pursue a transformative foreign policy in the face of an intolerable threat. John Gaddis has correctly observed that 'within a little more than a year and a half the United States exchanged its long-established reputation as a principal *stabilizer* of the international system for one as its chief *destabilizer*'. (Gaddis 2004: 101). However, this new US role will meet serious constraints. So a transformative strategy will be called for. But the only way to manage this situation is through a collaborative network of liberal nations. The model is the post-World War II situation confronted by Harry Truman, not the post-revolutionary world of J.Q. Adams, and not the post-World War I world which confounded Woodrow Wilson's vision of international affairs.

References

Bush, G. and Scowcroft, B. (1998) *A World Transformed*, New York: Knopf (for an account of the debates within the Bush Administration).

Daalder, I. and Destler, I. (2003) *America Unbound: The Bush Revolution in Foreign Policy*, Washington DC: Brookings.

Dickinson College (2004) *Visualizing a Mission: Artifacts and Imagery of the Carlisle Indian School*, Carlisle, PA, Trout Gallery Catalogue.

Fallows, J. (2004) 'Bush's Lost Year', *The Atlantic*, 294 (3): October.

Frum, D. and Perle, R. (2003) *An End to Evil: How to Win the War on Terror*, New York: Random House.

Fukuyama, F. (2004) 'The Neo-Conservative Moment', *The National Interest*, Summer.

Gaddis, J. (2004) *Surprise, Security and the American Experience*, Cambridge, MA: Harvard University Press.

Huntington, S. (1957) *The Soldier and the State: The Theory and Politics of Civil–Military Relations*, Cambridge, MA: Harvard University Press (remains the best account of the development of American military professionalism).

IISS (2002) *Strategic Survey: 2001–2*, London: International Institute for Strategic Studies.

Ikenberry, J. (2004) 'The End of the Neo-Conservative Moment', *Survival*, 46 (1): 7–22, Spring.

Judis, J. (2004) *The Folly of Empire*, New York: Scribner.

Kennedy, D. (1999) *Freedom from Fear: The American People in Depression and War, 1929–1945*, New York: Oxford University Press.

Kissinger, H. (1994) *Diplomacy*, New York: Simon and Schuster.

Kissinger, H. (2001) *Does America Need a Foreign Policy?*, New York: Simon and Schuster.

Krauthammer, C. (2004) 'Democratic Realism: An American Foreign Policy for a Unipolar World', 2004 Irving Kristol Lecture, American Enterprise Institute, posted on 2/12/2004 at www.aei.org/include/news_print.asp?newsID=19912

Lind, M. (2003) 'The Weird Men Behind George Bush's War', *New Statesman*, 7 April 2003.

McCullough, D. (2001) *John Adams*, New York: Simon and Schuster.

Mead, W. (2001) *Special Providence: American Foreign Policy and How It Changed the World*, New York: Knopf.

Merk, F. (1963) *Manifest Destiny and Mission in American History: A Reinterpretation*, New York: Knopf.

Ninkovich, F. (1999) *The Wilsonian Century: U.S. Foreign Policy Since 1900*, Chicago, IL: University of Chicago Press.

Pringle, H. (1931) *Theodore Roosevelt*, New York: Smithmark Books.

Steinfels, P. (1979) *The Neoconservatives: The Men Who Are Changing American Politics*, New York: Touchstone.

Stuart, D. and Tow, W. (1990) *The Limits of Alliance: NATO Out-of-Area Problems Since 1949*, Baltimore, MD: Johns Hopkins University Press.

Williams, W. (1962) *The Tragedy of American Diplomacy*, New York: Delta Books.

Wolfers, A. (1962) *Discord and Collaboration: Essays in International Politics*, Baltimore, MD: Johns Hopkins University Press.

4 What's the big idea?

Models of global order in the post-Cold War era

Richard Crockatt

Introduction

Fundamental structural change is a relative rarity in international politics. Wars have tended to mark the boundaries of particular systems, though not every war produces systemic change. The peace of Westphalia at the end of the Thirty Years War is conventionally held to be the beginning of the modern nation-state system since in that settlement were enshrined the ideas of national sovereignty and balance of power, as well as the beginnings of international law, which have been guiding principles of international politics since the seventeenth century – or at least until the late twentieth century (Watson 1992: Ch 17). Among scholars and observers of international affairs there is widespread agreement that the closing years of the twentieth century saw another of those great divides, even if the transition to a new system or a 'new world order' is not yet complete. At the centre of such discussions is the waning significance of the nation-state as the basic unit and organizing principle of the international system. The argument is not that the nation-state is disappearing but that, in the telling words of one analysis, it is being 'hollowed out' (Buzan and Little 1999: 93). According to this view, globalization and its attendant processes have undermined the nation-state both from above and below. Internally many states are splitting into pieces on the basis of ethnic, religious and/or linguistic differences; externally, numerous inter- or multinational organizations, especially large companies, have garnered powers larger than those of many nation-states, and even governments of large states are subject to forces, especially trade and financial fluctuations, which severely restrict their independence. Numerous Non-Governmental Organizations (NGOs) in a wide variety of fields play important roles which involve routinely working across national borders. 'Interdependence' is frequently described as the operating principle of international politics. Even the term inter*national* politics is often held to be a misnomer, 'world politics' being considered more apt (Baylis and Smith 2005: 2–3).

Deciding exactly how significant recent changes are in the light of long-term processes is difficult, if not at this stage impossible. It is easy, for example, to overstate the degree of continuity in the nation-state system between the seventeenth and twentieth centuries; the 'system', in so far as it can be described as such, accommodated numerous radical changes, not least the French Revolution, the Napoleonic wars and the World Wars of the twentieth century. The changes we observe now in international politics may simply be comparable shifts within a basically continuous system based as ever on the nation-state. After all, there is good evidence that the national principle is thriving as never before. In 1945 the world contained approximately 50 nation-states, while by 2005 the number was over 190. It would be paradoxical indeed if we should identify this multiplication with the death of the nation-state. On the other hand, can we really describe the United States and, say, Nauru as belonging to the same political species? Admittedly, these are extremes (the population of Nauru is 12,000) but there is sufficient variation in size, power and influence among the world's nations to throw some doubt on the notion that one model of the nation-state can encompass the variety of existing states. There are, of course, rejoinders to this claim and no doubt counter-rejoinders. There is evidently no sure way of measuring the long-term significance of the processes associated with globalization. What can be said is that traditional, or Westphalian, ideas of the nation-state have come under severe challenge.

Such notions have been reinforced by the global changes associated with the end of the Cold War. Globalization has been underway for decades, but the end of the Cold War brought it to a new stage. Indeed, it could be argued that the end of the Cold War was in part a *result* of globalization and the failure of the Soviet bloc economies to respond to its challenges, not least the revolution in information technology. As some theorists would have it, the end of the Cold War brought globalization to fruition on the basis of global capitalism and the all-but-universal acceptance of the idea of democracy. Even those who do not accept the strong or triumphalist version of this argument – most obvious in Francis Fukuyama's theory of the 'end of history' (1989 and 1992) – recognize that the removal of the communist challenge hastened the development of new levels of transnational activity, especially in the economic field.

Viewed from this perspective, the collapse of the Berlin Wall was of greater significance for the world political system than were the terrorist attacks of 11 September 2001. Devastating as these attacks were, they did not produce structural change, which is to say a fundamental change in the relationship between the units of the international system. Indeed, the attacks could be said to have been in part a consequence of the structural change brought about by the end of the Cold War. During the Cold War, mutual deterrence and the associated policies of containment served to check the behaviour not only of the superpowers but of insurgent groups whose activities might have influenced relations between the superpowers. International terrorism, while certainly not a new phenomenon, thrived on the new elements of instability and even 'turbulence' in world politics attendant on the end of the Cold War (Rosenau 1990).

Given that these events and processes are so close to us, there is no sure way of fully gauging their scale or significance. One possible measure of change, however, is the degree of consciousness of change as manifested in public discussion. What is indisputable at the beginning of the twenty-first century is the multiplicity of *models* of global politics available. Big ideas are in vogue. The period since the end of the Cold War has been immensely fertile in models of the global political system. It seems generally accepted that what happened in 1989–91 was not just the collapse of communism or even of antagonism between two opposing systems of ideology and government but something more abstract – the end of a particular conception of world order. That the ideas on offer were so varied and in many cases contradictory suggests that there were deep-lying processes at work. Furthermore, the centrality of the United States in many of these models, if in some cases only by implication, indicates something important about both the United States (or US) and the global political system: namely, their integral character. The US is often a factor in many situations where it is not apparently directly involved. Even a non-decision on the part of the US can have as much impact as a decision by many another power. Hence, the routine use of the term 'hegemony' to describe the United States even by those who have no particular ideological or theoretical axe to grind.[1]

In what follows I propose to examine a range of American 'big ideas' about the shape of the post-Cold War world and America's place in it with three ends in view. First, as has been indicated, the proliferation of models of world politics and their variety is itself suggestive of upheaval. Characteristically, attempts to understand the contemporary world on a grand scale, especially those associated with theories of historical development, achieve the widest audiences at times of crisis or fundamental change (Crockatt 2002). More particularly, in such circumstances debate focuses on the very terms of analysis, throwing basic assumptions about international order into question. An examination of the range of ideas about global order offers clues to the nature and scale of changes in the material world.

Second, it is surely no accident that the bulk of the influential big ideas about world politics should have originated in the US and in one way or another seek to understand and justify particular conceptions of America's place in the international order – and this includes the writing of those such as Noam Chomsky who are most critical of the United States (Chomsky 1997). Evidently, the success of a big idea depends not merely on its content but also on its provenance. To put it another way, America's hegemony operates in the theoretical as well as the practical realm. Third, I wish to suggest that, varied as the models of world politics are, they have in common that they miss, or perhaps take for granted, an important dimension of the global reality: namely, the distinctive character and salience of American nationalism. I will suggest that the connections between American nationalism and globalizing tendencies in the world system provide important clues to the workings of the system and help to explain the continuous contestation of American power.

The significance of big ideas

In order to lay foundations for discussion, two further preliminaries are necessary. First, it is important to distinguish this inquiry from debate about whether US foreign policy has a grand design and, more particularly, whether the US found itself 'bereft of strategy' with the end of the Cold War (Bacevich 2002: 1–6). This question is certainly related to the issue of conceptions of global order but is not identical with it. While the difficulty of creating a grand strategy for the United States in the 1990s was connected to the apparent indeterminacy of the international order, it also had other domestic sources. The concern in this inquiry is not with American policy as such, but with the intellectual problem posed by the end of the Cold War. I focus on answers to the question: 'What kind of global system do we live in?' not 'What kind of policies does America need in the post-Cold War world?' Where policy-makers contributed to debate about the shape of the international system – George H. W. Bush's New World Order is one example – these are discussed alongside those of foreign policy intellectuals and commentators. Where appropriate I shall indicate points where big ideas are reflected in government policies and where government policies have stimulated the production of big ideas.

Second, it is worth asking why big ideas are necessary and what functions they perform. In the first place they are designed to make sense of often complex and confusing situations which may have little obvious structure and few obvious ordering principles; in that sense they have an *explanatory* function. Second, they operate as general plans of action which indicate how best to achieve desired goals. Such schemes are therefore dynamic and have a *strategic* function. Big ideas do not of themselves constitute strategies but are preconditions for them. Third, they serve as *justificatory* mechanisms for possible courses of action. Even if particular courses of action or policies are not envisaged by the authors, conclusions about such actions can be drawn by readers and policy-makers. Above all, in their justificatory role such schemes of thought help to relate ideas of international order to key national values. In short, big ideas set many of the key terms of public discourse about foreign policy and international affairs. Finally, big ideas can be highly revealing in ways their authors are not always aware of, in that they betray unspoken assumptions, prejudices and preconceptions. We can thus use them as windows on the times, clues to tensions and conflicts which are generally unstated.

In order to keep the following analysis within bounds it will be useful to establish some criteria for comparing the schemes. I shall discuss them according to the following four categories.

- Assumptions about the basic unit of global politics (nation-state, civilization, etc.).
- Assumptions about the basic driving force in world politics (national interest, force, economic processes, culture, etc.).

- Judgements about the direction of global change (towards order, disorder, integration, disintegration, etc.).
- Assessments of the role of the US in global politics (the position it adopts towards other powers, whether America's role is fundamentally benign, etc.).

Needless to say, it will not be possible to offer comprehensive analyses of the many schemes under review here. The aim, rather, is to provide a schematic overview in order to provide means of comparison.

Big ideas in the post-Cold War era

President George H. W. Bush's New World Order

Among the most visible and earliest attempts to re-envisage the post-Cold War system was President George H. W. Bush's 'New World Order', announced in a series of speeches between January and March 1991 during the war in the Persian Gulf in response to Iraq's invasion of Kuwait. The war against Iraq, he declared in his 1991 State of the Union address, was about more than Iraq; it was about 'a big idea, a new world order where diverse nations are drawn together in common cause to achieve universal aspirations of mankind: peace, security, freedom, and the rule of law' (Bush 1991). The Wilsonian echoes in this statement are clear, yet Bush's adherence to Wilsonianism or 'liberal internationalism' was less complete than the rhetoric would suggest. Wilson was prepared to sacrifice all to his goal of embedding the League of Nations in the Treaty of Versailles and in the end he lost virtually all he had striven for. Bush's commitments were more equivocal, more conditional. While there is no reason to doubt that, other things being equal, he would prefer internationalist solutions across the board, were they achievable, it is also clear that these would not be pursued at the cost of compromising American national interests. Taking full advantage of the unusual climate of amity, most obviously with respect to the Soviet Union, which followed the collapse of communism, Bush seized the opportunity to declare a vision for the whole world which was at once universalist and American. In the coalition against Saddam Hussein, which included the Soviet Union and many Arab countries – unthinkable during the Cold War – all the traditional polarities of American foreign policy seemed neatly resolved: idealism and realism, internationalism and nationalism, moral consistency and the pursuit of national interest. The sequel, however, demonstrated that neither the Bush administration nor any other in the post-Cold War period would elevate internationalism consistently above nationalism. While the rhetoric of the New World Order continued until the end of Bush's administration, once the immediate goal of removing Iraqi troops from Kuwait had been achieved, the ring went out of the phrase when it became apparent that the element of consensus which had secured this immediate goal would not be forthcoming for more complicated or more controversial ventures. Among these were the establishment of the no-fly zones in Iraq and the crises in Bosnia and Somalia. This is not to say that the 'New World Order' was merely a political ploy, though it was undoubtedly that, but rather to acknowledge that the structure of the international system was insufficiently developed to sustain such a vision. The New World Order, in short, was testimony in part to a kind of euphoria consequent upon the shifting of the tectonic plates of international politics; as in the aftermaths of all wars, the times encouraged a certain expansiveness even arbitrariness of vision. Visions of world government and perpetual peace are never so prevalent as at the ends of wars, and the end of the Cold War was no exception. Indeed, one important interpretation of the post-Cold War order argues that it is best understood as a kind of peace settlement (Clark 2001). In Bush's case there was the added incongruity of such a grandiose vision coming from a man who, as he admitted, 'lacked the vision thing'.

In terms of our criteria for analysing the various schemes, it is clear that for Bush the primary unit of international politics remained the nation-state but in an internationalizing context in which there was the possibility of an enhanced role for international organizations such as the UN. Second, the driving force of international politics took the largely traditional form of conflict between national interests which in principle could be moderated by the promotion of cooperation through international organizations. Third, the tendency of the system, in principle at least, was towards greater harmony which, finally, would depend greatly on the United States as an enabling and guiding hand. There was nothing novel about Bush's vision; it was a compound of several elements, each of which could be traced to the American past. In any case, revolutions are not to be expected from sitting presidents. This did not stop his vision from being attacked. Each aspect of it could be and was questioned, largely because in practice there was a good deal less consistency than his principles would seem to suggest and because the actions and policies associated with the New World Order seemed designed to serve American national interests rather than the global collective good. Concerns, for example, were expressed inside the US about whether American leadership would be forthcoming (Nye 1990). Doubts, and even deep cynicism, were voiced from abroad about the Bush administration's commitment to internationalism, a widespread conclusion being that the New World Order was little more than a vehicle for American national interests (*Guardian Studies* 1991). Nevertheless, Bush's vision reflected one set of potentialities within the system and to that extent it remained a model with considerable appeal since it embodied global, cooperative principles, whatever its manifestations in practice.

From 'The End of History' to 'Clash of Civilizations'

Francis Fukuyama's vision pre-dated that of Bush. His most important contribution, 'The End of History', was published in the spring of 1989, before the Cold War can be said definitively to have ended, indeed at a time when the Bush administration was still highly sceptical about the Gorbachev revolution in the Soviet Union. As late as May 1989, Secretary of Defense Dick Cheney expressed the view that Gorbachev's *perestroika* was likely to fail and that he was likely to be replaced by a hardliner (*Guardian* 1989: 26). If nothing else, Fukuyama can be credited with a certain amount of foresight at a time when few were prepared to commit themselves to judgements about the direction of the Soviet Union and the Cold War itself. Fukuyama's 'End of History' has frequently been characterized as a triumphalist hymn to the Western liberal democracy which relies on an idiosyncratic and faulty notion of history. His definition of 'history' as the conflict of great ideologies, compared with which mere 'events' are outside history and apparently of little account, was widely greeted by academics with derision or incomprehension, although among a wider public it achieved considerable success. Viewed more dispassionately, Fukuyama's work appears firmly in the mould of post-Cold War models which expressed an essentially American vision of the world disguised as an internationalist theory.

Applying our criteria to Francis Fukuyama's 'End of History' (appearing first in article form in 1989 and then as a book in 1992) one finds that he is not specific about the basic constituents of world politics since the currency he deals in is ideas rather than institutions. His central notion of the 'triumph of the West' offers a broad notion of geography but he goes on quickly to add 'and of the Western idea', indicating that his is a theory less of world politics than of world ideologies. This also indicates that for Fukuyama the driving force in world politics is in the realm of consciousness, and also that his judgement about the direction of change is broadly positive (despite his professed 'sadness' about the consequences of the end of history). By implication the United States is a positive force, though he has very little to say about the US itself, save for some pages on the Civil War. 'United States' does not appear in the index of *The End of History and the Last Man*.

In many ways this was a curious candidate for a bestseller since it scarcely touched base with political realities; yet it was considerably more influential than more pragmatic and apparently grounded arguments. Why should this have been so? In part it is to be explained by the centrality of the idea of liberal democracy. Although in Fukuyama's scheme the US does not claim direct responsibility for bringing about the end of history, the association of liberal democracy with 'the West' and the association of the United States with both is enough to make clear the assumption about American leadership in these transformations. Furthermore, the very generality of the thesis enables people with many and often different ends in view to appropriate Fukuyama's ideas for their own purposes. Fukuyama was a signatory of the 'Statement of Principles' of the 'Project for a New American Century' which can be taken as a credo of the right in America; it was couched in direct opposition to the policies of the Clinton administration. However, the Clinton administration's idea of 'democratic enlargement' differed, if anything, only in tone from the belief of the right that the triumph of democracy was a necessary and desirable goal of American policy. Clinton's National Security Adviser, Anthony Lake, criticised the idea of 'the end of history' in a key policy paper of 1993 but embraced the idea of the 'enlargement' of democracy (Lake 1993). Clinton's policies were broadly consonant with the Fukuyama thesis. In short, Fukuyama's analysis helped to set the American agenda for the 1990s and beyond of spreading democracy.

Samuel Huntington's 'Clash of Civilizations' (1993) matched Fukuyama's 'End of History' in its currency in intellectual circles and was also followed up by the publication of a full-length book some years later. His thesis that cultural conflict between 'civilizations' was replacing conflict over economics and ideology between nations as the prime motor of global politics had the merit, like Fukuyama's, that it was easily reducible to a few simple propositions, however complex the exposition. Again, like Fukuyama, Huntington introduced new terminology and concepts – or rather reintroduced old ones in a new context – which addressed the widespread awareness of the fundamental character of the changes brought about by the end of the Cold War. Once again, it turns out that what is presented as an internationalist theory is largely a projection of anxieties about the survival of American national interests and goals in a dangerous world.

In Huntington's scheme the unit of international politics is the 'civilization', the driving force behind global politics is cultural conflict rather than economics, national interest or ideology, and Huntington's judgement is that conflict is likely to increase. Huntington focuses rather more than Fukuyama on the United States, albeit that the US is still generally subsumed under 'the West'. On a number of occasions Huntington notes America's special role in Western civilization as a crusader for democracy. 'The central problem in the relations between the West and the rest', he writes, 'is the discordance between the West's – particularly America's – efforts to promote a universal Western culture and its declining ability to do so'. Again: 'The West, and especially the United States, which has always been a missionary nation, believe that the non-Western peoples should commit themselves to the Western values of democracy'. And again: 'the collapse of the Soviet Union generated in the West, particularly in the United States, the belief that a global democratic revolution was underway' (Huntington 1996: 183, 183–84, 193). The United States features in Huntington's analysis as carrying a special interest in and responsibility for the values associated with 'the West'. It is for this reason that Huntington pays special attention to 'challenges' to the United States' capacity to continue with this exemplary function, the main challenge being immigration and the attendant idea of 'multiculturalism' which he believes threatens America's national identity by questioning the identification of America with Western civilization and undermining the unity of the United States (Huntington 1996: 305–8). The centrality of this theme for Huntington is indicated by the fact that he has since devoted a new book to this question – *Who Are We?* (2004).

Neither Fukuyama nor Huntington conform to 'realist' notions of international relations, although Huntington is closer to this approach in his vision of the international arena as one of chronic conflict. In a sense his 'civilizations' play the role which nation-states play in realist analyses of international relations. However, to the extent that the thrust of his analysis is towards cultural conflict between entities called civilizations which are considerably larger than nations and more shadowy in structure and organization, Huntington leaves a question mark over the implications his analysis might have for policy, particularly American policy. Indeed, the nation-state is almost wholly absent in his analysis despite the pro forma statement at the beginning that 'nation states will remain the most powerful actors in world affairs' (Huntington 1993: 22). And yet, Huntington's analysis provided both an explanation for emerging forms of global disorder and a rationale for national opposition to its most extreme and apparently dangerous forms. Huntington offered no policy recommendations but made clear the nature of the enemy in today's disordered world: the cultures of 'Islam' and 'Confucianism'. Given the salience of conflict in the Middle East, the growing level of 'Islamic terrorism' in the 1990s and then the terrorist attacks of 11 September 2001, it is not surprising that most attention should have focused on this feature of Huntington's analysis. His suggestion that Islam had 'bloody borders' was especially provocative. That his idea of civilizational conflict had penetrated deep into the popular psyche was apparent in the lengths to which George W. Bush and members of his first administration went – without, it has to be said, convincing critics of their sincerity – explicitly to deny that the war on terror involved a clash of civilizations (National Security Council 2002). The links Huntington made between global disorder and American domestic disorder indicated that American identity as a nation was at stake in the era of the clash of civilizations. The national perspective was implicit in his scheme; it was merely that the emphasis had switched from politics to culture.

Realist ideas and the national interest

We look now at a pair of analyses which are very different from those of Huntington and Fukuyama. What they have in common is a 'realist' bias in that both see nation-states as the primary units of global politics. The first is Charles Krauthammer whose article 'The Unipolar Moment' has entered the vocabulary of many who may never have read his article. His was another example of a memorable phrase which conveys a great deal more than the bare information contained in it. His thesis was that the global system was now oriented round a single pole – the United States – and that this nation provided the necessary ordering principle for the whole system. Indeed, it was an opportunity to be seized by the United States because the US was the only nation capable of establishing and enforcing order. The gap in power between America and the others was so large as to be unique in modern history. He believed therefore – bearing in mind our criteria for comparing these analyses – that the nation-state was the essential constituent of world politics, that national interest was the main driving force, that order was possible and that the United States was in a position to provide it. This was a vision which was easier to operationalize than those of Huntington and Fukuyama; it was also susceptible to critiques on various grounds, the main ones being arrogance and excessive optimism. It did, however, make sense to many American observers of that snapshot of a moment following the collapse of the Soviet Union, the first Gulf War against Iraq, and the heady sense that past policies had been vindicated. Moreover, it was hard to argue with the fact of American primacy, whatever judgments might be made of it. Krauthammer updated his ideas more than a decade on, insisting that the essentials of his vision had received further confirmation by events. Indeed, he declares that after 9/11, 'the unipolar moment has become the unipolar era' (Krauthammer 2003: 64). Significantly, Krauthammer insists that the realism he is arguing for is to be clearly distinguished from the selfish pursuit by America of its own narrow self-interest. Given its preponderant power, he writes, America should be prepared 'to self-consciously and confidently deploy American power in pursuit of ... *global* ends [emphasis added]' (Krauthammer 2003: 60). Nevertheless, Krauthammer's version of realism is strikingly narrow, based as it is on traditional realist notions of power and global order. There is little acknowledgement of the changes which are associated with globalization. Indeed, to the extent that he considers alternative outlooks to the one he proposes, he does so in terms of an outdated polarity between 'liberal internationalism' and 'realism', as if these were the only options available. While acknowledging the power of the American nation in the current context, his scheme does not offer a means of understanding either American nationalism or its global context.

John Mearsheimer's article 'Back to the Future: Instability in Europe After the Cold War' presented a very different vision of the global future (Mearsheimer 1990). His theme was what he believed to be the inevitable onset of instability, especially in Europe, in the absence of the old balances and restraints supplied by the Cold War – above all, nuclear deterrence which gave the bipolar system its characteristic stability. Mearsheimer's is a classically realist, indeed Hobbesian, vision in which international politics is conceived of as a war of each against all. The demise of bipolarity could produce only multipolarity and the pursuit of self-interest in a multipolar system could only produce instability. Fear was the driver of international politics. It was for this reason that Mearsheimer hatched the seemingly absurd idea that managed nuclear proliferation was the best way to recreate a climate of healthy anxiety about the motives of other nations and hence produce stability. In a separate analysis of the prospects for the newly independent Ukraine and its neighbouring powers, Mearsheimer applied the general thesis to a particular case. Using our criteria, for Mearsheimer the constituents of world politics were nation-states, national interest was the driving force, instability was the ever-present threat and most likely future, and the United States, in so far as it could be a force for order, could best secure it by managing the process of balancing up the potential antagonists. Mearsheimer is more determinedly anachronistic than Krauthammer in his insistence on the overriding significance of military power to the virtual exclusion of all other considerations. The limits of realism are nowhere more vividly demonstrated and this is testimony perhaps to the struggle of theorists to catch up with the reality of changes on global politics. The tendency is to describe the new in terms of the old; in this case to project Cold War nuclear deterrence onto a very different post-Cold War screen.

These were not the only realist models on offer but they were the most striking. Others saw the resurgence of less dangerous forms of multipolarity engendered by the rise of balancing powers, most notably Japan and the European Union, although there was a recognition that the EU did not yet act like a sovereign state. (It is worth recalling that the late 1980s and early 1990s was a time of anxiety in America about being overtaken by Japan. One of a succession of such analyses was entitled *The Coming War with Japan*, Friedman and LeBard 1991.) Behind such visions were traditional ideas of the balance of power, although the precedents were by no means all favourable. The descent of the Balkans in the 1990s into a succession of wars stimulated recollections of the way the First World War began. Moreover, Yugoslavia was a good example of a new and disturbing phenomenon – the disintegration of a nation-state, bringing in its train the threat of the spread of more general instability. Realist theories struggled to make sense of such cases because the precondition for the realist approach – the presence of legitimate governments presiding over sovereign states within clear borders – seemed not to exist.

It was some such sort of recognition no doubt which led the Clinton administration to adopt, if only as a loose framework, a model of global politics which its author, Madeleine Albright, called 'the four food groups'. It was, she said, her 'way of explaining the world in the absence of Cold War divisions'. The first group 'consisted of those who were full members of the international system' and they had governments, institutions and legal systems which functioned in ways which secured material well-being, domestic stability and protection of rights. The second group contained those nations, predominantly of the former communist bloc, which were making the transition to democracy and were essentially in the business of nation-building. The third group comprised 'countries with weak or nonexistent governments, often held back by poverty or mired in conflict', and the fourth 'was represented by governments that, for one reason or another, were hostile to the rules of the international system and sought to subvert or circumvent them'. These were, in the common parlance of the time (though Albright does not herself use the term), 'rogue states', of which Iraq and North Korea were prime examples. American policy towards the groups was 'to forge the strongest possible ties with the first', 'help the second group succeed', 'aid those in the third group who were most willing to help themselves' and 'strive to protect ourselves by reforming, isolating, or defeating those in the fourth group' (Albright 2003: 139–40).

It is perhaps characteristic of the practitioner to develop a model which serves directly in the formulation of policy. What is notable about this scheme is its openness to the untidiness of reality. While prescriptive in its own way, in the sense that there are clear judgements being made about the members of the various groups, it does acknowledge that the nation-state is a complex institution which takes a variety of forms. Being realistic here involves a sacrifice of the theoretical rigour of 'realism'. This scheme also remains open to the possibility that there are wider processes at work in the international system to which some nations are more subject than others. Among the most important of these are economic. Some nations and some governments have a good measure of control, even if not total, over the vital factors affecting their economic well-being; others are the playthings of the market and the more powerful players in it. For strong countries, inter-dependence can be a positive; for the weak it is often a negative. Albright's model allows for such conclusions to be drawn and in doing so it allows space for discussion of globalization and its uneven effects. If we apply our criteria, then we can say that for Albright the basic units of world politics remain nation-states but there are some qualifications and discriminations being made; nation-states are diverse in character and are affected differentially by global processes. The driving force behind global politics in this model is only in part national interest; there are cross-cutting pressures. As a practi-tioner with a reputation to defend, one would expect Albright to see the direction of world politics in a broadly positive light, not least because (moving to the last of our criteria) so much depends on the stance taken by the United States. America's influence, on Albright's reading, is predomi-nantly benign; America's motives and policies rise above self-interest to encompass the well-being of the larger international community.

Ideas of globalization and the American empire

The unspoken term in the above scheme is 'globalization' and indeed this is the next model of global politics which we need to examine. The most com-mon form of the argument says that the number and scale of transactions across the globe, whether in trade, finance, business operations (including manufacturing), information of all types and by all means, is now such as to have generated a qualitative change in the overall character of global rela-tions. Marshall McLuhan's 'global village' is now a reality; national bound-aries mean less and less, rendering the distinction between domestic and foreign policy of declining significance. Nation-states still exert a measure of influence; they are still the primary location for the bulk of the institutions which govern our day-to-day lives. However, they have diminished control over many of the activities inside their borders and are beholden to numerous transnational organizations and processes which scorn national borders (Scholte 2000; Giddens 1999).

There are many interpretations of this process, from fervent welcome for the extension of market capitalism to all corners of the globe to deep fears about its effects on those who for one reason or another are unable to participate as full members of global society or who see global society and do not want to be members of it. Anxieties about the excessive power of multinational companies, the homogenization of cultures, the marginalization of minorities, and many other features of what one sociologist has called 'the runaway world' abound. Some speak of 'uneven globalization', others of irreconcilable conflict between 'jihad' (using the word as a short-hand for various types of religious and political fundamentalism) and 'McWorld' (Giddens 1999; Holm and Sorenson 1995; Barber 2001).

What is clear in the many and diverse writings on this subject is that the units of international politics are much more difficult to specify because they are associated with processes and transnational bodies rather than with nation-states, identifiable cultures or regional groupings. We seem to be in a condition in which the traditional levers of power have no control. The internet symbolises the radical diffusion of power which is characteristic of globalization. There are some active agents but they are shifting and only loosely subject to controls. If the constituents of global politics are not clear, the chief driving force is perhaps more so – economic processes, the market. Judgements about direction are extremely diverse, as are ideas about America's role. For some, the whole process seems to be driven by the US – Americanization writ large – but from another point of view it is only incidentally a matter of government policy or national interest, more an outgrowth of the dynamism of the American economy and its culture. Even here qualifications have to be made since globalization has not been in the past and is not now a uniquely American process but has drivers in many other parts of the globe (Nye 2002: 77–81).

Given the indeterminate nature of these processes it is not surprising to find some analysts developing more or less complex syntheses which seek to integrate the great variety of phenomena discussed above, and others besides. John Gaddis, a leading historian of the Cold War who has also written a great deal about international affairs since then, sees an emerging competition between forces of integration and disintegration. He offers the arresting thought that, broadly speaking, the desire for satisfaction of intangible desires, such as freedom, tends to produce fragmentation in world politics while the satisfaction of material needs tends to produce integration. His preferred solution is for strategies which will seek to balance the forces of integration and disintegration and to this end he offers the US Constitution as a model: 'for what is our own Constitution if not the most elegant political text ever composed on how to balance the forces of integration against those of disintegration?' It is a neat solution, if overly abstract and schematic. Is it the case, for example, that attempts to satisfy material needs necessarily tend to produce integration? There are surely many situations in which pursuit of economic advantage will generate conflict. Moreover, this analysis reveals the immense difficulty of linking national interests – his article begins with a discussion of these – with abstract processes; it is as if two different vocabularies of international relations are in collision with each other. It is thus not easy to analyse Gaddis's article according to the criteria set out above. His unit of analysis shifts according to the subject under discussion; the world may be moving towards order or disorder, integration or disintegration; his vision is neither pessimistic nor optimistic but carefully hedges bets; finally, as far as America's place in this world is concerned, discussion is restricted to suggestions that the US must continue to adhere to its traditional goal of seeking a balance of power.

It may be that the indeterminacy of Gaddis's analysis is unavoidable because of the nature of the reality being analysed. However, Joseph Nye offers a different take on similar sorts of issues. After considering the merits of several schemes – multipolarity, three economic blocs, unipolar hegemony and multilevel interdependence – he concludes that 'the world order after the Cold War is sui generic … power is becoming more multidimensional, structures more complex and states themselves more permeable' (Nye 1992). Nye offers a developmental model which links the past with the future and a conception of national interest with globalization, unilateralism with multilateralism. In short, in terms of our criteria, Nye retains the nation-state as the primary unit of analysis while acknowledging the significance of new transnational institutions; he sees a complex of forces driving international relations forward, including traditional notions of national interest and globalization; he is cautiously optimistic about the direction of global change, concluding that 'in short, the new world order has begun'; his conception of America's role rests on the judgement that 'in realist terms the United States will remain the world's largest power well into the next century'. For this reason the US cannot 'leave the task of world order to the United Nations', although it must seek multilateral solutions wherever appropriate. In sum the US must steer a 'middle course between bearing too much and too little of the international burden' (Nye 1992: 95–6).

The final category of analysis to be considered here is the vogue for the idea of American empire, a concept which has been used to characterize not only American foreign policy but also the international order. The starting point for such analyses is the statement, which has assumed the status of a cliché, that 'the United States dominates the world as no state has' (Ikenberry 2004: 609). This is not a new theme but in the past has generally taken the form of critiques from the left, most notably in the writings of William Appleman Williams (Williams 1969; 1972). Such critiques still feature in the recent debate. Indeed, Andrew Bacevich's *American Empire* (2002) is in some respects an updated version of Williams' argument. However, there is a new edge to the debate in that the term 'empire' has been adopted, indeed embraced, by some analysts on the right. No longer arguing defensively that America is a nation with anti-imperial origins and in its growth as a republic anything but an empire, some conservatives point to the need for a *pax americana* to secure global order. 'Empires have unfairly got a bad name', writes Deepak Lal, which is 'particularly unfortunate, as the world needs an American *pax* to provide both global peace and security' (Lal 2003: 45). British historian Niall Ferguson echoes these conclusions and adds the comment that America is in 'imperial denial', to the detriment of the global order (Ferguson 2004: 294). In the debate as a whole, there is no longer a sense that the word 'empire' is being employed as a metaphor or a debating tool but rather as a scientific, descriptive term. America really *is* an empire – not just *like* an empire.[2]

Such views are much disputed on the grounds that a large element of distortion is required to fit the United States into the mould of empires such as those of Greece, Rome and Britain. James Chace, a firm (though critical) advocate of the view that America is now an empire, asks

> who would now deny that America is an imperial power? The American response to the attack on the World Trade Center and the Pentagon was swift and merciless. Thousands of troops swept down upon Afghanistan in an effort to capture or kill the terrorists and their protectors.
>
> (Chace 2003: 119)

However, in the aftermath of 9/11 and in the many other examples of American interventions in the past 40 years there are visible limits, not merely to American power itself but on the willingness to deploy that power and these are in part self-imposed. From Vietnam through the many interventions in the following years the US held back from the use of all-out military force. Indeed, insistence of Lyndon Johnson on fighting a limited war in Vietnam is commonly given by those on the political right as a reason for America's failure to win the war. Constraints on American action are supplied by domestic opinion, by America's native ideology of anti-imperialism and anti-colonialism, by global opinion, by anxiety about triggering war with another major power, and by accepted norms of international behaviour – indeed by the total context in which American power is deployed. America may possess the material might necessary to be an empire but, as Martin Walker writes, 'the United States does not rule, and it shrinks from mastery' (Walker 2003: 135). In fact, arguably it was more clearly an imperial power during the Cold War when its hold over allies and clients was firmer because of the need to meet the challenge of the common enemy of Communism. Furthermore, as one specialist in ancient empires notes, 'Athenians, Romans, Ottomans, and the British wanted land, colonies, treasure, and grabbed all they could get when they could. The United States hasn't annexed anyone's soil since the Spanish-American War' (Hanson 2003: 147). There is, needless to say, the rejoinder to this argument that, whatever the case after 1898, the territorial growth of the US during the nineteenth century was a story of classic imperialist land-grabbing (Cox 2004: 598–99).

There is no easy resolution to this debate. At worst, it becomes an empty exercise in definitional gymnastics; at best, it has stimulated important reflections about the nature of American power and its role in the global system. There surely is, however, a qualitative difference between the exertion of Greek, Roman or British imperial power in an age of dynastic states and an American hegemony in an age of democratic norms and institutions. The difference is in the form and level of political control as well as in the mind-set and ideology. To make the United States qualify as an empire we have, as Ikenberry points out, to loosen the definition of 'empire' from meaning direct political control to 'a hierarchical system of political relationships in which the most powerful state exercises decisive influence' (Ikenberry 2004: 619). We can call America a 'liberal empire' if we want to; but we still need the qualifier to make America fit into the frame of empire.

The US as a Westphalian state in a post-Westphalian system

Where do we go from here? Let us return to our criteria for understanding models of world order and set these against the salient events and processes of the post-Cold War period. What, then, can we take as the basic unit of international politics? In a theoretical sense and for many practical purposes nation-states remain the primary constituents of the world political system, if only because national governments are the responsible bodies to which most of the world's peoples are directly subject and to which they owe primary allegiance. Citizenship, which is at once political, legal, social and psychological, defines the relationship of individuals to governments. In most cases, furthermore, the governments of nation-states remain the chief vehicles for the representation of the interests of citizens at levels beyond that of the nation-state. For all the qualifications that can be made, and will be made below, to this mundane truth of international relations, there is no escaping its force.

Nevertheless, such a conclusion is misleading to the extent that it assumes that nation-states are the only constituents of consequence in the global political system. In international relations theory, 'pluralists' or 'neoliberal institutionalists' have for several decades noted the growing significance of non-state actors and transnational processes in global politics. 'We can imagine a world', wrote two of pluralism's leading proponents in the late 1970s, 'in which actors other than states participate directly in world politics, in which a clear hierarchy of issues does not exist, and in which force is an ineffective instrument of policy' (Keohane and Nye 1977: 24). The growing intensity of globalization has surely confirmed the essential insight of the pluralists regarding the increasing power and significance of non-state actors, whether multinational companies, bodies such as the IMF, or Non-Governmental Organizations and international 'regimes'. Moreover, there is growing recognition that the variety of types of nation-state undermines the notion that they are all essentially comparable with each other. Nation-states may all seek to maximize their power and effectiveness as international actors but they do so in many different ways and with widely differing results. Albright's 'four feeding groups' and the adoption of terminology such as 'failed states' and 'rogue states' indicates that it is practitioners as much as theorists who find it useful to make distinctions among nation-states. Robert Cooper, a British author who plays both roles, has introduced a tripartite distinction between 'pre-modern states' which are the product of post-imperial chaos and lack the attributes of genuine sovereignty and monopoly control of force within their borders; 'modern states', which pursue the classical realist goals of self-interest and tend to rely ultimately on the use of force as the guarantor of their security; and 'post-modern states' which operate in a cooperative environment where the boundary between internal and external affairs has broken down and groupings of states mutually agree to 'interfere' in each others' affairs (Cooper 2003: 16–18, 21–2, 26ff.). In effect, Cooper is talking about the coexistence of three state *systems* which promote and require different types of state behaviour. In the category of pre-modern states Cooper places Somalia, Afghanistan and Liberia. The United States, he suggests, is a characteristically modern state and the European Union a good example of the post-modern. In short, in trying to establish the basic unit of world politics it is apparent that the nation-state is an important but not exclusive constituent and also that the nation-state itself takes diverse forms.

Part of the usefulness of Cooper's model lies in his acknowledgement of the reality that there is no single world system of politics but rather the coexistence of several. It is evident also – moving to the second of our criteria for discussing ideas of world order – that the driving forces in world politics remain highly variegated. Contrary to the expectations of the pluralist theorists, the use of force has not been rendered 'ineffective' nor has it been displaced by the advent of new transnational actors and processes. Nevertheless, it could certainly be argued that force has changed its form in a number of ways in the past three decades. Terrorism and other forms of irregular fighting have become major weapons of insurgent groups, necessitating the development on the part of 'modern' nations such as the United States of new techniques of counter-terrorism and more flexible military methods, including the development of rapidly deployable mobile forces and increasing accuracy in airpower through the introduction of new technologies – everything that is implied by the phrase 'the revolution in military affairs (RMA)' which became current in the 1990s (Cohen 1996). The conclusion must be that the driving forces in world politics are multiple and complex; there can be no single driver such as cultural conflict or the working out of an idea of liberal democracy or the economic processes associated with globalization.

For this reason, looking at the third criterion for judging ideas of global order, there can be no certainty about the direction of change in the global system. Tendencies towards order and disorder, integration and disintegration, as Gaddis, Nye and others have observed, vie with each other. However, what can be said is that the global system does not exhibit either extreme orderliness or extreme disorderliness; the absence of global government does not mean that there is an absence of governance. Theorists posit that order is in part a property of the particular distribution of power in the system, whether it be some form of multipolarity, bipolarity, unipolarity, or even, according to one analyst, 'apolarity' (Ferguson 2004: 296–98). Different systems display varied patterns of balancing, according both to the structure of the overall system and the character of the units in the system. What can we say about the structure and balancing mechanisms of the current global system? Here we link consideration of the tendency of the system with our fourth criterion for assessing ideas of global order – the role of the United States. Indeed, a possibility worth pursuing is that the US can be seen as a link to all the other criteria: i.e. the units of the system, the driving force and the tendency of the system.

We can start with the observation that the US is both the largest and strongest nation-state in the system and also the chief agent of globalization which is purportedly leading to the demise of the nation-state. In a hybrid system in which the historic units of the system – nation-states – are being modified by processes of globalization, the United States plays a complex and often contradictory role. As the prime agent of globalization through the size of its economy and its global reach, the US has a stake in numerous multi-lateral organizations and in the universalization of certain rules and proce-dures, above all in the economic field. In this field it has been an advocate of breaking down barriers between nations in order to facilitate flows of goods, capital and information. In a globalizing world, furthermore, there are numerous other fields – environmental, legal, military and so on – in which there is pressure for internationally agreed protocols. There are limits, how-ever, to how far the US is prepared to go in the direction of cooperative multilateralism and these limits are defined in part by its historic national-ism. It is not simply the disparity in size and influence between the US and other nations but that America's national traditions disincline it to enter arrangements which might unduly compromise its sovereignty.

For all the attention given to the foreign policy of the United States, this feature of its history and current policy has been underestimated. Even where the domestic sources of American nationalism have been explored (Lind 1996; Lieven 2004), its implications for the structure of international politics have not been adequately assessed. Putting it perhaps over-schematically, America presents the paradox of a Westphalian state *par excellence* in a system which in important respects is post-Westphalian. The United States' origins and growth have inclined it to become the epitome of the Westphalian nation-state. There is no scope here for a full discussion of American nation-alism, far less its long and complex history (Greenfeld 1992: Ch. 5; Lind 1996; Lieven 2004). What can be said, as far as America's relations with the outside world are concerned, is that American nationalism historically is a compound of a missionary ideology of Americanism and dynamic economic growth and expansionism (Crockatt 2003: Ch. 1–2). At the heart of this history and also its current significance lies the theme of independence. The intensity of the American devotion to this principle is generally illustrated by reference to the Declaration of Independence but in some respects more telling is an arresting phrase in the text of the Treaty of Alliance with France (1778). Here, at the heart of a document in which the United States tied itself to another power, carrying the risk of compromising its new-won sovereignty, lay the assertion that 'the essential and direct End of the present defensive alliance is to maintain effectually the liberty, Sovereignty, and independence absolute and unlimited of the said united states [sic]' (Paterson and Merrill 2000: 38). America's will to independence – independence *absolute* – is visible not only in its separate declarations but also in the manner in which it enters into arrangements with others. The Treaty with France is the signal example. It is echoed in Woodrow Wilson's entry into the First World War as an 'associated' not an 'allied' power. It takes different forms in the period of American global power because now the US is the director and leader of the treaties and coalitions it enters. It has greater freedom of choice, has the power to set the terms and conditions under which it participates, and to a degree can dictate terms to others. The 'coalitions' formed for the wars in Afghanistan and Iraq illustrate the possibilities but also the limits of these powers: the US could ensure that the coalitions fought these wars on American terms but could not, in the case of Iraq, dictate who would become members of the coalitions. The determining factor in all cases was the maintenance of America's room to move, its 'independence'. As President Bush affirmed in the approach to the Iraq war, 'we will not seek a permission slip for our own security'. In short, independence is among the prime values in American foreign policy.

Moreover, the context in which this is now taking place is radically different from the setting in which the Westphalian system was established. American nationalism has always been a factor in American foreign policy, although its intensity has waxed and waned in response to perceived external threats. It has historically been compatible, as we have seen, with multilateralism. It continues to be a factor as the international system undergoes fundamental changes in the direction of interdependence, globalization and efforts to institutionalize cooperation in a range of fields from economics, trade, environmental protection, justice, aid and many others. As has been observed by Menzies Campbell, British Liberal Democrat party spokesman on foreign affairs, 'for America, NATO and the other alliances are a matter of choice; for Europe and the UK, multilateralism remains a necessity'. 'We should be under no illusion', he added, 'as to the force of American pragmatism and the determined pursuit of its national interest' (Campbell 2004: 29).

Conclusion

These points have a bearing on the issue of American unilateralism in the policies of the Bush administration. In the light of the framework developed here, discussion of American unilateralism has been conducted on far too narrow a basis. What is at issue is not only a policy choice or a party programme or even a presidential philosophy but a political culture with deep historical roots. George W. Bush has exploited to the full the potentialities of both the American tradition and the international context in which he found himself. Amidst the shock of 9/11 the United States was able to draw on a deep vein of historical tradition which linked the moral and the national with the security challenge. The times offer scope for the US to command greater sovereignty than other nations, to be less beholden to other nations and international institutions, more able to maintain freedom of action – in a word, more *independent*. The word connects present policies and behaviour with a core idea which is as old as the nation itself. Whatever the reigning orthodoxy or slogan, at whatever time in its history, whether it be non-entanglement, isolationism, manifest destiny, making the world safe for democracy or ensuring the survival of liberty, the notion of independence has never been far from the surface.

Of course, all nations cultivate nationalism and also independence to one degree or other. The difference is that America's nationalism generally has greater consequences. America's peculiar privilege is old-fashioned nationalism at a time when most other nations cannot afford it or reserve it for football matches and the Olympic games. For all its role as the arch-globalizer, for all its commitment to what a nineteenth-century advocate of manifest destiny called the 'expansive future' (Paterson and Merrill 2000: 250), the United States at the beginning of the third millennium is also committed to a future based on its own past. And there are few nations with a longer or more continuous past. This, indeed, is one of the key ingredients of American nationalism. This is nowhere more visible than in George W. Bush's second inaugural address, although the point could be substantiated with reference to such speeches by virtually any American president.

> From the day of our Founding we have proclaimed that every man and woman on this earth has rights, and dignity, and matchless value, because they bear the image of the Maker of Heaven and earth. Across the generations we have proclaimed the imperative of self-government, because no one is fit to be a master, and no one deserves to be a slave. Advancing these ideals is the mission that created our Nation. It is the honorable achievement of our fathers. Now it is the urgent requirement of our nation's security, and the calling of our time.
>
> (Bush 2005)

The encounter between an intensified American nationalism and a world moving in the direction of interdependence is ripe for conflict and dissension. This is so in part because the aspirations of American nationalism, particularly as expressed by the administration of George W. Bush, are so extensive. Indeed, they are couched as universals. The biggest and most potent idea among the many big ideas which have been spawned since the end of the Cold

War is the idea of the American nation and its peculiar destiny. Americans need to understand this as well as others. They will then understand why American power is so fiercely contested.

Notes

1 'Hegemony' was a term adopted by Marxist analysts, following Gramsci, but soon became familiar among international relations theorists in the form of 'hegemonic stability theory'. It is now routinely used by empirical scholars as well as theorists to describe the United States in the contemporary international system. See, for example, Foot, MacFarlane and Mastanduno (2003). A comparable evolution has been followed by 'empire'. This is discussed below.
2 There is now a large body of literature on American empire. A useful guide to the range of issues involved is a *Review of International Studies* Forum with contributions by Michael Cox, G. John Ikenberry and Michael Mann (2004).

References

Albright, M. (2003) *Madam Secretary: A Memoir*, New York: Macmillan.
Bacevich, A.J. (2002) *American Empire: The Realities and Consequences of U.S. Diplomacy*, Cambridge, MA: Harvard University Press.
Barber, B.R. (2001) *Jihad v McWorld: Terrorism's Challenge to Democracy*, New York: Ballantine Books.
Baylis, J. and Smith, S. (eds) (2005) *The Globalization of World Politics: An Introduction to World Politics*, 3rd edn, Oxford: Oxford University Press.
Bush, G.H.W. (1991) State of the Union Address, 29 January 1991. Online at http://bushlibrary.tamu.edu/research/papers/
Bush, George W. Second Inaugural Address, 20 January 2005. Online at http://whitehouse.gov
Buzan, B. and Little, R. (1999) 'Beyond Westphalia? Capitalism after the "Fall"' *Review of International Studies*, 25, December, 93.
Campbell, M. (2004) *Independent on Sunday*, 7 November 2004, p. 29.
Chace, J. (2003) 'In Search of Absolute Security', in A.J. Bacevich, *The Imperial Tense: Prospects and Problems of American Empire*, Chicago, IL: Ivan R. Dee, pp.119–33 (first published 2002 in *World Policy Journal*).
Chomsky, N. (1997) *World Orders Old and New*, London: Pluto Press.
Clark, I. (2001) *The Post-Cold War Order: The Spoils of Peace*, Oxford: Oxford University Press.
Cohen, E. (1996) 'A Revolution in Warfare', *Foreign Affairs*, 75 (2) March/April: 37–54.
Cooper, R. (2003) *The Breaking of Nations: Order and Chaos in the Twenty-First Century*, London: Atlantic Books.
Cox, M. (2004) 'Empire, Imperialism and the Bush Doctrine', *Review of International Studies*, 30 (4): 585–608.
Crockatt, R. (2002) 'Challenge and Response: Arnold Toynbee, The United States and the Cold War', in D. Carter and R. Clifton (eds), *War and Cold War In American Foreign Policy, 1942-1962*, Houndmills: Palgrave, pp. 108–30.

Crockatt, R. (2003) *America Embattled: September 11, Anti-Americanism and the Global Order*, London: Routledge.

Ferguson, N. (2004) *Colossus: The Price of America's Empire*, London: Allen Lane, Penguin Books.

Foot, R., MacFarlane, S. and Mastanduno, M. (eds) (2003) *US Hegemony and International Organizations*, Oxford: Oxford University Press.

Friedman, G. and LeBard, M. (1991) *The Coming War with Japan*, New York: St Martin's Press.

Fukuyama, F. (1989) 'The End of History', *National Interest*, Summer, 3–18.

Fukuyama, F. (1992) *The End of History and the Last Man*, London: Hamish Hamilton.

Giddens, A. (1999) *Runaway World: How Globalisation is Reshaping Our Lives*, London: Profile Books.

Greenfeld, L. (1992) *Nationalism: Five Roads to Modernity*, Cambridge, MA: Harvard University Press.

Guardian (1989) May 3, p. 26.

Guardian Studies (1991) *New World Order?: Seven Writers in Search of an Ideal*, London.

Hanson, V.D. (2003) 'What Empire?' in A.J. Bacevich, *The Imperial Tense: Prospects and Problems of American Empire*, Chicago, IL: Ivan R. Dee, pp. 146–55.

Holm, H.-H. and Sorensen, G. (eds) (1995) *Whose World Order?: Uneven Globalisation and the End of the Cold War*, Boulder: Westview Press.

Huntington, S.P. (1993) 'The Clash of Civilizations', *Foreign Affairs*, 72 (3) Summer: 22–49.

Huntington, S.P. (1996) *The Clash of Civilizations and the Remaking of World Order*, New York: Simon and Schuster.

Huntington, S.P. (2004) *Who Are We? America's Great Debate*, New York: Free Press.

Ikenberry, G.J. (2004) 'Liberalism and Empire: Logics of Order in the American Unipolar Age', *Review of International Studies*, 30 (4): 609–30.

Keohane, R. and Nye, J.S. (1977) *Power and Interdependence: World Politics in Transition*, Boston, MA: Little Brown.

Krauthammer, C. (2003) 'The Unipolar Era', in Andrew J. Bacevich, *The Imperial Tense: Prospects and Problems of American Empire*, Chicago, IL: Ivan R. Dee, pp. 47–65 (first published in *The National Interest*, Winter 2003).

Lake, A. (1993) 'Remarks to Johns Hopkins School of Advanced International Studies', United States Information Service, US Embassy, London, 22 September, 22 pp.

Lal, D. (2003) 'In Defense of Empires', in A.J. Bacevich, *The Imperial Tense: Prospects and Problems of American Empire*, Chicago, IL: Ivan R. Dee, pp. 29–46 (first published 2002).

Lieven, A. (2004) *America Right or Wrong: An Anatomy of American Nationalism*, London: Harper Collins.

Lind, M. (1996) *The Next American Nation: The New Nationalism and the Fourth American Revolution*, New York: Free Press.

Mann, M. (2004) 'The First Failed Empire of the 21st Century', *Review of International Studies*, 30 (4): 631–53.

Mearsheimer, J. (1990) 'Back to the Future: Instability After the Cold War', *International Security*, 15 (2): 191–222.

National Security Council (2002) 'Security Strategy of the United States', September. Online at http://www.whitehouse.gov/nsc/

Nye, J.S. (1990) *Bound To Lead: The Changing Nature of American Power*, New York: Basic Books.

Nye, J.S. (1992) 'What New World Order?', *Foreign Affairs*, 71 (2) Spring: 83–96.

Nye, J.S. (2002) *The Paradox of American Power: Why the World's Only Superpower Can't Go it Alone*, New York: Oxford University Press.

Paterson, T.G. and Merrill, D. (eds) (2000) *Major Problems in American Foreign Relations*, Vol. 1, Boston, MA: Houghton Mifflin.

Rosenau, J.N. (1990) *Turbulence in World Politics: A Theory of Change and Continuity*, Hemel Hempstead: Harvester/Wheatsheaf.

Scholte, J.A. (2000) *Globalization: A Critical Introduction*, Basingstoke: Palgrave.

Walker, M. (2003) 'An Empire Unlike Any Other', in Andrew J. Bacevich, *The Imperial Tense: Prospects and Problems of American Empire*, Chicago, IL: Ivan R. Dee, pp. 134–45.

Watson, A. (1992) *The Evolution of International Society: A Comparative Historical Analysis*, London: Routledge.

Williams, W.A. (1969) *The Roots of American Empire: A Study of the Growth and Shaping of Social Consciousness in a Marketplace Society*, New York: Random House.

Williams, W.A. (1972) *The Tragedy of American Diplomacy*, New York: Dell (first published 1959).

Part II

The European discontent: a new anti-Americanism?

5 Anti-Americanism in Europe

What's new? An appraisal and personal account

Rob Kroes

Introduction

'Nous sommes tous américains.' We are all Americans. Such was the rallying cry of the French newspaper *Le Monde*'s editor-in-chief, Jean-Marie Colombani, published two days after the terrorist attack against symbols of America's power. He went on to say: 'We are all New Yorkers, as surely as John Kennedy declared himself, in 1962 in Berlin, to be a Berliner.' If that was one historical resonance that Colombani himself called forth for his readers, there is an even older use of this rhetorical call to solidarity that may come to mind. It is Jefferson's call for unity after America's first taste of two-party strife. Leading opposition forces to victory in the presidential election of 1800, he assured Americans that 'We are all Federalists, we are all Republicans', urging his audience to rise above the differences that many at the time feared might divide the young nation against itself. There would clearly be no need for such a ringing rhetorical call if there were not at the same time an acute sense of difference and division. Similarly in the case of Colombani's timely expression of solidarity with an ally singled out for vengeful attack, solely because it, more than any of its allies, had come to represent the global challenge posed by a shared Western way of life. An attack against America was therefore an attack against common values held dear by all who live by standards of democracy and the type of open society that it implies. But, as in Jefferson's case, the rhetorical urgency of the call for solidarity suggests a sense of difference and divisions now to be transcended, or at least temporarily to be shunted aside. This sense of difference had always been there during the years of the Cold War, but was contained by the threat of a common enemy. With the end of the Cold War, though, the need for a reorientation of strategic thinking was felt on both sides of the Atlantic that, if anything, only sharpened differences and divisions.

The end of the Cold War

Undeniably, many changes that occurred during the 1990s are direct consequences of the end of the Cold War. To mention just a few of the obvious examples, the expansion of the European Union and of NATO into areas under the sway of the Soviet Union during the Cold War are attempts at reconfiguring the world that were clearly occasioned by the Soviet Union's collapse. Similarly, the Balkan wars of the 1990s or Saddam Hussein's invasion of Kuwait would probably not have occurred in the absence of the breakdown of an international balance of power and ideology and of patterns of clientism, typical of the Cold War world. Most dramatically, perhaps, transatlantic tensions, never absent during the Cold War but contained by the imperative of a joint defence against the Soviet bloc, now appear as clashing visions of the post-Cold War new world order. The words – 'New World Order' – were coined by George H.W. Bush, at the time of the first Gulf war, when briefly it seemed as if the framework of international institutions, centring on the United Nations (UN), could finally come into its own. But the world has moved a long way away from those early hopes and visions. And we may well be asking ourselves the question whether the terrorist attack on symbols of American power on 11 September 2001, may not have been a greater sea change than the end of the Cold War. Or was it merely the catalyst that led America to implement a foreign policy approach that had been in the making since the early 1990s? If so, and it seems to be likely, America's current foreign policy is clearly a response to its unique position of the one hegemon in a unipolar world, intent on safeguarding that position. A group of neoconservative foreign policy analysts took their cue from a White Paper produced in 1992 at the behest of William Cheney, then Secretary of Defense, entitled 'The New American Century'. In 1997, they coalesced around the Project for a New American Century and founded a think-tank under that name. Their thinking hardened around a view of American foreign policy, centring on military strength. Now, in the current George W. Bush administration, they are in a position to implement their views. Parallel to this gestation of a foreign policy view, in American society throughout the 1990s national rituals such as the Super Bowl increasingly blended the appeal of mass spectator sports with displays of military prowess and martial vigour.[1] It may herald a militarization of the public spirit, propagated through the mass media. To some it is eerily reminiscent of earlier such public stagings, as at the time of the 1936 Olympics in Nazi Germany. It may have readied the American public's mind for the later curtailment of democratic rights through the Patriot Act and the emergence of a national security state at the hands of the current George W. Bush administration. In a recent article, American philosopher Richard Rorty (2004) warned Europeans that institutional changes made in the name of the war on terrorism could bring about the end of the rule of law in both the United States (US) and Europe. Remarkably, he forgot to mention that many of these changes had already come to the US, without much public debate or resistance.[2]

Much as the entire world may have changed in the wake of the Cold War, my focus shall be on the particular ways these changes have affected Europe and the US, internally as well as in their transatlantic relation. An important aspect is the way Europeans and Americans have begun to redefine each other, in response to a creeping alienation that has affected public opinion and public discourse on both sides of the Atlantic. If increasingly each side appears to the other as 'Other', as more alien than at any point during the Cold War, the construction of such a perspective is not entirely new. It draws on older repertoires of anti-Americanism in Europe, or of anti-Europeanism in the US, as illustrated by Secretary Rumsfeld's snide reference to 'old Europe'. Yet there may be a new, and more ominous, ring to these revived repertoires. They may also strike responsive chords among people who previously thought they were free from such adversarial sentiments.

In what follows I wish to explore this new resonance. It is partly a personal account, an attempt at introspection, tracing emotional and affective shifts in the way I perceive and experience America. Let me begin with a necessary proviso. Recently, in a piece in the French newspaper *Le Monde*, Alfred Grosser (2003) reminded us that one need not be anti-American for opposing America's foreign policy, nor an anti-Semite or anti-Zionist for taking Israeli government policy to task. He is not the first to make the point, nor will he be the last. The point bears making time and time again. Too often the cry of anti-Americanism or anti-Semitism is used as a cheap debating trick to silence voices of unwelcome criticism. Like Grosser, I have studied forms of anti-Americanism for years, trying to understand what triggers it, trying to understand the logic of its inner structure, while looking at it from a rather Olympian height. More often than not the subject had seemed more meaningfully connected to the non-American settings where it appeared than to America itself. But, like Grosser, I now feel the need to make a point that had for so long seemed obvious. He and I and many others now feel a stronger urge to take our distance from the directions that American foreign policy is taking, and ironically are now confronting the charge that we have become anti-American. A topic of intellectual and scholarly interest has now assumed the poignancy of a private dilemma. Grosser and I and others know we have not turned anti-American, while having become critical of the turn American policies have taken. We are now facing the question of when a stance critical of specific American policies becomes anti-American. For that shift to occur, more is needed than disagreement, however vehement. Anti-Americanism typically proceeds from specific areas of disagreement to larger frameworks of rejection, seeing particular policies or particular events as typical of a more general image of America. Anti-Americanism in that sense is mostly reductionist, seeing only the simplicity of the cowboy and Texas provincialism in President George W. Bush's response to terrorism, or the expansionist thrust of American capitalism in Bush's Middle East policies, and so on, and so forth. Entire repertoires of stereotyped Americas can be conjured up to account for any contemporary transatlantic disagreements.

To the extent that, for people like Grosser and myself, the topic of anti-Americanism has come home to roost, the following section illustrates the before-and-after quality of my involvement with the topic. It is in part a personal account of my attempts to keep my feelings of alienation and anger over recent trends in America's foreign policy from alienating me from America more generally. It is the report of a balancing act.

9/11 and the American turn to unilateralism

I happened to be in the US on the dismal day of 11 September 2001. I had flown in from Washington DC to Logan Airport in Boston the previous evening, hours before knife-wielding terrorists hijacked civilian airplanes taking off from Logan. I stood transfixed in front of the television screen, impotently watching the second plane crash into the second of Manhattan's Twin Towers, then seeing them implode – almost in slow motion, as I remember it. A year later I was back in the US, watching how Americans remembered the events of the year before in a moving, simple ceremony. The list of names was being read of all those who lost their lives in the towering inferno of the World Trade Center. Their names appropriately reflect what the words 'World Trade Center' conjure up: they are names of people from all over the world, from Africa, the Middle East, the Far East, the Pacific, Latin America, Europe and, of course, North America – people of many cultures and many religions. Again, the whole world was watching, and I suddenly realized that something remarkable was happening. The American mass media recorded an event staged by Americans. Americans powerfully re-appropriated a place where a year ago international terrorism was in charge. They literally turned the site into a *lieu de mémoire*. They were, in the words of Lincoln's Gettysburg Address, read again on this occasion, consecrating the place. They imbued it with the sense and meaning of a typically American scripture. It is the language that, for over two centuries, has defined America's purpose and mission in the ringing words of freedom and democracy.

I borrow the words 'American scripture' from Michael Ignatieff. He used them in a piece he wrote for a special issue of *Granta* (Ignatieff 2002). He is one of 24 writers from various parts of the world who contributed to a section entitled 'What We Think of America'. Ignatieff describes American scripture as

> the treasure house of language, at once sacred and profane, to renew the faith of the only country on earth … whose citizenship is an act of faith, the only country whose promises to itself continue to command the faith of people like me, who are not its citizens.
>
> (Ignatieff 2002)

Ignatieff is a Canadian. He describes a faith and an affinity with American hopes and dreams that many non-Americans share. Yet, if it was the point of *Granta*'s editors to explore the question of 'Why others hate us, Americans', Ignatieff's view is not of much help. In the outside world after 9/11, as *Granta*'s editor, Ian Jack, reminds us, there was a widespread feeling that

'Americans had it coming to them', that it was 'good that Americans now know what it's like to be vulnerable'. For people who share such views, American scripture deconstructs into hypocrisy and wilful deceit. They may well see their views confirmed now that America is engaged in an occupation of Iraq, advertised as an intervention to bring democracy to that country, while in fact engaging in acts that may well be war crimes in terms of international treaties that count the US among its co-signatories.

There are many signs in the recent past of people's views of America shifting in the direction of disenchantment and disillusionment. Sure enough, there were fine moments when President Bush rose to the occasion and used the hallowed words of American scripture to make it clear to the world and his fellow-Americans what terrorism had truly attacked. The terrorists' aim had been more than symbols of American power and prowess. It had been the very values of freedom and democracy that America sees as its foundation. These were moments when the President literally seemed to rise above himself. But it was never long before he showed a face of America that had already worried many long-time friends and allies during Bush's first year in office.

Even before September 11th, the George W. Bush administration had signalled its retreat from the internationalism that had consistently inspired US foreign policy since World War II, if not before. Ever since Woodrow Wilson, American scripture had also come to imply the vision of a world order that would forever transcend the lawlessness of international relations. Many of the international organizations that now serve to regulate inter-state relations and give legitimacy to international actions bear a markedly American imprint and spring from American ideals and initiatives. President George H.W. Bush., in spite of his avowed aversion to the 'vision thing', nevertheless deemed it essential to speak of a New World Order when, at the end of the Cold War, Saddam Hussein's invasion of Kuwait seemed to signal a relapse into a state of international lawlessness. George W. Bush takes a narrower, national interest view of America's place in the world. In an unabashed unilateralism he has moved US foreign policy away from high-minded idealism and the arena of international treaty obligations. He is actively undermining the fledgling International Criminal Court in The Hague, rather than taking a leadership role in making it work. He displays a consistent unwillingness to play by internationally agreed rules and to abide by decisions reached by international bodies that the US itself has helped set up. He squarely places the US above or outside the reach of international law, seeing himself as the sole and final arbiter of America's national interest.

After September 11th this outlook has only hardened. The overriding view of international relations in terms of the war against terrorism has led the US to ride roughshod over its own Constitutional protection of civil rights, as well as over international treaty obligations under the Geneva Convention in the ways it handles individuals, US citizens among them, suspected of links to terrorist networks. Seeing anti-terrorism as the one way to define who is with America or against it, President Bush takes forms of state terrorism, whether in Russia against the Chechens, or in Israel against the Palestinians, as so many justified anti-terrorist efforts. He gives them his full support. He calls Sharon a 'man of peace' and has pre-empted future negotiations between the Palestinians and the Israelis by supporting strategic Israeli positions regarding the Palestinians' rights of return under international law, or Israeli settlement of occupied Palestinian land, which is against international law. If Europeans beg to differ and wish to take a more balanced view of the Israeli–Palestinian conflict, the George W. Bush administration and many op-ed voices in the US blame European anti-Semitism.

The Palestinian–Israeli divide

This latter area is probably the one where the dramatic, if not tragic, drifting apart of America and Europe comes out most starkly, notwithstanding the Israeli withdrawal from the Gaza Strip in the summer of 2005. It testifies to a slow separation of the terms of public debate. Thus, to give an example, in England the chief rabbi, Jonathan Sacks,[3] said that many of the things Israel did to the Palestinians flew in the face of the values of Judaism. '[They] make me feel very uncomfortable as a Jew.' He had always believed, he said, that Israel 'must give back all the land [taken in 1967] for the sake of peace'. Peaceniks in Israel, like Amos Oz, take similar views. Even more remarkably, in the wake of a rampage of the Israeli army in the Gaza Strip that left 1600 Palestinians homeless, Tommy Lapid, the justice minister and the only Holocaust survivor in the Israeli government, declared that the house demolitions were inhumane. As the *Guardian Weekly* quoted him, he said:

> The demolition of houses in Rafah must stop. It is not humane, not Jewish, and causes us grave damage in the world. At the end of the day, they will kick us out of the United Nations, try those responsible in the international court in The Hague, and no one will want to speak to us.[4]

Many in Europe, Jews and non-Jews alike, would agree. And they have the chance to do so, because Israeli voices like Lapid's are being aired in the European press. Leading quality newspapers, in France, in England, in Germany and Italy as well as in other European countries, do what top-notch journalism is all about: write contemporary history as it unfolds, with all its welcome and unwelcome sides. Leading journalists as well as editorial writers are not loath to say the unwelcome things, such as the Gaza withdrawal did not change the Israeli attitude towards Palestinians.

Yet it would be hard to hear similar views expressed in the US other than in the American equivalent of the Soviet Samizdat voice of dissent: an equivalent that avails itself of the internet for the spirited exchange of dissenting views. In the public realm there is a closing of ranks, among American Jews, the religious right, opinion leaders and Washington political circles, behind the view that everything Israel does to the Palestinians is done in legitimate self-defence against acts of terrorism. Yet, clearly, if America's overriding foreign policy concern is the war against terrorism, one element tragically lacking in public policy statements of its Middle East policy is the attempt to look at themselves through the eyes of Arabs, or more particularly Palestinians. A conflation seems to have occurred between Israel's national interest and that of the United States, as in the case of Richard Perle, foreign policy guru in Washington government circles, who did not see any conflict of interest (personal or national) in drafting policy documents for Benjamin Netanyahu's Likud Party in Israel in 1997. Both countries, at the official level, share a definition of the situation that blinkers them to rival views more openly discussed in Europe.

Among the pieces in *Granta* is one by a Palestinian writer, Raja Shehadeh. He reminds the reader that

> today there are more Ramallah people in the US than in Ramallah. Before 1967 that was how most Palestinians related to America – via the good things about the country that they heard from their migrant friends and relations. After 1967, America entered our life in a different way.
>
> (Shehadeh 2002: 72)

The author goes on to say that the Israeli occupation policy of expropriating Arab land to build Jewish settlements and roads to connect them, while deploying soldiers to protect settlers, would never have been possible without 'American largesse'. But American assistance, Shehadeh continues, did not stop at the funding of ideologically motivated programmes. In a personal vignette, more telling than any newspaper reports, Shehadeh writes:

> Last July my cousin was at a wedding reception in a hotel on the southern outskirts of Ramallah when an F16 fighter jet dropped a hundred-pound bomb on a nearby building. Everything had been quiet. There had not been any warning of an imminent air attack. ... Something happened to my cousin that evening. ... He felt he had died and was surprised afterwards to find he was still alive. ... He did not hate America. He studied there. ... Yet when I asked him what he thought of the country he indicated that he dismissed it as a lackey of Israel, giving it unlimited assistance and never censoring its use of US weaponry against innocent civilians.
>
> (Shehadeh 2002: 74)

The author concludes with these words:

> Most Americans may never know why my cousin turned his back on their country. But in America the parts are larger than the whole. It is still possible that the optimism, energy and opposition of Americans in their diversity may yet turn the tide and make America listen.
>
> (Shehadeh 2002: 74)

The current Bush administration, with its pre-emptive strategy of taking out opponents before they can harm the US at home or abroad, in much the same way that Israeli fighter jets assassinate alleged Palestinian terrorists, in their cars, homes and backyards, without bothering about due process or collateral damage, is not an America that one may hope 'to make listen'. Who is not for Bush is against him. Well, so be it. Many Europeans have chosen not to be bullied into sharing the Bush administration's view of the world. They may not command as many divisions as Bush, but they surely can handle the 'divisions' that Bush – the man who in the 2000 election campaign had portrayed himself as a uniter, not a divider – has inflicted on the Atlantic community, if not on Europe itself.

If there is division now in the way that many Europeans 'read' the events in the Middle East compared to Americans, it is surely a matter of different exposure to the daily news, which in Europe is presented less selectively and in a less biased way. Even today, a full year after President George W. Bush declared the Iraqi mission 'accomplished', many American reporters in Iraq voluntarily embed themselves for their own safety in US Marine encampments. As one correspondent, Pamela Constable of *The Washington Post*, described her experience: 'I quickly became part of an all-American military microcosm' (Massing 2004). As Michael Massing argues in a piece in *The New York Review of Books*, if US news organizations truly want to get inside events in Iraq, there is a clear step they could take: incorporating more reporting and footage from international news organizations. Arabic-language TV stations have a wide presence on the ground. European outlets like the BBC, the *Guardian*, *The Financial Times*, *The Independent* and *Le Monde* have Arabic-speaking correspondents with intimate knowledge of the Middle East. Reuters, The Associated Press and Agence France-Presse have many correspondents stationed in places where US organizations do not. As Michael Massing writes in conclusion of his piece:

> In the current climate, of course, any use of Arab or European material – no matter how thoroughly edited and checked – could elicit charges of liberalism and anti-Americanism. The question for American journalists is whether they really want to know what the Iraqis themselves, in all their complexity, are thinking and feeling.
>
> (Massing 2004: 10)

It is a charge against a blinkered and parochial American journalism that is more generally made in European attempts at fathoming the depths of the divide between American and European public discourse.[5] A free press, as the highly regarded author and war correspondent Philip Knightley noted in *Index on Censorship*, would not reduce the post-9/11 debate to 'abuse, incitement, personal attacks, inflammatory accusation and intimidation until many a commentator and intellectual, the very people whose voices we want to hear, have been cowed into silence' (Knightley 2002). Or driven underground, we might add, into the American internet form of Samizdat dissent.

But there may also be a deeper force at work. Tellingly, the *Guardian* referred to Tommy Lapid as the sole Holocaust survivor in the current Israeli government. If World War II memories may have resurfaced in his reading of the Gaza events, something similar may be at work on a more general scale among European audiences. Photographs from Palestine or Iraq may well bring back memories of German retaliatory action against villages in Europe, they may also bring back remembered photographs of World War II atrocities used so powerfully in the education of Europeans regarding the enormity of Nazi rule. They trigger a submerged reservoir that Europeans do not share with Americans. Yet this basic difference need not drive the two sides of the Atlantic apart. When Europeans saw their tragic history repeat itself in the Balkan wars of the 1990s, in the end united action under NATO auspices put an end to the atrocities perpetrated there. Americans and Europeans could eventually share a reading in terms of crimes against humanity. Precisely such a shared reading of events in the Middle East and their implications for foreign policy seems to be lacking. A widely shared sense of outrage among Europeans, fed by the daily exposure to pictures and news reports from the Middle East, translates into impotent anger at an American Middle East policy seen as lacking balance and fairness.

Divided America and anti-Americanism

There has been a resurgence of open anti-Americanism in Europe and elsewhere in the world, not least in the Middle East, the area that has brought us Osama Bin Laden and his paranoid hatred of America, and of the West more generally. But if he can still conflate the two – America *and* the West – why can't we? If Raja Shehadeh still holds hopes of an America that one can make listen, why don't we? Let us face it: we are all Americans, but sometimes it is hard to see the Americans we hold dear in the Americans that hold sway. Those are the dangerous moments when clashing policy views may assume the contours of deeper, more fundamental differences – when difference translates into incompatibility, and the face of just one president may seem to reflect an America that has changed its face more permanently and fundamentally.

What different kind of face could that be? As some see it, it may have begun to show the effects of long-term cultural trends that increasingly set America apart from Europe. According to the World Values Survey, a long-term survey research project of the University of Michigan, the overall picture is ambivalent.[6] America consistently scores as high as or higher than European countries when it comes to values to do with political or economic freedoms. Americans and Europeans share ideas of democracy and freedom and have a common interest in defending those ideas. But the Michigan project also looked at a different set of values and ranks countries along a conceptual axis ranging from traditionalism to secularism. Traditionalism comprises those views that give central place to religion, family and country. At the other end we find the secular-rational values that emphasize individual choice in matters of life-style and individual emancipation from older frameworks of affiliation such as the church or the fatherland. America's position on this scale is exceptional among Western countries. It leans much more strongly towards the traditionalist end of the scale than European countries (with the exception of Ireland). Americans are the most patriotic of Western nations: 72 per cent claim to be 'very proud' of their country, thus putting themselves alongside such countries as India and Turkey. Religion – according to the survey the single most important gauge of traditionalism – positions Americans closer to Nigerians and Turks than to Swedes or Germans. And the differences with North-Western European countries have, if anything, only increased. Since the first survey, in 1981, America has grown more traditional, Europe less. Yet in terms of the other set of values, those of democracy and freedom, they have moved in tandem.

From these survey data America appears as a country of a cultural ambivalence all its own, in an evolving idiosyncratic symbiosis of traditionalism and modernism. The historical dynamics of this symbiosis, with the growing influence of traditionalism, may well have contributed to the mutual alienation between Europe and America. Public discourse on either side of the Atlantic is losing its shared terms of reference. America's political establishment has long been the safe haven of a secular, Enlightenment world view which it shared with political elites in Europe. Slowly but surely, however, traditionalism has made inroads into America's centres of policy-making. Of the two main political parties, the Republican Party has targeted its political strategy towards the incorporation of the traditionalist segment among the electorate. The strategy is two-pronged. Contemporary traditionalism has thrived on the ongoing culture war against anything connected to the life-style revolution of the 1960s. Its anti-modernism may remind us of an earlier high-water mark of traditionalism in the 1920s, forever epitomized in the anti-Darwinian Scopes (or 'monkey') trial. At the time it may have seemed like traditionalism's last hurrah. Yet with great organizational acumen it has made a remarkable come-back, waging a cultural war on the forces of moral relativism and libertarianism unleashed in the 1960s. Having got its act together politically, it offers itself as a tempting electoral bloc to the Republican party. Yet the Republican party is not solely the passive recipient of such support. It has chosen actively to play on the cultural fears of the traditionalists, posturing as the champion of all those who see gay marriage, abortion, divorce and more such moral issues as defining the political agenda, while casting the Democrats as representing moral depravity.

If we can discern two different Americas – the one modern and secular, the other centred on traditional values – they seem to coincide with one or the other of the two main parties. America seems to be split down the middle, with its two halves cohabiting in delicate balance. Visiting Europeans, journalists and diplomats among them, cannot fail to notice the widespread alienation from the George W. Bush administration precisely based on a cultural rift as outlined here. This view has become common coinage in press commentaries, in *Le Monde* in France, in *The Guardian* in England, in the *Frankfurter Algemeine* in Germany, to name just three of the more influential, opinion-forming newspapers in Europe.

Affiliating with the urbane and modern America, as many Europeans are wont to do, they may tend to exaggerate the 'moral issues' divide as the single most important determining factor in the Republican party's electoral strength. However, exit poll and public opinion data may well suggest that fear of a different sort has assured Bush's re-election.[7] Against the backdrop of the war on terror, keeping its ugly face from the general public, yet cynically manipulating alarm stages, casting Bush as the decisive war leader while painting the opponent as a flip-flopper, the Republican party's electoral strategy has successfully managed to rally those voting on their fears behind it. There is an Orwellian *1984* quality about this, with ongoing low-level warfare and scare-mongering preparing a population to surrender their democratic freedoms.

Cultural and political anti-Americanism

The highly partisan nature of such recent trends may remind Europeans that anti-Americanism is not the point. We may believe we recognize a generic Americanism in any particular American behaviour, be it cultural or political. Yet the range of such behaviour is simply too wide – ranging in culture from the sublime to the vulgar, and in politics from high-minded internationalism to narrow nationalism – to warrant any across-the-board rejection. Anti-Americanism, if we choose to retain the term at all, should be seen as a weak and ambivalent complex of anti-feelings. It only ever applies selectively, never extending to a total rejection of both forms of Americanism: the cultural and the political. Thus, we can have either of two separate outcomes: an anti-Americanism rejecting cultural trends which are seen as typically American, while allowing admiration for America's energy, innovation, prowess and optimism, or an anti-Americanism in reverse, rejecting an American political creed that for all its missionary zeal is perceived as imperialist and oppressive, while admiring American culture, from its high-brow to its pop varieties. These opposed directions in the critical thrust of anti-Americanism often go hand in hand with opposed positions on the political spectrum. The cultural anti-Americanism of those rising in defence of Europe's cultural identities is typically on the conservative right wing, whereas the political anti-Americanism of the Cold War and the war in Vietnam typically occurred on the left. Undoubtedly, the drastic change in America's position on the world stage since World War II has contributed to this double somersault. Since that war, America has appeared in a radically different guise, as much more of a potent force in everyday life in Europe and the larger world than ever before.

As we all know, there is a long history that illustrates Europe's long and abiding affinity with America's daring leap into an age of modernity. It shared America's fascination with the political modernity of republicanism, of democracy and egalitarianism, with the economic modernity of progress in a capitalist vein, and with an existential modernity that saw Man, with a capital 'M' and in the gender-free sense of the word, as the agent of history, the moulder of his social life as well as of his own individual identity and destiny. It was after all a Frenchman, Crèvecoeur, who on the eve of American independence pondered the question of 'What, then, is the American, this new Man'. A long line of European observers have, in lasting fascination, commented on this American venture, seeing it as a trajectory akin to their own hopes and dreams for Europe.[8] Similarly, French immigrants in the US, in order to legitimize their claims for ethnic specificity, have always emphasized the historical nexus of French and American political ideals, elevating Lafayette alongside George Washington to equal iconic status (Foucrier 1999).

But as we also know, there is an equally long history of a French, and more generally European, awareness of American culture taking directions that were seen as a threat to European ways of life and views of culture. Whether it was Tocqueville's more sociological intuition of an egalitarian society breeding cultural homogeneity and conformism, or later views that sought the explanation in the economic logic of a free and unfettered market, the fear was of an erosion of the European cultural landscape, of European standards of taste and cultural value. As I have argued elsewhere, the French were not alone in harbouring such fears (Kroes 1996), but they have been more consistently adamant in making the case for a defence of their national identity against a threatening process of Americanization. The very word is a French coinage. It was Baudelaire who, on the occasion of the 1855 *Exposition Universelle de Paris*, spoke of modern man, set on a course of technical materialism, as 'tellement américanisé ... qu'il a perdu la notion des différences qui caractérisent les phénomènes du monde physique et du monde moral, du naturel et du surnaturel' (Lacorne *et al*. 1986: 61). The Goncourt brothers' *Journal*, from the time of the second exposition in 1867, refers to 'L'exposition universelle, le dernier coup à ce qui est l'américanisation de la France' (Lacorne *et al*. 1986: 62) As these critics saw it, industrial progress ushered in an era where quantity would replace quality and where a mass culture feeding on standardization would erode established taste hierarchies. There are echoes of Tocqueville here, yet the eroding factor is no longer the egalitarian logic of mass democracy but the logic of industrial progress. In both cases, however, whatever the precise link and evaluating angle, America had become the metonym for unfettered modernity, like a Prometheus unbound.

These longer lines of anti-Americanism, cultural and political, are alive and well today. And often the two blend into one. Whenever Europeans, particularly young ones dressed in blue jeans and T-shirts, rise in protest against

American interventions on the world stage, they go out and smash the windows of a nearby McDonald's (and there is always a McDonald's nearby). As an icon of America's global presence, it represents in the eyes of protesters America's cultural imperialism, but it serves equally well as an emblem of political imperialism. The protest is facile and inarticulate, yet it serves to make a point against American power which is seen as overbearing and unresponsive. But how about the recent surge of anti-Europeanism in the US?

Given Europe's daring post-World War II venture in the construction of a European Union, inventing proto-federalist forms in the search for a supranational Europe, how do we account for the recent resurgence of anti-Europeanism in the US? Having promoted and supported this European evolution for many decades, why have so many American opinion leaders now turned anti-European? In the vitriolic vituperation that has recently set the tone of transatlantic exchanges, leading American voices discard as the 'Old Europe' those countries that criticize the drift of American foreign policy, while hailing other countries as the 'New Europe' that are willing to follow in America's footsteps. Robert Kagan contributed to this rising anti-Europeanism in the US when he paraphrased the dictum that men are from Mars, women from Venus. As he chose to present the two poles, Americans now are the new Martians, while Europeans are the new Venusians. Never mind the gendering implied in his view that Europeans are collectively engaged in a feminine endeavour when they pursue the new, transnational and cosmopolitan Europe. He does make an astute point, though, when he describes the European quest as Kantian, as an endeavour to create a transnational space where laws and civility rule. As Kagan sees it, though, the Europeans are so self-immersed that they are forgetful of a larger world that is Hobbesian, not Kantian, and is a threat to them as much as to the US. To the extent that Europeans still involve themselves in the larger world they tend to emphasize peace-keeping operations rather than pre-emptive military strikes (Kagan 2003).

Kagan and many others tend to forget that it has taken the US about one hundred years to find and test its institutional forms and build a nation of Americans from people flooding to its shores from all over the world. It could only have done so while turning its back to the world, in self-chosen isolationism, under the protective umbrella of a *Pax Britannica*. Europe has had only some 40 years to turn its gaze inward when it engaged in shaping the contours of a new Europe. During those years it enjoyed in its turn the protection of an umbrella, provided this time by the *Pax Americana*. This constellation came to an end along with the Cold War (Fabbrini 2004). Yet only then could the European construction fully come into its own, conceiving of the new Europe on the scale of the entire continent. It is a tremendous challenge and Europe needs time to cope with it. If it succeeds it may well serve as a model to the world, a rival to the American ideal of transnationalism, of constituting a nation of nations. If they are rival models, they are at the same time of one kind. They are variations on larger ideals inspiring the idea of Western civilization and find their roots in truly European formative moments in history, in the Renaissance, the Reformation and the Enlightenment. Larry Siedentop (2000: 190, 195, 198) places the formative moment even earlier in time, coinciding with the rise of a Christian view of the universal equality of mankind vis-à-vis God. As he presents it, the formative moment consisted in universalizing a religious view that in Judaism was still highly particularist, claiming an exceptionalist relation between God and the people of Israel. This shared heritage inspired the first transatlantic readings of what the terrorist attack of 9/11 signified. It was seen as an onslaught on the core values of a shared civilization. How ironic, if not tragic, then, that before long the US and Europe parted ways in finding the proper response to the new threat of international terrorism.

As for the US, the first signs of its farewell to internationalism in foreign policy – to its Wilsonianism, if you wish – and to its pioneering role in designing the institutional and legal framework for peaceful inter-state relations in the world, had, as I pointed out before, actually preceded 9/11. No longer does the George W. Bush administration conceive of the US as the *primus inter pares*, setting the guidelines for collective action while seeking legitimacy for action through treaties and UN resolutions. As the one hegemon on the world stage it now feels free to pursue its national interest through policies that one can only describe as unilateralist. It may seem like a throwback to the time of nation-state sovereignty, a stage of history that Europe is struggling to transcend. Unspectacular and cumbersome as the European project may seem, it is already rich in achievement. It has brought together long-time enemies like Germany and France, it has admitted as democratic member states nations that quite recently knew fascist dictatorships, like Italy, Spain and Portugal, or that were under the heel of military dictators, like Greece. It recently admitted nations that had lived under Communist rule since World War II. Turkey, a long-time member of NATO and since 1949 a member of the Council of Europe and subscriber to the European Convention on Human Rights, is now busy getting its house in democratic order so as to qualify for membership of the European Union.

If the European project is successful – and this means the inclusion of Turkey – Europe, I strongly believe, would offer a model to the world, particularly the world of Islam or for that matter the state of Israel, of a civil and democratic order, multinational and multicultural, far more tempting than the version of democracy brought under American auspices through pre-emptive military invasion. Those in support of what the US are pursuing in Iraq, blithely call it a neo-Wilsonianism. I beg to differ. If there is a neo-Wilsonian promise, it is held by the new Europe, not the current Bush administration.

Conclusion

In the European repertoire of the cultural critique of America, one observation may have gained in poignancy. Albert Camus and Jean-Paul Sartre in France, or Oswald Spengler in Germany, have been among those who noted an absence in America of the European sense of the tragic. In the blithe meliorism of the American project to bring democracy to the Middle East, what is lacking is the awareness that the active pursuit of good ends may well result in achieving its opposite. As in classic Greek tragedy, the Gods may strike with blindness those they wish to destroy. In the case of America's forward defence of democracy in Iraq, however, the blindness may be self-inflicted, as if its leaders were in a pathological state of denial. When the shocking pictures of systematic humiliation of Iraqi prisoners entered the public realm, President Bush and Secretary Rumsfeld dismissed the acts as un-American. If this is what Americans did, it is not what Americans would do. America is inherently good.[9] Among many others, Romano Prodi, then president of the European Commission in Brussels, begged to differ. Never one to mince words, he affirmed that the Iraq tortures were war crimes, which, for him, made it difficult to see the American presence in Iraq as a peace mission. Others, of a subtler cast of mind, expressed similar views. Thus, in an interview in the *Süddeutsche Zeitung* on the occasion of his 75th birthday,[10] German philosopher Jürgen Habermas testified to his disillusionment and disenchantment with the current US administration and its standard bearers. The experience was all the more painful since, as he acknowledged, he could not have come into his own as a philosopher of public space and democratic debate without the impact of America's pluralist liberalism and its philosophy of pragmatism. Ever since he was 16, his political ideas had been nourished by the American enlightenment ideals, thanks to a sensible re-education policy in the post-war years of American occupation in Germany. But now, in a recent book on the divided West, he has this to say: 'Let us not delude ourselves: the normative authority of America lies in tatters.'[11] The official manipulation of public opinion and the rampant patriotic conformism he said he would not have deemed possible in the liberal America that he envisions.

Let me return to the editor-in-chief of *Le Monde*, Jean-Marie Colombani. Like Habermas his feelings about America have followed a curve from affiliation all the way to alienation, only in a shorter time span. In a May 2004, editorial entitled 'Are We All Un-American?',[12] he comments on Rumsfeld's facile dismissal of the Abu Ghraib abominations as un-American. If this implies a definition of true Americanism, it is one that Colombani refuses to share. As Colombani put it: 'In the wake of September 11, we all felt ourselves to be Americans. Donald Rumsfeld would make us all un-American.' I tend to agree. If the George W. Bush administration shows us the face of a self-righteous, arrogant and unbridled Americanism, it is an Americanism that I oppose.

Notes

1 On this topic see Kooijman (2004).
2 In a spirited response, as yet unpublished, Tomas Mastnak, currently a fellow at the International Center for Advanced Studies at New York University took Rorty to task for ignoring recent trends in the United States.

3 See the interview in the *Guardian* on 27 August 2003.
4 *Guardian Weekly*, 28 May–3 June 2004, p. 7.
5 See, for example, the chapter 'America and the World as America', in Sardar and Wyn Davies (2002). Similar best-selling indictments, in languages other than English, of America's recent course in world politics and the failure of the American press to take an independent and critical position, are, for example, Leyendecker (2004), van Wolferen (2003) or Artaud (2004).
6 See Ronald L. Inglehart (2004).
7 Ira Chernus, available online at http://www.tomdispatch.com/index.mhtml? pid=2068_
8 May I refer the reader to my survey of such French views of American modernity. See Kroes (2000: Ch. 9).
9 I am paraphrasing the comic Rob Corddry on *The Daily Show with Jon Stewart*: 'It's our principles that matter, our inspiring, abstract notions. Remember: just because torturing prisoners is something we did, doesn't mean it's something we *would* do.' Quoted by Danner (2004: 74)
10 *Süddeutsche Zeitung*, 138 (18 June 2004): 15.
11 J. Habermas (2004). The quotation is from the interview in the *Süddeutsche Zeitung*.
12 *Le Monde Sélection Hebdomadaire*, 22 May, 2004. The French caption reads: 'Tous non-américains?'.

References

Artaud, D. (2004) *L'Amérique des néoconservateurs: L'Empire a-t-il un avenir?*, Paris: Editions Ellipses.
Danner M. (2004) 'The Logic of Torture', *The New York Review of Books*, LI (11) 24 June 2004, p. 74.
Fabbrini, S. (2004) 'America and Europe in the Post-Cold War Era', in R. Janssen and R. Kroes (eds), *Post-Cold War Europe, Post-Cold War America*, Amsterdam: VU University Press, pp. 87–100.
Foucrier, A. (1999) *Le rêve californien: Migrants francais sur la côte Pacifique (XVIIIe–XXe siècles)*. Paris: Belin.
Grosser, A. (2003) 'Les hors-la-loi', *Le monde*, Friday, 18 April 2003 (reprinted in *Le monde, Sélection hebdomadaire*, no. 2842, 26 April 2003, p. 8).
Habermas, J. (2004) *Der gespaltete Westen*, Frankfurt am Main: Suhrkamp Verlag.
Ignatieff, M. (2002) 'What We Think of America', *Granta*, 77 (Spring 2002): 47–50.
Inglehart, R.L. (ed.) (2004) *Human Values and Social Change: Findings from the World Values Surveys*. International Studies in Sociology and Social Anthropology, vol. 89. Leiden: Brill.
Kagan, R. (2003) *Of Paradise and Power: America and Europe in the New World Order*, New York: Alfred A. Knopf.
Knightley, P. (2002) 'Losing Friends and Influencing People', *Index on Censorship*, January, 31 (1): 146–55.
Kooijman, J. (2004) 'Bombs Bursting in Air: The Gulf War, 9/11, and the Super Bowl Performances of "The Star-Spangled Banner" by Whitney Houston and Mariah Carey'. In R. Janssens and R. Kroes (eds), *Post-Cold War Europe, Post-Cold War America*, Amsterdam: VU University Press, pp. 178–94.

Kroes, R. (1996) *If You've Seen One, You've Seen the Mall: Europeans and American Mass Culture*, Urbana, IL: University of Illinois Press.

Kroes, R. (2000) *Them and Us: Questions of Citizenship in a Globalizing World*, Urbana, IL: University of Illinois Press.

Lacorne, D., Rupnik, J. and Toinet, M.F. (eds) (1986) *L'Amérique dans les têtes*, Paris: Hachette.

Leyendecker, H. (2004) *Die Lügen des Weissen Hauses: Warum Amerika einen Neuanfang braucht* [The Lies of the White House: Why America Needs a New Start], Reinbek bei Hamburg: Rowohlt.

Massing, M. (2004) 'Unfit to Print?', *New York Review of Books*, LI (11) 24 June 2004, p. 8.

Rorty, R. (2004) 'Post-Democracy', *London Review of Books*, 1 April 2004.

Sardar, Z. and Wyn Davies, M. (2002) *Why Do People Hate America?*, Cambridge: ICON Books.

Shehadeh, R. (2002) 'What We Think of America', *Granta*, 77 (Spring 2002): 71–5.

Siedentop, L. (2000) *Democracy in Europe*, London: Penguin Books.

van Wolferen, K. (2003) *De ondergang van een wereldorde* [The Demise of a World Order], Amsterdam: Uitgeverij Contact.

6 Anti-Americanism and the European peace movement

The Iraq war

Carlo Ruzza and Emanuela Bozzini

Introduction

Like other anti-war movements, the movement against the second Gulf war articulated a range of grievances against governments in favour of military intervention. Among these grievances, several issues were identified for an oppositional stand against the first George W. Bush administration – the dominant interventionist administration – and combined together amounted to a justification for the substantial anti-Americanism of this movement. Anti-Americanism constitutes a cultural current which is a recognized and recurrent component of some European national cultures and of several social movements (SMOs) in particular. Social movements mobilize on the basis of an array of connected grievances that constitute their ideological system of reference. A central ideological core that defines the movement – typically principled opposition to wars – is connected to a set of peripheral ideological elements that are more likely to vary across situations and over time. Anti-Americanism is one such contingent element that has arguably increased in recent years.

The specific meaning and impact of this cultural current has been commented upon by several observers who have noted how it has allowed a broadening of the potential movement's constituency beyond the traditional peace advocates. Its relevance and impact does however merit a more detailed investigation. In particular, as a territorially-related concept, anti-Americanism sets itself in relation to European identities – a connection that needs to be investigated in detail. This chapter will examine these concepts in the activist materials of European peace movements.

The second Gulf war (started with the military occupation of Iraq in the Spring 2003) developed in the context of widespread protests organized in several countries by large peace movements. In Western Europe, anti-war protests have increasingly been marked by anti-American sentiments. In recent years tensions between the United States (US) and Europe have been noted on several topics, ranging from trade disputes to attitudes towards the environment and genetically modified organisms, to security issues in relation to topics such as the Israeli–Palestinian conflict. They are therefore not limited to contrasting views on matters implicated in the war. Nonetheless, the war has made differences visible and peace movements have taken the role of popularizers of contrasts with the US administration. Different conceptions on approaches ranging from Islamic terrorism to security in Iraq have seen peace movements engaged in a cultural battle with the first Bush administration, reflecting a public opinion view as regards transatlantic relations which parallels geopolitical tensions.

The impact of peace movements has been viewed as depending on the political legitimacy that they have been able to acquire in public discourse and more broadly the credibility of the interrelated advocacy coalitions that in different Western countries opposed the second Gulf war. This is in turn related to their ability to appear defenders of universally supported ideas. In an era of global communications, their impact is also dependent on their ability to present a unified message and relate it to the moralization of international politics, therefore framing the war as a 'violation of binding international law'. In this chapter we will address these issues through a content analysis of European peace movements' activist materials of the period.

We investigate the uses that European peace movements made of anti-Americanism and in this context we examine whether and how anti-Americanism came to constitute a new political opportunity. First a short discussion on the nature, relevance and political prospects of peace movements is necessary.

Anti-Americanism and recent peace movements' cycles

In general, peace movements are amongst the most visible and widespread social movements in Western societies, although they tend to be short-lived. They have tended to register peaks of activity and long phases of demobilization and abeyance. They rarely completely cease to exist as they rely on a small, morally motivated activist base which keeps them alive even in the absence of viable political opportunities. However, the limited size of their permanent activist base means that they redefine themselves when they re-emerge and do so using the cultural materials available and strategically appropriate at the time more freely than other movements.

The fact that, more than other movements, they vary widely in size and expand when anti-war sentiments spread implies that their composition is more articulated. Their forms of protest are supported by coalitions of like-minded actors which are broader than the left-liberal families of new social movements typically promoting other campaigns. These are coalitions of both institutionalized and non-institutionalized actors who belong to a variety of social and political institutions and who therefore express a relevant sector of public opinion – a set of social attitudes with a degree of stability and coherence.

To attract support these coalitions have to be able to connect their objectives – typically to halt a war or avoid its beginning – to commonly held views in public opinion. They also have to be able to identify elements of a common platform. However, this is not an easy task. Peace movements' features are affected by the political context in which they emerge and the nature of the grievances they express. Their ideology of reference, protest tactics, supporting institutional allies and outcomes vary. Their ideological referent can make processes of discursive connection to prevalent opinion problematic and their internal differences are difficult to overcome. As a result their mobilization capability is highly variable. Anti-Americanism as a stable if limited set of attitudes has generally constituted a discursive resource for peace activists.

In the past 50 years, four cycles of international peace mobilization can be identified. Opposition to atmospheric nuclear tests in the 1950s gave international visibility to peace movements; opposition to the deployment of Pershing 2 and Cruise missiles marked a second cycle that lasted from 1980 to 1985 (Kaltefleiter and Pfaltzgraff 1985). Opposition to the Gulf war constituted another cycle which lasted from December 1990 to March 1991. After a short cycle of opposition to the intervention in Afghanistan, opposition to a new conflict in Iraq also emerged at the end of 2002. In addition there have been movements concerned with local wars such as mobilizations against wars in the Balkans which did not achieve wide support. Before and during the second Gulf war of 2003, peace movements increased significantly in size and their views were widely echoed in media and public opinion, more so than in previous waves. We will seek to explain this increase in their capability to mobilize with reference to anti-Americanism as a political opportunity.

The four mobilization waves of the 1950s, the 1980s, the 1990s and the beginning of the new century share some common features. They called into question issues of imperial behaviour and specifically the role of the US in matters of international security. But there were also substantial differences. The first mobilization episode focused on the issue of nuclear weapons and was therefore directly connected to the anti-nuclear mobilizations of the 1950s against atmospheric tests. In the 1950s, peace movement mobilizations were often dominated by the Communist left which gave them a strong and univocal anti-imperialist characterization. The US was often seen as an aggressive superpower intent on repressing popular struggles throughout the world and utilizing nuclear blackmail to that purpose. Movements were fairly organized and connected to existing general-purpose organizations of the left. A tradition of committed leftists emerged whose anti-Americanism was anti-imperialist, radical and directed against the US and not only against its government. It re-emerged in successive waves but gradually lost importance with all-encompassing changes in the social movement sector.

Anti-Americanism re-emerged in each successive wave, but to the old anti-imperialist themes new themes were added. Anti-Americanism in the 1980s also related to a rejection of dangerous technologies masterminded by a superpower neglectful of environmental concerns and operating on a scale so large that it diminished individuals' power to control their physical environment. Despite massive mobilizations, the controversial missiles which spurred the movement of the 1980s were deployed. However, soon afterwards the international situation changed radically. The Soviet Union under Gorbachev began a programme of reforms which, over time, led to substantial reduction of the nuclear arsenal of both superpowers. Perceptions of threat began to diminish and former activists became increasingly difficult to mobilize. Established goals of the movements which related to global war between the superpowers became less relevant, or were actually achieved in the context of the East–West superpower summits, which to many symbolized the end of the Cold War.

On 2 August 1990 the relevance of the European peace movement increased radically with Iraq's invasion of Kuwait. Soon afterwards a multinational military contingent was assembled. Western European movements soon began to grow and mobilize (Brittain 1991) and steadily increased in intensity reaching the high mobilization level of the early 1980s. Anti-Americanism reappeared and new concerns began to emerge about the emergence of a single 'arrogant' superpower, in addition to the existing anti-imperialist, environmentalist and anti-technological concerns. In this new situation the Catholic Church and other churches entered the arena of pacifism more decisively, an arena which they were previously somewhat reluctant to join when the peace movements were dominated by the left. With the participation of churches, the doctrine of the just war reacquired relevance. In addition, a juridical frame appeared and gradually grew in importance among peace movement grievances. It appeared convincing to a broad advocacy coalition and to large sectors of the European population. Against a backdrop of continuing demonstrations, a '100 hours' war crushed the Iraqi military. Soon after the war ended, the movement quickly demobilized.

In connection with the events of 11 September 2001 a situation of tension re-emerged in the same geopolitical area. The first George W. Bush administration declared a 'war on terrorism'. A new anti-Americanism emerged as a reaction to what came to be seen in movement circles as a misguided and self-serving emphasis of US politicians. Anti-Americanism once again became a central focus of movement framing. The first intervention took place in October 2001 in Afghanistan with the objective of dismantling the Taliban regime and its Al Qaeda supporters. Subsequently, attention turned to Iraq – seen by the US administration as in some way associated to the Al Qaeda network. The US thus sought to mobilize a coalition to disarm it.

The situation reached a turning-point after the November 2002 United Nations (UN) resolution (no. 1441) which reinstated UN inspections in order to verify the destruction of weapons of mass destruction, though activists could claim some success in pressurizing the Bush administration into seeking a UN mandate for its campaign against Iraq in the first place. According to the resolution, should 'material breach' of the disarmament process take place, military intervention would ensue. However, a majority of the peace movement continued to oppose intervention whether or not a UN mandate was secured. The movement coalition against the war continued to grow rapidly. Notable early manifestations included protest marches in London in September 2002. This new movement became even more visible in Europe at the European Social Forum held in Florence in November 2002 and then more massively in February 2003 on the eve of a possible military intervention in the region.

On 15 February 2003, millions turned out in more than 600 cities around the world. As mentioned above, participation was particularly strong in Europe, reaching one million in London and Rome. Participation in Asia and the US was more muted with about 20,000 joining a rally in New York. The event was extensively prepared throughout Europe and its preparation produced a host of activist materials which reflect the wealth of concerns and ideological backgrounds of the movements and have been sampled for analysis.

The peace movement's attempt to stop the war failed. On 20 March 2003, the US–British military coalition attacked Iraq, bombing Baghdad and other cities in Iraq. On 7 April the American army entered Baghdad, and at the end of April President Bush declared the war over, the US-led coalition victorious and a regime change in Iraq as having been effected. On 12 April a last substantial demonstration took place in several European cities. After this event, the peace movement rapidly demobilized. Observers noted that although ultimately unsuccessful this movement had an unprecedented effect on public opinion, emerging on the international scene as a relevant actor distinct and often counterposed to governments.

In the following months, however, new events spurred a gradual resurgence of the movement. First, the frequency of episodes of political violence increased. This included suicide attacks of Muslim fundamentalists against military targets, Western hostage-taking and their execution, the bombings of Madrid, and a deterioration of the situation in Palestine. The pacification of Iraq by the coalition forces was largely unsuccessful. A year after the nominal end of the war, killings of Westerners continued unabated on the streets of Iraqi cities and pocket of armed resistance were not defeated.

The movement reacted by attempting to revive mobilization but failed to achieve relevant results. There was a sporadic re-emergence of protest and cultural activities against the war. Concerted efforts focused on organizing a demonstration on 20 March 2004 – a year after the beginning of the war. This achieved only moderate support throughout all European capitals, and failed to attract significant media attention.

To sum up, it emerges that anti-Americanism has always been present in peace movement framing but has been defined differently and connected in different ways to other dominant movement frames such as Christian pacifism, romantic anti-modernism and Western European nationalism (Rochon 1988). In recent mobilizations, additional factors played a role: in particular a new articulation of the North–South issue and a focus on the importance of international law emerged. Nonetheless Anti-American arguments previously played a marginal role, and were emphasized mainly by leftist sectors of the movement. They were therefore viewed as a liability, given their internally divisive nature and potential to undermine the impact of the movement on moderate public opinion.

However, in recent years, in relation to its position as the world's sole remaining superpower, the role of the US in world politics and economy has become an even more central issue in public debate. Discussion of America's role is connected to central concerns as regards the impact of globalization and related concerns for economic and cultural dominance and marginalization of local cultures. America is more and more identified as the most important actor in influencing domestic policies as well as lifestyles. The identification of globalization as Americanization seems to be common among people. In reaction, anti-Americanism has developed an increasing salience among European publics. Survey data shows that criticism of the US has been growing among European public opinion since 1999, and that the war in Iraq significantly increased this trend (see Chapter 7 by Pierangelo Isernia).

The role of America is also widely debated in relation to the post-Cold War period and in relation to Islam and the causes of terrorism. There is a growing literature, academic and non-academic, which investigates these topics and highlights the problematic nature of US dominance. After 11 September 2001, several observers tried to explain the reaction against America and its foreign policy. For instance, Ziauddin Sardar and Merryl Wyn Davies in *Why do people hate America?* examine the nature of US hegemony in different areas: political, economic and cultural (Sardar and Davies 2003).

Media discourses also focus on these arguments. In particular, the opposition to war in European countries has been widely debated in terms of eroding support for traditional alliances with US. These attitudinal changes proved a potential political opportunity for peace movements – an opportunity that was, however, time-related and therefore likely to change as events developed on the ground. In this chapter we examine how anti-Americanism has been utilized by peace movements at two crucial points in time: during the largest mobilization before the military intervention and a year after.

Frame analysis of peace movements' documents

In order to identify peace movement objectives and the dominant ideological frames and their relation to anti-Americanism a content analysis was performed of activist documents collected from the large demonstrations of 15 February 2003 and 20 March 2004. We concentrated on four large countries – Italy, the UK, France and Germany – which we selected both for their relevance and in order to maximize variation in terms of attitudes of the ruling coalitions towards the war. We posited a different structure of political opportunities as two of the governments were in favour of war and sent troops, therefore constituting a clear target to local activism, and two were against. We then concentrated on documents produced by large anti-war networks to address the concerns of the dominant peace coalitions rather than smaller movement organizations. In each country we identified 20 documents which united all the peace groups in a common platform. We then proceeded to examine them utilizing a frame analysis approach.

Useful insights into movements' ideologies are provided by the framing tradition in the social movements' literature.[1] The concept of frame and frame alignment proposed by Snow and colleagues (1986), facilitates description of the nature of the ideologies and ideological alliances that developed among advocacy groups of the 2003 and 2004 peace movement. Snow points out that a movement needs a 'master frame' that condenses the grievances of its members into a single concept. By means of a 'master frame' certain aspects of reality are identified and given prominence while others are omitted. Certain connections between elements are highlighted and others are ignored. For a social movement to achieve wider support, its master frame must resonate with the priorities of sectors of the general public. Movements attempt to enhance this resonance by means of 'frame alignment' strategies whereby their frames become aligned with dominant cultural frames.

Movements borrow the discourse of powerful institutions and attempt (strategically or because of a cognitive merging of taken-for-granted frames) to modify it in order to legitimate activism or other forms of support for a social movement. This modification can take different forms. The linkages among the discourses of different organizations are of special interest. Snow and Benford (Snow and Benford 1988) and the tradition of social movements research that developed from their work have asserted the centrality of processes of frame alignment between dominant social frames and movements' frames which attempt to reinterpret prevalent societal discourse and reorient it along the political positions that they advocate.

Methodologically, this approach entails a group of competent readers scoring key documents to identify and count typical themes and ideological positions. Utilizing this approach, peace movement frames were examined within activist documents through a conceptual lens that initially focused on the frames described in the literature previously reviewed. The sample of texts considered consisted first of a small sample of documents from Italy, Germany, Belgium, the UK, Spain, Portugal, France and Austria. On these documents an initial qualitative frame analysis was conducted. We then concentrated on four countries – Italy, France, Germany and the UK – and identified relevant documents from the main peace networks. These documents were analysed in detail utilizing a computer-assisted methodology.[2]

Documents considered are common platforms of umbrella organizations, speeches and official statements of peace networks and individual transnational organizations involved in the organization of the demonstrations. These networks include a large number of organizations – for instance 'Stop the War' numbers in Italy and in the UK 200 organizations – and the documents analysed therefore reflect the body of opinions of European peace movements.

Anti-Americanism within European peace movements

This section begins with an overview of the contents of documents analysed and is then followed by an assessment of empirical evidence of the relevance of anti-American arguments. The first important finding is that the documents generally appeared to be similarly constructed in terms of their structure, themes represented and their importance. Typically, documents contained self-definitions of the movements, arguments against the war, actions that needed to be taken to prevent it, views on the causes of the war, its implications and consequences, and views of the American government, its motives and responsibilities. In the next paragraphs we focus on five themes: differences in anti-American arguments, the prognosis on the consequences of war, the self-definition of the peace movement as a new global actor, the role of national governments and the role of Europe.

We define anti-Americanism very broadly as the movements' intentional use of discursive frames that blame the American people, American politicians or even generally aspects of the US polity for negative consequences resulting from interventions in world affairs. This broad definition is then refined by identifying, describing and quantifying specific discursive frames. This implies that we sought to identify both ad hoc arguments against specific American stances in world affairs as well as the adoption of general moral arguments which were utilized instrumentally to blame America.

Anti-Americanism has been very prominent in the European peace movement: within our sample 34 per cent of quotations contain an anti-American statement. A content analysis of anti-American quotations highlights that three main forms of anti-Americanism can be distinguished: legalistic, political and economic. Each version of anti-Americanism presents a coherent set of arguments to oppose the war and to blame the US administration for its decisions.

1   Legalistic anti-Americanism: the war against Iraq is illegal, and the US is seen to epitomize a fundamentally illegal and immoral behaviour, linked to the violation of international norms. US immorality is identified with the doctrine of Preventative War, which is a deviation from the established international political rules and is a threat to the right to self-determination recognized in international law: 'The preventive War is the death of international law. The preventive war is the dominion of the stronger' (*Fermiamo la Guerra* – Italy, 2003). Bush was strongly criticized because in 2003 he had already decided on war without having consideration for UN resolutions and all pretensions to the contrary were considered simply deceitful. Thus, in this case we see the violation of a universalist legal principle being selectively stressed by peace activists, and we would like to argue that this amounts to an implicit form of anti-Americanism.

2   Political anti-Americanism: opposition to war is framed in political terms. This means that activists stress that war is not the solution to international

threats and that it is counterproductive for a democratic global order. For instance:

> [The war] should be opposed by everyone who believes in democra-
> tic, political solutions to international conflicts because it will be a
> war without resolution with the potential to lead to global disaster.
>   (European Social Forum, The Anti-war Call, 2003)

In analysing the international situation activists stress that the US is politically isolated, as it tends to act unilaterally without considerations for
Western allies and other countries. In addition, the US is criticized because
it does not take into account public opposition to war:

> the majority of people in the majority of countries in the world
> oppose this war and the 15 February demonstrations are expected to
> be the largest mass mobilizations ever seen. On February 15 we will
> say to Bush and his allies that the war against Iraq can not be con-
> ducted in the name of the people of the world.
>   (Fermiamo la Guerra, Italy 2003)

3   Economic anti-Americanism: the opposition to war is framed in economic
    terms, in particular activists stress that the US interest in Iraqi oil is the
    most important factor in explaining American strategies and decisions.
    President Bush is accused of being linked to oil companies and reflecting
    their priorities. The US is seen as seeking world hegemony in military and
    economic terms.

The legalistic version of anti-Americanism is the most frequently used and
represents 44.5 per cent of anti-American quotations. Four out of ten sentences refer to the political form of anti-Americanism and a minority of
sentences (15 per cent) refer to the economic version. Table 6.1 illustrates
the differing incidence of the use of these three different forms of anti-
Americanism by country.

It is interesting to note that there is a difference in emphasis among countries:[3] German and British activists focus mainly on the legal dimension of
anti-Americanism, whereas Italian and French activists provide their readers

Table 6.1 Incidence of type of anti-Americanism expressed within countries (number
of quotations = 405)

	France	Germany	Italy	UK	Total
Legalistic anti-Americanism	24.2	53.3	33.7	56.9	44.4
Political anti-Americanism	38.7	37.7	51.9	34.3	40.8
Economic anti-Americanism	37.1	9.0	14.4	8.8	14.9
Total	100	100	100	100	100

with a detailed political analysis of the international situation. We would like to argue that this difference is largely due to the different internal composition of peace networks in the countries analysed. Traditionally, in France and Italy peace movements have been strongly linked to Communist and left-wing parties and trade unions, which tend to frame the issue in directly political terms. In the cycle of mobilization here examined, leftist organizations and leftist local administrations have been very active in promoting public demonstrations and in mobilizing their constituencies. As a result political arguments and analyses play a central role in the framing strategy and in absolute terms have prominence. In other contexts the stronger impact of civil society organizations lead to arguments less focused on international politics and more on moral issues, which are often framed in legal terms.

However, the concept of the war as illegal was the most widespread within peace movements, as all organizations adopted it to blame the US administration, and it generally constituted the first reason mentioned for opposing the war. In this sense it is important to note that it constitutes a shared frame that allows an overcoming of differences among leftist, religious, anti-globalization, civil society organizations and NGOs. Adopting a legalistic version of anti-Americanism, these organizations have been able to submit common documents based on the idea that the US was challenging established international norms and is getting involved in an illegal war.

In addition, this strategic framing has been successful in bridging movements' conception of anti-Americanism with prevalent societal conceptions of legitimate international order. Opinion polls show that opposition to military intervention in Iraq was strongly influenced by the existence of UN resolutions, revealing public support for established international rules. The use of military force was seen as plausible only when nation-states followed recognized institutional deliberative norms. Consequently, the violation of international rules by the US administration constituted the most important political opportunity for the peace movement, allowing it to articulate anti-American claims in a legitimate fashion. Peace activists stressed their role as defenders of universally recognized norms and of human rights.

In 2004, anti-Americanism based on the international legality perspective was still present. In reviewing the full story of the war against Iraq, activists sought to remind the public that the US acted unilaterally and in violation of international dispositions. However, we note a shift in emphasis, as in late 2004 activists focused mainly on the concept of 'occupation' in describing the presence of US troops in the country. This frame is important because of its legal consequences: in defining the US as an occupying power, activists still referred to evidence of illegality in their negative assessment of the US administration. For instance, we found statements like: 'Just as the invasion had no legal basis, the occupation and privatisation of Iraq is contrary to international law and must be opposed' (Stop the War – UK, 2004).

The legalistic focus of anti-Americanism and the focus on the doctrine of preventative war were useful as they allowed criticism to focus on the Bush

Administration rather than America in general. In this sense the legalistic anti-Americanism seemed to be an important discursive strategy, as only a minority of West Europeans blamed the US as a whole. For instance, in France and Germany 15 per cent and 30 per cent of people respectively thought that the US as a whole has a negative impact in the global governance, but about three-quarters of people in France and two-thirds in Germany blamed President Bush personally. This data confirms anti-Americanism to be a controversial topic, which presents different degrees of acceptance among citizens, and the emphasis on international norms appears a successful strategy in order to gain consensus among different national publics.

The theme of consequences of war was another important topic for peace activists. In documents drafted in February 2003, at a time when activists were trying to avert the beginning of the war, they sought to widely diffuse to the public the message of the dangers of war and its human costs. In this context three main arguments can be found:

- the humanitarian disaster that the war would create,
- the risks of global instability, and
- the ineffectiveness of war in combating terrorism.

The most frequently reported argument in 2003 was that innocents are victims and that the conflict will lead to a catastrophe for the Iraqi people. All organizations made reference to the economic and trade embargo on Iraq and its consequences, underlining the fact that the living conditions of the population would get worse should a conflict ensue. One year later this argument had been reinforced by references to the concrete situation faced by Iraqi people, and it was still the most frequently used frame for describing the consequences of the war. In comparison to 2003, activists expanded the list of victims, referring to coalition soldiers, journalists and hostages. Activists strongly stressed the emergency in the country and the need to support humanitarian aid.

Second, all networks stressed the dangers of war – that it would provoke instability, would lead to further conflicts and to a weakening of established norms. In 2003 these arguments were connected to reflections on the future of international institutions. As far as the doctrine of the preventive war represents a shift from shared international rules and practices, activists blamed the US for renouncing 50 years of effort to establish peaceful resolution of conflicts, thus weakening the role of the United Nations in global governance. In addition activists expressed concern about the situation in the Middle East. In common platforms SMOs stated that the American concept of 'preventive war' had been an opportunity for the Sharon government to execute the 'permanent war' against the Palestinians and in this sense they affirmed that the war against Iraq brought heavy consequences with regard to global governance. Additionally, we note an emphasis on the dangers and immorality of war in absolute terms. After all, Catholic associations and the no-global movement are explicitly involved in the construction of a better world, and they aim to abolish war from history.

Finally, there was the view that the war would be ineffective: it is not the right answer to terrorism and it is expected to increase the power of Islamic fundamentalists and the number of fundamentalist adherents. As a result war will lead to the clash of civilizations and will provoke intercultural tensions. In 2003 the ineffectiveness argument was shared by all organizations except the no-global networks. In as far as they focus mainly on the economic interests of the US government, they regard the war as necessary for American hegemony and for global capitalism more generally, and significantly, the no-global movement affirmed that it was impossible to stop the war.

In recent common documents war is not framed as ineffective: SMOs stress that it worsened the situation in Iraq and more generally in the entire world. Activists focus their analysis on terrorism, in the light of the March 2004 attack in Madrid and with reference to increasingly prevalent taking of Western hostages in Iraq. In this sense a new theme is added to the interpretative framework. On the whole in 2003 references to terrorism were rare. There were no mentions of the attack on the Twin Towers, and in terms of relevant actors Osama Bin Laden and Al Qaeda were absent. In 2003 terrorism was not perceived as a direct threat to Western countries. The theme of terrorism emerged in 2004, and was mostly used to confirm the diagnosis that activists proposed the year before. As noted above, the American attack on Iraq was expected to exacerbate relations with Islamic people, more generally to strengthen anti-Western attitudes in Arab countries, and consequently to increase risks for European and American citizens. The increasing strength of terrorism was linked to the presence of American troops in Iraq and with the errors made by the Bush administration in governing the country. In this sense peace movement organizations criticize the entirety of American policy and decisions and – as we will see in the next paragraph – the anti-war mobilization proposed and sustained an alternative way for conducting international relations, presenting itself as a new actor on the global scene.

Peace movement as a new global actor

Within our sample, 16 per cent of quotations refer to a self-definition of the anti-war movement. The worldwide demonstration of 15 February 2003 and the adoption of common frames and symbols allowed peace movement networks to define themselves collectively as a new powerful transnational actor, which has been able to gain consensus across all countries in the world (26 per cent among quotations that refer to self-definition of the movement) and represent an event of historical relevance (10 per cent among quotations that refer to self-definition of the movement).

Activists were aware of the composite structure of the movement, and organizations themselves made reference to the internal differences that characterize the peace movement (17 per cent among quotations that refer to self-definition of the movement). Their view is that differences within indicate that support for peace was gaining consensus independent of and across social, religious and political beliefs. In particular broad coalitions stress this argument, and affirm that diversity enriches and strengthens the movement. Peace movement organizations continue to stress that their power is based on their clarity of purpose. They have a well-defined priority: in 2003 they aimed at avoiding the beginning of the war (33 per cent among quotations that refer to goals and appeals), in 2004 they wanted troops to be withdrawn from Iraq (25 per cent among quotations that refer to goals and appeals). On the occasion of the worldwide demonstration of 15 February 2003 frames were coherently constructed in order to blame the US administration for the war. Prognostic frames were mainly coherent to diagnostic frames, and focused on the role of international law. In order to stop the war it would have been sufficient to obey the established norms. In this sense they appealed for a negotiated solution that could take into account the role of the United Nations, and that could oblige the US government to respect international institutions and their decisions. They strongly stressed the role of global public opinion in supporting this solution. SMOs emphasized their links with public opinion and they present themselves as expressions of the collective will of citizens.

All organizations emphasized public opinion support for their initiatives and arguments, and mentioned opinion polls widely. Interestingly, activists tended to equate polls with public opinion, and in this sense they aligned their strategy to the contemporary political tendency to make extensive use of statistical methods in estimating consensus and in orienting political decisions. In 2004 the new goal 'to withdraw troops from Iraq' seemed to be more difficult to achieve; on the one hand SMOs still proposed to involve the UN in order to press the first Bush administration in a generic way, on the other hand the lack of international mobilization forced activists to focus on the humanitarian consequences of the war. The decline in mobilizing capability forced peace organizations to stress their positive role in delivering concrete goods to the Iraqi people. In this light we note a stronger identification and support for civil society organizations, especially for those involved in humanitarian projects.

This emphasis on humanitarian work has represented a fundamental change in the peace movement. Peace activity has for more activists than before come to mean work in support of refugees, trips to locations of conflict to make clear their dissent and put pressure on state authorities, collections of food, medicines and other resources to send to areas of conflict, etc. These activities were by no means new but they have expanded to the point where they constituted a fundamental change. Evidence of the importance of linking anti-war mobilization to humanitarian work emerged in calls for action. All networks invited people to join a rally or to organize a public demonstration, and they all called for support for humanitarian efforts. There were

Table 6.2 Percentages of calls for actions to be undertaken
(N = 150)

To join a demonstration	29.1
Symbolic actions	19.7
Resistance	14.1
To sustain humanitarian aid	13.1
To press institutions	11.2
General strike	7.3
Civil disobedience	3.7
To pray	0.9
To boycott	0.8
Total	100

calls for civil disobedience and resistance (for example, conscientious objectors sought to halt trains that transported military supplies), invitations to put pressure on national and international institutions, prayers and symbolic actions such as the display of flags and other symbols. Finally, there were plans to boycott multinational American companies, proposed only by no-global networks (see Table 6.2). In 2004 this frame was enhanced by references to daily life: calls for action were mainly based on support for humanitarian aid and involvement in actions promoting peace in workplaces, schools and in other public places.

Views on national governments and Europe

The transnational nature of the European peace movement was also highlighted by its vision on how to check US power. For its activists, this role had to be played by the EU rather than the single national governments. The national governments of the four countries analysed expressed different attitudes towards the war against Iraq. British Prime Minister Tony Blair was the most important ally of the US, together with Mr Berlusconi who has been strongly supportive of American decisions in relation to the war. On the opposite side, President Chirac and Chancellor Schroeder actively opposed the American attack on Iraq, influencing the course of events in the UN assembly.

In this light one might expect that peace networks expressed a strong opposition to Italian and British governments and a positive attitude towards French and German administrations. Our results provide evidence that this is only partially true. Although peace networks expressed their concern for the Italian and British involvement in the 'illegal war', on the whole they addressed national governments only marginally. It appears that – coherently with their discursive strategy based on the legalistic version of anti-Americanism – anti-war networks focused their criticisms on President Bush and tried to gain influence over the American administration, thus by-passing national governments.

Activists blamed Mr Blair and Mr Berlusconi for being subordinate to American decisions, and condemned Italian and British participation in military operations, but in general terms national Prime Ministers were not held directly responsible for the Iraqi situation; rather they have been regarded as accomplices and British activists accused Blair of being a liar because of statements regarding the presence of weapons of mass destruction in Iraq. PM Berlusconi was seldom mentioned in documents and normally he was listed together with Mr Blair and Mr Aznar.

More importantly, there were no references to the potential role of domestic institutions in achieving peace and in influencing American decisions on war. Although in 2003 peace networks supported President Chirac because of the role of France within the UN Council, our results suggest that peace networks clearly regarded national governments as ineffective for delivering peace. These results confirm the transnational character of the anti-war movement. According to Keck and Sikkink (1998), transnational mobilizations are more likely to emerge where domestic institutions appear to be unsuccessful or useless in resolving a problem. In such cases social actors by-pass their domestic institutions and activate a network at the transnational level, which targets international institutions directly and applies pressure on national governments from the outside. In anti-war mobilizations, European national governments were not expected to be able to exercise influence over the US administration and consequently activists relied on worldwide public support for achieving their goals and trying to stop the war. However, interestingly enough, what emerges from the data is a strong concern with a political future for Europe. This was in part a response to the coincidence of the war and of the European constitutionalization process. It was possibly also an activists' decision – moving the debate on Europe to the future – that reflected the internal division of the movements on assessments of the present. For some, the EU is an irretrievable creation of capitalists without legitimacy and to them it would appear illogical, illegitimate and of no utility to use the war as a reason to advocate its stronger weight. To others, however, Europe is an ally that needs to be involved. The EU parliament is a well known supporter of several movements' causes (Ruzza 2004) and if one grants it a modicum of legitimacy, its involvement is a valuable opportunity. By moving most of the emphasis onto a future Europe, this debate could be postponed whilst the definitions of states as moral entities could be reaffirmed.

Empirical researches highlight that, in general, social movement organizations are aware of the importance of the supranational level, but they continue to be based on national and subnational level, and often have only a weak level of engagement in EU policy-making. Of course, this frame differs depending on the policy involved (Rucht 2001). In the case of the peace movement Europe has been conceived as a positive but still unaccomplished political project. Peace networks stressed their interest in the construction of a new Europe, which should be characterized by a strong support for human rights, solidarity and international cooperation. In this sense Europe will have the opportunity to differentiate itself from America. An example of this argument emerges in an Italian document of 2003:

> *Tavola della pace* aims at contributing to the construction of the Europe of citizens, open and responsible, non-violent, an instrument for peace and justice in the world. Europe should be able to reject war, and to create a global system for security; to discuss the western model of development, to eradicate the roots of economic inequality and poverty, and to promote a sustainable human development, to promote international democracy, and to give an impulse to the democratisation of the United Nations, the centre of global governance.
>
> (Tavola della Pace, 2003a)

In sum, a political Europe was considered the only potential check on the US, given that the main European governments were divided on what position to take on the Iraqi war. As noted above, the interventionist coalition led by the UK and the US was counterposed to a coalition led by France and Germany which argued its case in the name of an alleged alternative vision of Europe, less inclined to use military force. In doing so the traditional French and German governments' concern for an independent European political identity could be supported while remaining faithful to the preference of their voters. In other words, a strong stand on a specific issue had the double objective of reasserting a universally valued goal – European identity – and at the same time taking an electorally useful stand.

In relation to the Persian Gulf war, the existence of a common vision of Europe was even more contested and the need to reassert it crucial, with an EU internally divided and unable to agree on a common position. But the movements found in this cultural fragmentation of political elites, as regards the meaning of Europe, a political opportunity. Elite allies emerged and their support was connected to a framing of anti-Americanism that created space for an alternative vision of a European identity – an identity that connects principled politics and European identity – and in doing so created new opportunities for the elite realignments that benefited the movement.

Conclusions

This chapter has argued that anti-Americanism characterized European peace movements' framings of their campaigns in 2003 and 2004 and denotes new opportunities that the movements exploited with reference to the context that characterized international relations during and before the second Persian Gulf war, and also with regard to factors pertaining to the relationship between the movements and their institutional environments. In particular, this analysis shows that a number of key themes emerged, and gave specific meaning and a voice to a diffused anti-Americanism as well as engendering hostility towards the first Bush administration among large sectors of the European population.

Through anti-Americanism, the European peace movement mobilized a wider set of constituencies than in previous cycles of peace mobilization. We pointed to the connection between anti-Americanism and dynamics of political identity connected to the process of European integration which are increasingly topical for both ruling coalitions and the social movement sector. We emphasized the impact of the widening of the movement's strategy in terms of utilizing a juridical focus and emphasizing morality as framing strategies which were predominant and alternative to previous anti-imperialist framings of anti-Americanism. We pointed to the impact on political systems that anti-Americanism had as a movement's enabling construct, therefore contributing to new political opportunities. We documented an emphasis on moral behaviour and principled politics which the US administration was accused of neglecting, and an attempt to counter this with an idealized view of a moralized European identity set in the future. An alternative vision of Europe therefore became an element in the movements' mobilizing efforts and the benchmark against which to judge and indict the interventionist ethos of the pro-war coalition.

Anti-Americanism had also emerged as a reflection of the growing influence in the peace movements of the no-global movement and the increasing importance of activists connected to churches and other third-sector organizations and engaged in voluntary work.

Notes

1 For a summary of this tradition, which emphasizes socially constructed ideas in collective action see McAdam, McCarthy and Zald (1996).
2 The programme 'Atlas ti' for text analysis was utilized. Documents have been organized keeping track of background variables which included nationality, types of organizations and known institutional affiliations. The unit of analysis was the sentence. Within sentences a frame analysis which allowed for one or more frames was conducted. Results were examined by extrapolating all similar frames and relating them to background variables. 120 frames were identified. Only the major ones and the ones relating to anti-Americanism are discussed here.
3 Pearson chi-square value 44.6, df $= 6$, $p = 0.00$.

References

Brittain, V. (1991) *The Gulf Between Us: The Gulf War and Beyond*, London: Virago Press.
Kaltefleiter, W. and Pfaltzgraff, R.L. (1985) *The Peace Movements in Europe and the United States*, New York: St. Martin's Press.
Keck, M.E. and Sikkink, K. (1998) *Activism Beyond Borders*, Ithaca, NY: Cornell University Press.
McAdam, D., McCarthy, J.D. and Zald M.N. (eds) (1996) *Comparative Perspectives on Social Movements*, Cambridge: Cambridge University Press.
Rochon, T.R. (1988) *Mobilizing for Peace*, Princeton, NJ: Princeton University Press.

Rucht, D. (2001) 'Lobbying or Protest? Strategies to Influence EU Environmental Policies', in S. Tarrow (ed.), *Contentious Europeans*, Lanham, MD: Rowman & Littlefield Publishers, Inc.

Ruzza, C. (2004) *Europe and Civil Society: Movement Coalitions and European Governance*, Manchester: Manchester University Press.

Sardar, Z. and Davies, M.W. (2003) *Why Do People Hate America?*, London: Icon Books.

Snow, D.A. and Benford, R.D. (1988) 'Ideology, Frame Resonance, and Participant Mobilization', *International Social Movement Research*, 1: 197–217.

Snow, D.A., Rochford, E. Burke, Worden, Steven K. and Benford, Robert D. (1986) 'Frame Alignment Processes, Micromobilization and Movements Participation', *American Sociological Review*, 51: 464–81.

7 Anti-Americanism and European public opinion during the Iraq war

Pierangelo Isernia

Introduction

The spectre of anti-Americanism is hovering again about Europe.[1] In the past three years, politicians and commentators, on both sides of the Atlantic, have denounced its rapid resurgence in Europe.[2] In their view, the spread of anti-Americanism would contribute towards explaining Europe's lukewarm solidarity with the United States' (US) fight against terrorism and rogue states, such as Iraq. However, as is often the case, the existence and the relevance of the phenomenon is taken for granted, and little effort is spent on trying to understand its precise contours, interrelationships and consequences. Is anti-Americanism a manifestation, a cause or a consequence of the present transatlantic rift? Any analysis of the dimensions, nature and consequences of anti-Americanism is difficult for at least three reasons: its 'essentially contested' nature; its loose empirical referents and the variety of its manifestations. Not surprisingly, different answers are offered to the question on who is and what it means to be anti-American.

Here, I interpret anti-Americanism as a general feeling towards America rather than more specific beliefs towards this or that attribute of American political, cultural and socio-economic system. I will therefore define anti-Americanism as the *psychological tendency to evaluate negatively the US*. Such a definition of anti-Americanism leaves open for empirical assessment the issue of whether its sources are rational or irrational, 'visceral' or thoughtful. As such, anti-Americanism can be seen either as a manifestation of what are fundamentally internal, intra-psychic, needs and problems, a form of 'symbolic scapegoating' similar in its function to ethnocentrism,[3] or as a reaction, perceptually and cognitively mediated, but still a reaction to what America is or does.

Given the powerful position occupied by the US in the world system, people tend to pass evaluation of American policies and action on their own merits, quite distinct from their feelings towards the political object. Following the prevalent consensus in the literature (e.g. Haseler 1985) I would not define this kind of criticism as a form of anti-Americanism, but rather as a critical attitude towards it, whose connection with beliefs and feelings has to be empirically assessed, rather than assumed.

Given the problems one incurs in handling the concept of anti-Americanism, as Sergio Fabbrini argues in Chapter 1, let me state as clearly as I can from the beginning the exact purport of my chapter. Here, I will focus my attention on mass-level anti-Americanism in four European countries – France, Germany, Italy and the United Kingdom. My analysis has therefore three characteristics. First, it is limited to Western European forms of anti-Americanism; for some (e.g. Hollander 1995; Haseler 1985) the less mercurial and resentful ones, as compared to those in the Third World. I selected France, Germany, Italy and the UK because of their different national cultures and because these are countries for which a rich set of long-term data is available. Second, this is an analysis of anti-Americanism at the mass level. Not many studies on anti-Americanism are available at the mass attitudinal level (among the few see Smith and Wertman 1992: 91–128; more recently, Johnston and Ray, 2004 and, for South Korea, Larson *et al.* 2004). But if elites use anti-Americanism 'to socialize conflict' (Schattschneider 1960: 11), it is crucial to see what impact this use has at the mass level.

Third, my analysis is based exclusively on a secondary analysis of available mass survey data. Survey data form a useful complement to the traditional methods that look at the cultural, literary or political manifestations of anti-Americanism. Since available survey data on anti-Americanism go back to the 1950s, they constitute a very rich, differentiated and often underutilized stock of material that can contribute to shedding some light on the phenomenon over a long period of time. Of course, being a secondary analysis, it is limited by the kind of questions others asked for their own purposes. In trying to turn this variety of questions to my own advantage, I will move across surveys conducted in different time periods, so as to exploit the variety of indicators available, at the expense of some of the rigour offered by strict comparability over time of identically worded questions.

In an attempt to give an order to the different meanings of anti-Americanism in what is an admittedly murky terrain,[4] I will make a distinction between two fundamentally different sets of attitudes towards the US: feelings and policy attitudes. People can hold different affective or emotional feelings towards the US and different evaluations of what America does; and they can vary quite independently among themselves. Following this bipartite distinction of attitudes towards the United States, my chapter is organized in two parts. First, I will present how anti-Americanism has been measured, using attitudinal data, and its evolution over time. Then, I will move to anti-Americanism as an independent variable to explain policy attitudes. More specifically, I will examine whether the present critical European stance vis-à-vis the American decision to attack Iraq is driven by anti-Americanism, or rather by other factors, such as attitudes towards the first George W. Bush administration, the beliefs in the wisdom of American foreign policy or ideology.

Anti-Americanism on the rise?

To measure anti-Americanism at the mass level, three sets of indicators have been used over time (see also the discussion in Smith and Wertman, 1992: 93–103). A first set of questions asks about the respondent's feeling or opinion towards the United States. These questions come in two formats. The most frequent format is a standard five-point Likert-scale question, asking the respondent to choose between four options:[1] very good opinion, good opinion, fair (or alternatively neither good nor bad),[2] bad opinion, or very bad opinion. An alternative way of assessing people's feelings towards a country is the so-called 'feeling thermometer'.[3] A second set of questions, also asked repeatedly over time, demands the level of *trust* in the American *people*, rather than in the United States.[4] The third, and probably the most direct way of obtaining an insight into anti-American feelings, was in fact tried twice, in Eurobarometer 17 (April 1982) and 22 (April 1984): 'How would you describe your feelings towards the United States? Strongly anti-American, somewhat anti-American, somewhat pro-American, strongly pro-American or neither pro- nor anti-American (only volunteered)'.

There are just two crucial differences in the questions whose impact on the aggregate level of negative orientation towards the US is worth exploring here: the sentiments which are called into the questions (of feelings, opinion, trust) and the referent object (US and/or American people). Is there any difference in asking about opinion or trust for the US and the orientation towards the US or rather the American people? Or are all these trends tapping the same underlying dimension of anti-Americanism?

The general reference to the US has been criticized because 'it does not refer to an explicit set of national characteristics or attributes and therefore we have no way of knowing which symbols and associations serve as referents to the respondent prior to his expression of feeling' (Abravanel and Hughes, 1973: 113). On the other hand, Abravanel and Hughes continue, just because it is so clueless, the feeling question taps a general and basic attitude towards the referent object, an 'anchoring dimension of people's images of the international environment' (Abravanel and Hughes, 1973: 114) hierarchically superior to beliefs and policy attitudes, through which the respondents filter their perceptions of the international environment. Moreover, an explicit reference to American people could be criticized as an indicator of anti-Americanism, given the fact that anti-Americanism is commonly assumed to be a critical orientation towards what US is and not an ethnocentric distaste for its people. Finally, the attempt to solve the problem as in the feeling thermometer, in which respondents are invited to rate their feelings towards 'countries, institutions and people', is affected by a triple-barrel problem. We simply do not know which of these three elements the respondent has in mind when rating the United States.

In order to explore what differences these individual wordings produce, one needs to examine some available evidence. It shows four things: first, respondents are able to distinguish between the people of a nation and their governments, if invited to do so, and more than ready to blame the latter rather than the former when called upon to evaluate policies; also in situations, such as a war, in which such a distinction is less obvious and less likely to be expected. Second, the distinction between the people and their government is more relevant when political tension exists between the respondent's own country and the US. Third, the simple reference to the US is more likely to evoke the country rather than the American people in the respondent's mind. Fourth, the different questions eventually produce similar and consistent results and they are quite highly intercorrelated.

The fact that people are able to distinguish between governments and their subjects, when explicitly asked to do so, does not tell us, however, what is in the people's minds when the only reference is the US. Are they thinking of the government, the people or both? Table 7.1 sheds some light on both these points. The table compares the difference made by asking for feelings towards a 'country' or its 'people', keeping constant other possible sources of variation. And, it assesses this difference for our four countries in quite different periods. In both cases, a split-half experiment was tried, in which one-half of the sample were asked about their feelings towards the US and the other half about the Americans. In the 1958 USIA question, there is no difference in the two distributions and in the 2002 PEW question there is a slight difference, with the respondents being more likely to have a good opinion of the people than the nation.[9]

The slight difference between sympathy towards the US and the American people in 2002, as compared to 1958, might be a consequence of the state of political relationships between the respondent's country and the US in the two periods. In other words, the tendency to distinguish between the people

Table 7.1 Feelings towards Americans and the United States (%)

| | October 1958 | | June 2002 | |
	Nation	People	Nation	People
Very good/very favourable	15	15	13	14
Good/favourable	43	41	52	59
Fair	22	27	na	na
Bad/unfavourable	8	7	24	17
Very bad/very unfavourable	2	2	5	4
DK	10	8	5	6
Total	100	100	100	100
	(2475)	(2404)	(2516)	(2516)

Sources: 1958: XX-11, USIA; 2002: PEW Global Attitudes Survey. Pooled countries: France, Germany, Italy and United Kingdom.

and the government – and the differential impact of a clear reference to one or the other – becomes more evident when the level of tension between the countries involved is higher, as it was the case in 2002 in comparison with 1958. This is confirmed by the fact that, once we consider the entire set of 44 countries surveyed by PEW in 2002, clear differences do exist between the overall feelings towards a country and those towards the American people in some countries, but not in others. The difference is relevant among the Western European countries, where favour towards Americans is seven points per cent higher than towards the US, and even higher (16 points difference) in the three Middle East countries surveyed (Egypt, Jordan and Lebanon), while it is insignificant in all the other countries. These two pieces of information put together seem to indicate that, in a period of tension, the distinction between the US and Americans is more relevant and that the question asking about feelings towards the US taps the general orientation towards the country rather than towards the American people.

The Eurobarometer on 17 March–April 1982 allows us to explore more systematically the impact these differences in wordings produce on the pattern of responses. In that survey, most of the questions discussed here were asked. A first question, placed at the beginning of the questionnaire, asked about the level of trust in Americans.[10] Then, in the middle of the question-naire, a set of five different questions measured the opinion towards the US,[5] the confidence in the American Administration's ability to deal wisely with world problems,[6] whether it is better for the respondent's own country to coordinate with the US or not,[7] the extent to which the US takes the respon-dent's own country's interests into account when they make a decision,[8] the effects for peace or war of US policies in the past year,[9] and, finally, the anti-American feelings of the respondent.[10] Table 7.2 reports the Pearson correlation coefficients among these different indicators. They are all highly intercorrelated, and in particular the affective indicators, such as the general opinion of the US, the feelings of anti-Americanism and trust towards Americans. It is possible that the strength of some of these correlations was inflated by the fact that all questions (but one) were asked in a sequential order, one after the other. But still the correlation between the only question that was asked earlier on in a separate section of the questionnaire (the level of trust towards Americans), also shows a high correlation with all the other items. These results are corroborated by a principal component analysis of the five variables that produces only one factor (eigenvalue of 4.18, explaining 59.8 per cent of the variance and an average factor loading of 0.772).[11]

My data is in line with the conclusions reached by Smith and Wertman (1992: 94) ten years ago, in the sense that these different ways of measuring the overall opinion of the US, although with different formats and wording, produce very similar results. This is true over time and across countries. In conclusion, general opinion towards the US – usually measured using a feeling question – appears to be a reliable and a valid indicator of anti-Americanism. Given the long time-series available for this question, one is in

Table 7.2 Correlation coefficients among indicators of attitudes towards the United States

	General opinion of US	Confidence in US	Foreign policy and US interests	National security and US decisions	US effects on peace	Pro/anti-American
Trust in Americans	0.638* (3620)	0.560* (3686)	0.426* (3345)	0.460* (3567)	0.414* (3133)	−0.495* (3570)
General opinion of US		0.678* (3676)	0.456* (3338)	0.494* (3537)	0.499* (3102)	−0.596* (3523)
Confidence in US			0.468* (3405)	0.531* (3646)	0.526* (3173)	−0.543* (3598)
Foreign policy and US interests				0.493* (3363)	0.433* (2928)	−0.430* (3307)
National security and US decisions					0.453* (3512)	−0.411* (3115)
US policy effects on peace						−0.502* (3085)

Source: Eurobarometer 17, March–April 1982 (pooled data for France, (West) Germany, Italy and United Kingdom). Only the cross-section sample has been used.

* = p significant > .01

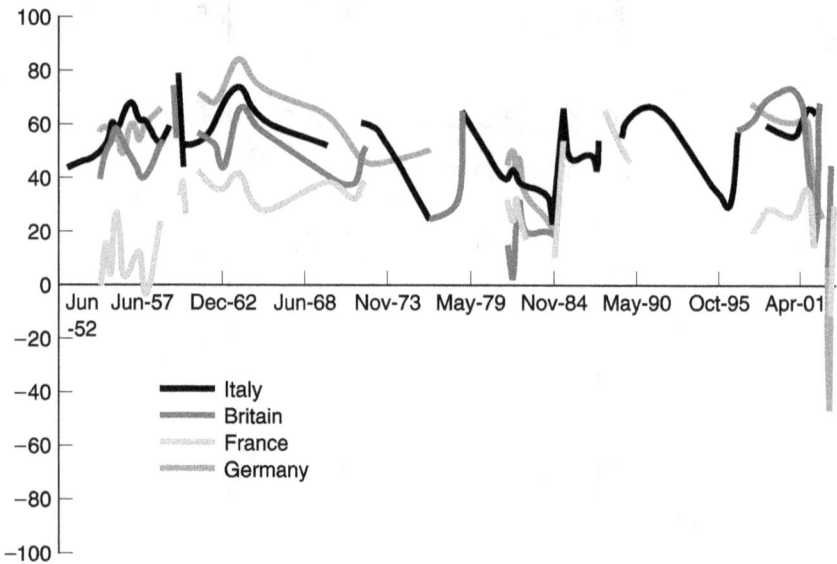

Figure 7.1 Trends in the net attitudes towards the United States. The vertical line
reports the net favour towards the United States, measured subtracting
those who have a bad opinion of the US from those who have a good
opinion. A positive number means that the percentage of those who hold
a positive opinion is higher than that of those having a bad opinion and a
negative sign the opposite.

Sources: USIA XX-series 1952–1967, Eurobarometer series 1970–2000, Pew Global
Attitudes Survey 2002 and Transatlantic Trend Survey 2002–2004.

a position to assess the level of anti-Americanism over a long time span.
Figure 7.1 shows, for these four countries, the trend in the net general
feeling towards the US between 1952 and 2003, obtained by subtracting
those with a negative opinion from those with a favourable one. The figure
points to three main results.

First, in all four countries sentiments towards the US are prevalently positive. This long-term view confirms once again what also other authors have
stressed, that 'anti-Americanism has been the view of only a limited minority in most Western European countries throughout the post-war period'
(Smith and Wertman 1992: 101). Second, although substantially positive,
the aggregate level of anti-American sentiments is systematically different
across countries. The French public is always more anti-American in its orientation, while the Germans and Italians are less so than the overall average.
The net average feeling towards the US in France is 20 points, while in
Germany and Italy it is respectively 50 and 48, with Britain at a slightly
lower 43 points. This confirms the image of the French public as less pro-
American (it is probably too strong to say more anti-American given the

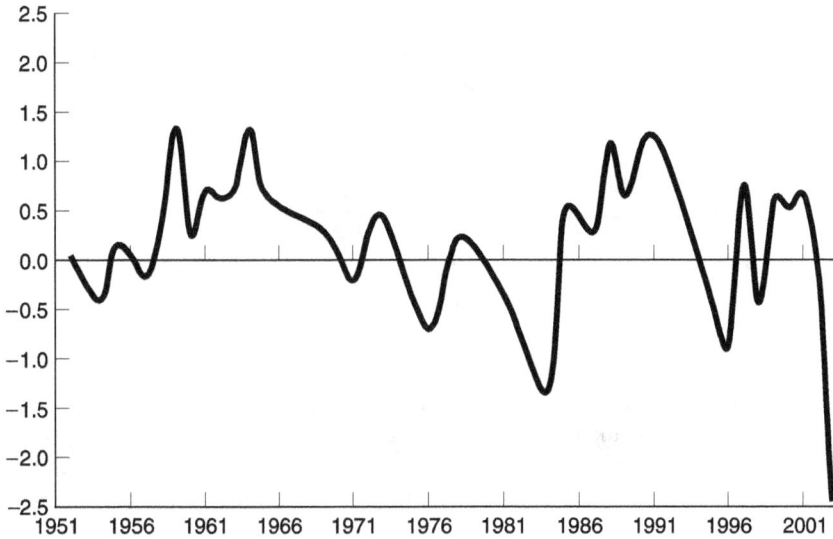

Figure 7.2 Trends in the net attitudes towards the United States (normalized average, yearly base). For the details of how this figure has been computed see text.

Sources: USIA XX-series 1952–1967, Eurobarometer series 1970–2000, Pew Global Attitudes Survey 2002 and Transatlantic Trend Survey 2002–2004.

systematically positive sign of the net feeling indicator) compared to the other European countries. Third, the figure also reports some fluctuations over time in the net level of anti-Americanism.

To give a plainer view of these fluctuations of anti-Americanism over time, I proceeded to smooth the four trend lines, using the same procedure that Stimson (1991: 36–39) applied to develop his measure of mood.[12] Since I am interested here in examining the movement of anti-Americanism in time, the differences between countries can be ignored. In fact, the four series move quite in parallel, with an average correlation between pairs of 0.617, with only the British–France pair less than 0.5 (at 0.377) and one pair higher than 0.8 (Italy–Germany, at 0.865). Once forced to vary around the same average and range of variation, the series flattens a bit and shows the clearer picture in Figure 7.2.

The level of anti-Americanism, as measured by the net favour indicator, appears to be related to the nature of the international political environment. The increases in anti-Americanism (as measured by dips in net favour) are all related to crises in transatlantic relations. The first dip was in October 1954 due, however, exclusively to the French data point, as a consequence of the Franco–American crisis followed by the failure to ratify the European Defence Community by the French National Assembly. A second downturn, in the second half of the 1950s, coincided with the Suez crisis, which lasted until November 1957, as reported from the available survey data. A third surge in anti-Americanism materialized between 1971 and 1976, as a consequence of the turbulent state of transatlantic relations in connection with the Vietnam War and the monetary crisis due to the stop in dollar convertibility and the economic crisis ensuing the Arab oil embargo. The following surge of anti-Americanism manifested itself in the early 1980s, in connection with the collapse of détente, the controversial NATO Euro-missiles decision and the acrimonious debate about the Reagan's foreign policy towards the Soviet Union. Things started to improve again in 1985, with the arrival of Gorbachev and the changes in policies which he introduced. The next dip, in 1994–95, must be interpreted with caution, as this data was only available for Italy. It probably occurred as a consequence of the reluctance of the United States to be embroiled in the Balkans' turmoil and the uncertainty about the American willingness to intervene there in support of European troops on the ground.

Finally, we arrive at 2003, which has the highest increase in anti-Americanism in all four countries since survey data has been available. In 2003, a net favour in these four countries not only reaches the lowest level ever, but for the first time becomes negative in Germany and Italy and reaches the bottom lowest +8 points for the UK. However, as in the past, sympathy towards the US quickly recovers. Already in July 2003, positive feelings in France outmatch negative ones by 29 percentage points. This rapid upswing in positive feeling is quite characteristic of attitudes towards the United States for the entire 40-year period. However, as Figure 7.2 also emphasizes, the range of oscillations in levels of anti-Americanism becomes wider and wider over time.[13] Now that the general trend in anti-Americanism in the past 40 years has been established, I will explore whether this general feeling is related to evaluations about American foreign policy.

Anti-Americanism and US foreign policy in the 2000s

The period 2002–2004 (see Figure 7.2), witnessing the most dramatic increase in anti-Americanism ever, is particularly useful in this respect. In order to detect if anti-Americanism plays any role, a period in which the American image is tarnished is the most appropriate focus of study. To do so, I will first describe in some detail what impact the events unfolding between 9/11 and the war in Iraq had on sentiments towards the US. Then, I will examine the influence of anti-American sentiments on attitudes towards Iraq, as compared to other factors, such as the antipathy towards the first Bush administration and harsh judgment of the American foreign policy.

Anti-Americanism in the wake of 9/11

In the wake of the 9/11 Al Qaeda attacks against the World Trade Center and the Pentagon, sympathy towards the United States was aroused immediately in all the four countries here examined.[14] In France, a country whose positive feelings towards US are systematically lower than in other European countries, the terrorist attack produced an upward pulse in sympathy of more than 20 percentage points. To the SOFRES question 'Do you have sympathy for the US or rather antipathy, or neither of these?' in 16–18 May 2000 (French-American Foundation), 41 per cent answered 'sympathy', 10 per cent 'antipathy' and 48 per cent 'neither one nor the other' (1 per cent were 'don't know's). On 1–2 November 2001, to this same question (SOFRES for *Le Nouvel Observateur*), 65 per cent answered 'sympathy', 5 per cent 'antipathy' and 29 per cent 'neither one nor the other' (1 per cent were 'don't know's). However, already by August 2002 the percentage of those having sympathy for the US had declined to 39 per cent, while those having feelings of antipathy towards the US increased to 16 per cent and the indifferents to 44 per cent. In Germany, to an EMNID question for the Ministry of Defence asking 'The United States has been hit most strongly by the terrorist attacks of 11 September. Do you personally feel solidarity with the USA?' on 12–15 November 2001, 79 per cent of the 2000 interviewed answered 'Yes', and only 19 per cent 'No' (with 2 per cent having no opinion).

Immediately after 9/11, some commentators stressed questions asking about the possible relationships between the American foreign policy and the 9/11 events as an indicator of anti-Americanism. In general, public opinion in the countries in which a question of this sort has been asked appears divided over the responsibility of American foreign policy in bringing about the 9/11 attack. The alternatives offered seem also to have an effect on the distribution of answers. Immediately after the event, on 26–27 September 2001, SOFRES asked in France 'What are, in your opinion, the principal reasons for the terrorists to attack the United States of America?' A plurality (49 per cent) chose the option 'because the US are the leading economic power in the world', and another 42 per cent (the question allowed multiple response) mentioned either 'American foreign policy in general' or 'American policy towards the Arab states' in particular. Another 38 per cent mentioned 'support for Israel' and 29 per cent being a 'symbol of the West'. In Italy, to a question (SWG/*Famiglia Cristiana*, September 2001) asking 'With respect to the terrorist attacks that occurred in New York some say that the terrorists are entirely responsible for these attacks, others say that the United States are also partly responsible because of their policies around the world. With which view do you most agree?', 45 per cent picked the first option and 46 per cent agreed that 'the United States shares part of the responsibility' (with 10 per cent who did not know). In the UK, to the question 'Some people are saying that the Americans brought these attacks on themselves because of their policies on the Middle East. Do you agree or disagree?' (GALLUP/*Daily Telegraph*, 17–18 September 2001) only 23 per cent agreed with the statement, while 66 per cent disagreed and 11 per cent did not answer. The only truly comparative question on this matter has been asked by MORI for the GMFUS in June 2002 (Table 7.3) and it shows that in France, 63 per cent

Table 7.3 Has American foreign policy contributed to the 9/11 attack? (June 2002)

	Strongly agree	Agree somewhat	Somewhat disagree	Strongly disagree	Don't know	N
UK	24	33	17	19	7	1000
France	19	44	17	15	6	1001
Germany	17	35	24	20	5	1000
Italy	19	33	20	23	7	1000

Source: MORI for GMFUS.

Note: Question wording: 'Some say American foreign policy has contributed to the September 11 attacks. Do you agree or disagree with this statement? Strongly or somewhat?'.

agree (strongly or somewhat) with the statement 'American foreign policy has contributed to the September 11 attacks', while in the UK the percentage of those in agreement with this statement is 57 per cent, and in Germany and Italy 52 per cent.

Although it is not clear exactly what this question is measuring, the conviction that American foreign policy has contributed to the 9/11 attack is not strongly related to anti-American feelings. Correlating the standard feeling thermometer, as an indicator of anti-Americanism, with the agree–disagree statement mentioned right above in Table 7.6 produces a significant but weak correlation in all the four countries surveyed: 0.281 in Britain, 0.280 in Italy, 0.307 in France and 0.250 in Germany.

The increase in sympathy towards the US in the wake of the 9/11 attack, not surprisingly, passed on support for the military action undertaken by the US in Afghanistan to oust the Taliban regime, found to be an accomplice of the Al Qaeda ring. The data on the degree of support for the American military action in Afghanistan in a set of 63 countries surveyed in November–December 2001 by Gallup International, show that France, Germany, Italy and the UK, together with most of the other NATO members, Albania, Israel, India and Kosovo are the only countries in which a clear majority in support of the American military action in Afghanistan is found. In the UK, France, Germany and Italy, two-thirds of the public were supportive of the action. All other countries were either divided, with only a slim majority or a plurality in favour of the American military operation (e.g. Japan, Switzerland, Ireland and Sweden) or resolutely hostile to the American military operation in Afghanistan (with Pakistan, Greece, Azerbaijan, Malaysia, Argentina, Turkey, Mexico, Bolivia, Bosnia, Uruguay, Yugoslavia and the Ukraine in descending order of opposition). In another survey, carried out by IPSOS/REID in 12 countries in the same period (Global Express Monitor, 19 November–17 December 2001), asking whether the respondents did 'support or oppose these US-led air strikes on Afghanistan', including 'military sites of the Taliban government, and training camps of the Al Qaeda group led by Osama bin Laden', a majority of the public in France (60 per cent), Germany (60 per cent), Italy (58 per cent) and the UK (65 per cent) supported 'these US-led air strikes on Afghanistan', while Argentina, Turkey, China and Spain opposed and South Korea and Japan showed mixed feelings.[15]

The high level of support for the United States is confirmed by a different way of tackling the same issue. Asking how justified were the American attacks, as a response to the 9/11 events, 77 per cent of the Germans believed on 12 October 2001 (ENMNID/n-TV) that they 'were justified'; 61 per cent of the Italians thought in September 'that the terrorist attacks justify a military response by the US' (SWG/Famiglia Cristiana, 16–25 September 2001) and 51 per cent of the British in November were ready to go as far as to justify 'the allied bombing campaign against the Taliban in Afghanistan, including the use of carpet bombing and "daisy cutter" bombs' (ICM/*The Guardian*, 16–18 November 2001). On the contrary, in countries like Morocco and Palestine the American reactions were seen as unjustified by three out of four people (Everts and Isernia, 2002).

Some evidence points to the fact that support for the American war on terrorism in France, the UK, Germany and Italy stemmed from a test of pro-Americanism and a willingness to demonstrate support for a friendly country rather than from a shared diagnosis of the best way to deal with terrorism. Scattered but convergent pieces of evidence from survey data point to the fact that military force was not perceived by the Europeans, at that time, as the preferred option to deal with the terrorist threat. An Environics survey, carried out in October–November 2001 in 16 countries (Global Issues Monitor Survey) asked whether the respondent agreed 'that military force is the most effective way of dealing with international terrorism'. 59 per cent of the French agreed with this statement, while 39 per cent of the Germans, 36 per cent of the Italians and 46 per cent of the British were also in agreement. On the contrary, in America, 76 per cent subscribed to this view. In the Gallup International Survey on 14–17 September 2001, only in India and Israel were clear majorities found in favour of a military option. In the US, only a bare majority of 54 per cent of the public would have preferred that only 'once the identity of the terrorists is known, should the American government launch a military attack on the country or countries where the terrorists are based'. Firm majorities in all the other 34 countries surveyed (and 30 per cent of the Americans) would rather have seen that 'the American government seek to extradite the terrorists to stand trial'. In France, only 29 per cent whould have approved an attack rather than extradition, in Germany 17 per cent, in Italy 21 per cent and in the UK 18 per cent. Extradition was chosen respectively by 77 per cent of the Germans, 67 per cent of the French, 71 per cent of the Italians and 75 per cent of the British.

However, the support for the use of force might be even lower as the last question examined hints at. Apparently, the way in which the question was phrased may have led to overestimating the degree of support for military action. Whenever the question was not asked in the form of a simple dichotomy of 'yes' and 'no', but in the form of presenting alternative options including non-military ones, the outcomes were often rather different and support generally went down. Thus, for instance, in one German poll (EMNID) 58 per cent preferred to use diplomatic means in the struggle against terrorism with 40 per cent saying that only military force could be effective. In an SWG survey in Italy in September 2001, only 10 per cent preferred 'bombing' and 20 per cent 'send ground troops' among alternative options, while 49 per cent preferred 'economic sanctions'. In one YOUGOV poll in the UK, to a question asking 'Which of the following do you think should be the main focus for action taken against countries that knowingly harbour terrorist organizations?', 33 per cent preferred 'diplomatic negotiations', 26 per cent 'economic sanctions' and 34 per cent 'military action'. However, to a question, by the same institute YOUGOV asking in two different occasions in the Autumn of 2001 if 'there should be no military retaliation and that any action should be limited to economic and/or diplomatic sanctions against countries knowingly harbouring terrorist organizations?', a strong majority answered that actions should include 'military retaliation'. And to a Gallup/Daily Telegraph question asking 'Should the United States and its allies, or should they not, be prepared to take military action against countries believed to be giving aid and comfort to last week's terrorists?', 70 per cent of the sample interviewed on 17–18 September 2001 answered they 'should'.

Feeling that the American counteractions were justified and having sympathy for the American situation did not imply automatically, however, that one wanted one's country to become involved too. But again, here, France, Germany, Italy and the UK stand out, together with most of the NATO members, Israel and India, in their willingness to cooperate with the American military strategy in Afghanistan. To a Gallup International question asking 'Some countries and all NATO member states have agreed to participate in the military action against Afghanistan. Do you agree or disagree with that [your country] should take part with the United States military action against Afghanistan?' in September–October 2001 73 per cent of the French, 53 per cent of the Germans, 66 per cent of the Italians and 79 per cent of the British agreed. To a slightly different question, asked by EOS Gallup in the 15 EU countries in the second half of November (13–23 November 2001), in which an explicit reference to ground troops rather than to the more generic 'take part with the United States military action' was made,[16] among the NATO members only in France, Germany, Italy, the Netherlands and the UK could majorities be found, but not in Belgium, Denmark, Portugal, Spain, let alone Greece. In France, 54 per cent answered 'yes', national 'troops should be sent to fight with the US forces', in Germany 55 per cent, in Italy 51 per cent and in the UK 66 per cent.

This affirmation of support for the US did not, however, last long. In November–December 2001 the percentage of those supporting the proposition that the respondent's country 'should take part in the US military action against Afghanistan' was slightly eroded in respect of the identical question asked two months before (in France positive responses went down from 73 to 67 per cent, in Italy from 66 to 57 per cent, in the UK from 79 to 68 per cent and only in Germany slightly increased from 53 to 58 per cent) but still remained a majority. This being the second survey carried out once the operations in Afghanistan had truly begun, when the US government had made clear that it wanted the allies to support and cheer them on, but not their participation in the fighting if that would enable them to claim a say in the way the battle was being fought, the lack of increase, if not downright decrease, of support shows an erosion of the opening of goodwill among those allies of the US who had been staunchest up to this point.

The slight, but unequivocal, decrease in support for – and presumably sympathy towards – the American position in the fight against terrorism can be traced back to the resurfacing of a set of differences between European countries and the US over the best way to fight terrorism. A PEW survey in April 2002 compared attitudes across the Atlantic (the United States on the one hand and France, Germany, Italy and the UK on the other) on a number of issues related to the terrorist attacks and the problem of how to respond to them (Table 7.4). On a number of important aspects of the terrorist issue a growing gap appears between the American and European views; elements, incidentally that will loom large in the troubles to come in the following years due to the Iraqi crisis. While in 2002 a majority of the public in our four European countries still approved 'The US led military campaign against' Afghanistan, no more than one-third in France, Germany and Italy and slightly less than 40 per cent in the UK approved the 'axis of evil' reference in the 'State of the Union' speech by President Bush in January 2002; and only a similar percentage approved the American Middle East policy. In contrast, overwhelming majorities of Europeans, but only a slight majority of Americans, approved Bush's decision 'to increase US foreign aid to poor countries'.

Remarkably enough, these different assessments of American policies are not accompanied by a different degree of concern and fear about the dangers of Islamic terrorism. In this respect there is hardly any transatlantic divide. 60 per cent of the French (18 per cent 'very' and 42 per cent 'somewhat'), 63 per cent of the Germans (17 per cent 'very' and 46 per cent 'somewhat'), 59 per cent of the Italians (21 per cent 'very' and 38 per cent 'somewhat') and 56 per cent of the British (16 per cent 'very' and 40 per cent 'somewhat') are worried 'about the possibility of Islamic terrorism in [their own country] these days'. In the US, 67 per cent are 'very' (22 per cent) or 'somewhat' (45 per cent) worried about terrorism (PSRA/PEW Survey, 2–10 April 2002).

It is not surprising then that to a PEW question in 2–10 April 2002 asking 'How do you see the US-led war on terrorism: do you think the US is taking into account the interests of its allies in the fight against terrorism or do you think the US is acting mainly in its own interests?' 80 per cent of the French, 85 per cent of the Germans, 68 per cent of the Italians and 73 per cent of the British thought America was 'acting mainly in its own interests'

Table 7.4 Attitudes towards terrorism, axis of evil and US policies in Middle East (2–10 April 2002, % approve)

As I read some specific US policies tell me if you approve or disapprove of them.

	France	Germany	Italy	United Kingdom	United States
The US-led military campaign against the Taliban and Al Qaeda in Afghanistan	64	61	59	73	83
President Bush calling Iraq, Iran and North Korea an 'axis of evil'	27	17	29	37	56
President Bush's decision to increase US foreign aid to poor countries	90	86	95	90	53
US policies in the Middle East[a]	26	25	39	36	55

Source: PSRA/PEW.
Note:
a Asked in form 2 only.

and only 17 per cent of the French, 12 per cent of the Germans, 28 per cent of the Italians and 22 per cent of the British thought the US was 'taking into account the interests of its allies'.[17]

In conclusion, the review of the available evidence on support for the US and its foreign policy in the crucial period between 11 September 2001 and the 'axis of evil' speech in February 2002 shows that the conspicuous endowment of sympathy and support for the United States generated in our four countries by the eventful attacks in New York and Washington began to be eroded well before the Iraq war of 2003, and for reasons related to both differing views on how best to deal with terrorism and an increasing uneasiness with the developments taking place in the United States foreign policy after the Afghan war. In this context of increasing wariness and puzzlement over the direction American foreign policy was taking, the issue of an intervention in Iraq was brought into the agenda by Bush's administration.

Anti-Americanism and Iraq

It is not my intention here to review the available evidence on attitudes towards the war in Iraq in 2003 (on which, for more details please see, Everts and Isernia, 2005), but rather to explore in some depth whether, and to what extent attitudes towards Iraq can be explained by anti-American feelings in Europe. Using the comparative Transatlantic Trend Survey conducted in 2002, 2003 and 2004, I will examine the impact of anti-Americanism on attitudes towards the war in Iraq, as compared to with four other possible explanations of the tepid support for the Iraq war: attitudes towards the first

Table 7.5 Attitudes towards a US attack on Iraq (June 2002, in %)

There has been some discussion about whether the US should use its troops to invade Iraq and overthrow the government of Saddam Hussein. Which of the following positions is closest to yours?

	UK	Italy	France	Germany	US
The US should not invade Iraq	20	32	27	27	13
The US only invade Iraq, with UN approval and the support of allies	69	54	63	56	65
The US should invade Iraq even if they have to do it alone	10	10	6	12	20
DK	1	3	3	4	2
Total	100	100	100	100	100
(N)	1000	1000	1001	1000	1000

Source: CCFR-GMF Worldviews 2002.

Bush administration's handling of foreign policy, attitudes towards the American leadership, orientation towards international relations and the ideological predispositions of the respondents. Given the fact that questions are not exactly identical before and after the war, the results of the comparison among the different surveys have to be interpreted with caution.

To measure attitudes towards the war in Iraq I used two different sets of questions. In June 2002, when the discussion on Iraq was still at the beginning and no clear war plan had yet been made public (although some sources, e.g. Woodward 2002, claim that the Bush administration had already made up its mind on what to do with Iraq much earlier than that), I used a question asking about what the United States should do in Iraq.[18] As shown in Table 7.5, a clear majority of the public in the four European countries (and in the United States as well) was in favour of attacking Iraq 'only … with UN approval and the support of allies'. Only one-tenth of the public in Europe, and one-fifth in the US would have approved it 'even if they [i.e. US] have to do it alone'. One-third in the four European countries and slightly more than one-tenth of the American public supported the idea that the 'US should not invade Iraq' anyway. In 2003 and 2004 the question was in the 'worth the costs' format.[19] In 2004, a methodological twist was added in the question. Half of the sample was asked the standard 2003 version, while the other half was submitted to a differently worded question, in which a reference to the idea of 'liberating the Iraqi people' was included, to test the impact on support.[20] To account for this change in wording, I used a dummy variable that had value 1 when the reference 'to liberate the Iraqi people' was present in the question, and zero otherwise.

Besides anti-American feelings, measured through the feeling thermometer, I examined four major alternative determinants of orientation towards the

United States policy towards Iraq. A first, very obvious, one was the pure and simple antipathy towards Bush's administration entertained by the European public. George W. Bush's first administration's image in Europe was tarnished even before the war in Iraq. Eichenberg (2004) has assembled data on British opinion on three American presidents: Carter, Reagan and George W. Bush. Figure 7.3 shows clearly how Bush's popularity was low even before the Iraqi crisis broke out. In August 2001, net favour towards Bush was at the level of Reagan's popularity during the Euromissiles crisis. In this connection, an up-shift – though not dramatic – occurred with the 9/11 attack. But already in 2003, Bush's net opinion was again negative, touching the lowest popularity score of the three presidents reported in the Figure. The indicator I used in my analysis is the assessment of the foreign policy job performance.[21] The hypothesized relationship is in the positive direction. A positive assessment of the performance of Bush's job should positively affect attitudes towards the war in Iraq.

A second variable is the perception of American leadership, an indicator of the public assessment of the American foreign policy. The question asks 'how desirable is it that the US exert strong leadership in world affairs? Very desirable, somewhat desirable, somewhat undesirable, or very undesirable?' This question has been asked several times over the past decades and it is sensitive to the evolution of American foreign policy in a pattern quite similar to the one shown by the anti-Americanism indicator reported in Figure 7.1. Also, here I hypothesize that those who deem it desirable that the United States exert a strong leadership are more likely to be in favour of the Iraqi operation.

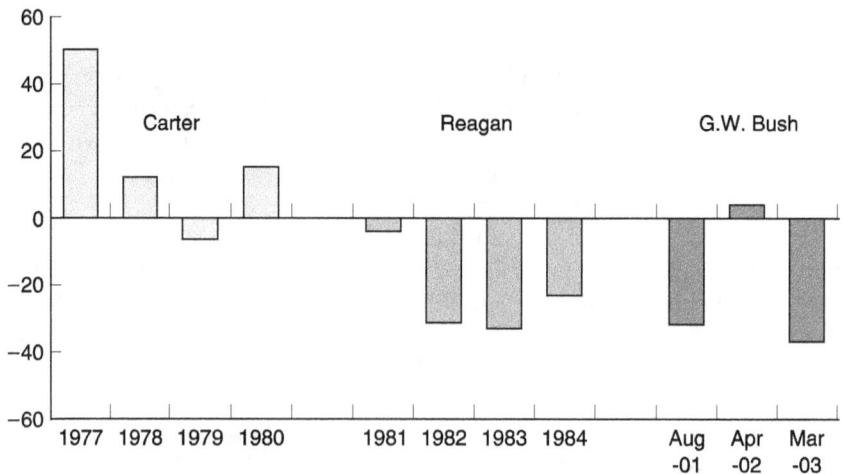

Figure 7.3 Net favourable opinions of three American presidents.

Source: Richard Eichenberg, personal communication. Data from British Gallup, various years, and Pew Research Center.

While the two previous variables measure the attitudes towards concrete American administration and political actors, as symbolized by the President of the United States or by the American leadership role in the world, the feeling thermometer is an indicator of anti-Americanism. The assumption here is that if people assess the merit of the Iraqi crisis according to anti-American lenses, this should emerge in this variable, once controlled for the short-term, policy-sensitive and event-reactive attitudes, as measured by the two previous variables. In other words, if anti-Americanism is behind the present harsh judgment of the American policy in Iraq, this should manifest itself with a strong and positive impact of the coefficient of anti-Americanism on attitudes towards the war. Otherwise, a negative and insignificant result should imply that most of the differences can be traced back to different judgments on the merit and nature of the American foreign policy in the Iraqi war.

I also included two measures of the general orientation towards international politics, to take into account the argument, put forward by some analysts (e.g. Kagan, 2003), that Americans and Europeans have a different image of the world and of its threats. In this connection, I included first an indicator of internationalism, to assess whether opposition to the war might arise by a desire on the part of the Europeans to isolate themselves from present world politics' turbulence. The question asking whether we should 'take an active part or stay out' of world affairs has been used. I expect that those who are more internationalist are also more likely to be in favour of a military operation against Iraq. The second indicator taps another potential source of ideological difference between Europeans and Americans: the greater importance attributed by the Europeans to 'soft power' (Nye 2004), and economic power in particular. In fact, available data shows that Europeans are more likely to agree with the statement that economic power is nowadays more important than military power in international relations. Other studies have also shown (see Asmus *et al.* 2004a; 2004b) that this is also an important predictor of foreign policy attitudes and quite stable over time, even in turbulent times such as the present ones. The question in 2002 asked directly 'Which of the following do you think is more important in determining a country's overall power and influence in the world – a country's economic strength, or its military strength?' In 2003 and 2004 the question was an agree–disagree statement on a four-point scale: 'Economic power is becoming more important in world affairs than military power'. I hypothesize that those who think that economic power is becoming more important than military power in world politics are also less inclined to support a military attack against Iraq or to deem the Iraq war worth the costs.

In 2002, a variable measuring the perceived threat from Iraq was also included, in order to assess whether this perception played any role in explaining attitudes towards a prospective military operation against this country. The assumption being here that those who were convinced that Iraq was a crucial threat were also more likely to subscribe to the idea of attacking it.

I included also a set of background variables, such as age, gender, education,[22] and the ideological predisposition, as measured on a 7-point left–right continuum. I expect the younger generations, the women, the better educated and the left-wing oriented to be more reluctant to use force and therefore less eager to support the Iraqi operation.

The results of the OLS regression here reported (Table 7.6) shed some doubts on the argument according to which anti-Americanism is the groundswell of the present source of tension between Europe and the US, at least as far as the war in Iraq is concerned. By far, the assessment of Bush's first administration and of American leadership in world affairs are the two most important determinants of attitudes towards the war both before and after the American attack, and in this order. As to anti-Americanism, it plays no systematic role across countries and over time. It has a minor influence in the UK before the war, in France immediately after the toppling of Saddam Hussein's regime and in Italy in both periods, while it has no significance for the entire period in Germany. Moreover, in 2004 the variable is not significant in any of the four countries. From these results, a major source of differences in explaining attitudes towards the Iraq war is the assessment of the US foreign policy, both in general – in terms of 'world leadership' – and in connection with the person at the helm of power, President George W. Bush. No other variable plays such a systematic role across the four countries here considered. In 2002, threat perception apparently had an impact, in the expected direction, only in the UK. Internationalism has no impact whatsoever in any country. As to the more general ideological dimension of the importance of soft power, it has a significant influence, and in the expected direction, in Germany and Italy in 2002, and in the UK in 2004.

One should also note the role played by the reference to 'liberating the Iraqi people' in the 2004 survey. The coefficient has the right sign in all four countries and it is relevant in three out of four (the only exception being Italy where it is statistically barely insignificant). The results indicate the importance of the goals of the action for the public in three out of the four countries here considered. In France, Germany and the UK a reference to the goal of 'liberating' the Iraqi people increases support for the war.

Conclusion

Anti-Americanism is an elusive phenomenon. In this chapter I have distinguished between a general affective orientation towards the US, which I suggest may properly be defined as anti-Americanism, and policy attitudes about American foreign policy. Although related, they are not necessarily part of the same syndrome. In fact, one of the results of this analysis is the discovery that people can entertain quite complex and critical views of what the US does, and still have a generally positive affective orientation towards it.

If anti-Americanism is a psychological predisposition to negatively evaluate the United States, available data over more than 40 years has led us to

Table 7.6 OLS-estimate of determinants of attitudes towards the Iraq war (standardized beta coefficient, *t*-ratio in parentheses)

	UK			France		
Model	*2002*	*2003*	*2004*	*2002*	*2003*	*2004*
Feelings US	0.033	0.096	-0.050	0.092	-0.024	-0.052
	(0.868)	(2.537)*	(-1.285)	(2.315)*	(-0.636)	(-1.445)
US leadership	0.111	0.069	0.106	0.112	0.110	0.006
	(2.999)**	(1.722)	(2.586)**	(2.922)**	(2.898)***	(0.170)***
Assessment Bush's foreign policy	0.113	0.311	0.334	0.092	0.266	0.225
	(2.998)**	(7.839)***	(8.133)***	(2.403)*	(6.957)***	(6.186)***
Threat Iraq	-0.142	na	na	-0.002	na	na
	(-4.240)***			(-0.050)		
Economic power	-0.025	0.038	0.078	-0.02	-0.021	-0.037
	(-0.748)	(1.129)	(2.235)*	(-0.769)	(-0.628)	(-1.116)
Internationalism	0.039	-0.053	-0.008	0.008	0.023	-0.014
	(1.160)	(-1.507)	(-0.233)	(0.220)	(0.695)	(-0.431)
Dummy liberate Iraqi people	na	na	-0.114	na	na	-0.075
			(-3.292)***			(-2.298)*
Adjusted R^2	0.129	0.200	0.173	0.091	0.117	0.100
SEE	0.53	0.87	0.43	0.57	0.64	0.29
N	(829)	(714)	(702)	(792)	(824)	(860)

	Italy			Germany		
Model	*2002*	*2003*	*2004*	*2002*	*2003*	*2004*
Feelings US	0.123	0.110	-0.010	-0.041	0.068	-0.003
	(2.905)**	(2.849)**	(-0.233)	(1.072)	(1.870)	(-0.086)
US leadership	0.082	0.067	0.155	0.079	0.048	0.123
	(2.056)*	(1.527)	(3.549)***	(2.097)*	(1.207)	(3.267)***
Assessment Bush's foreign policy	0.094	0.273	0.285	0.077	0.360	0.241
	(2.359)*	(6.122)***	(6.333)***	(2.020)*	(9.500)***	(6.480)***

(*Continued*)

Model	Italy			Germany		
	2002	2003	2004	2002	2003	2004
Threat Iraq	-0.079 (-2.140)*	na	na	-0.061 (-1.744)	na	na
Economic power	0.080 (2.212)*	-0.013 (-0.409)	-0.053 (-1.506)	0.071 (2.063)*	-0.032 (-1.003)	0.021 (0.647)
Internationalism	0.006 (0.170)	-0.019 (-0.587)	0.018 (0.516)	-0.040 (-1.154)	-0.011 (-0.354)	0.005 (0.155)
Dummy liberate Iraqi people	na	na	-0.056 (-1.613)	na	na	-0.070 (-2.122)*
Adjusted R^2	0.112	0.240	0.235	0.077	0.194	0.097
SEE	0.63	0.80	0.35	0.68	0.65	0.28
N	(699)	(715)	(636)	(802)	(832)	(844)

Notes: Socio-demographic factors and left–right continuum not reported here.

Dependent variables: 2002: 'There has been some discussion about whether the US should use its troops to invade Iraq and overthrow the government of Saddam Hussein. Which of the following positions is closest to yours: 1 The US should invade Iraq, 2 The US should only invade Iraq with UN approval and the support of its allies, 3 The US should invade Iraq even if they have to do it alone.' 2003 and 2004: 'Do you think the war in Iraq was worth the loss of life and the other costs of attacking Iraq, or not?' In 2003, 1 No, 2 Uncertain and 3 Yes, worth the costs. In 2004, in half of the sample the question was worded 'Do you think the war in Iraq *to liberate the Iraqi people* was worth the loss of life and the other costs of attacking Iraq or not?' 1 Worth, 2 Not worth. To account for this change a dummy variable was inserted with value 1 when 'to liberate the Iraqi people' was present in the stem and 0 otherwise.

Independent variables: *Feelings thermometer towards United States*: 0–100. *US leadership*: 'From your point of view, how desirable is it that the US exert strong leadership in world affairs? Very desirable, somewhat desirable, somewhat undesirable, or very undesirable?' 1 Very desirable, 2 Somewhat desirable, 3 Somewhat undesirable, 4 Very undesirable. *Assessment of Bush's foreign policy*: 2002: 'How do you rate the George W. Bush administration's handling of the following problems? Would you say the American administration's handling of [overall foreign policy] has been excellent, good, fair or poor?' 1 Excellent, 2 Good, 3 Fair, 4 Poor; 2003: 'Do you approve or disapprove of the way the President of the United States George Bush is handling international policies: very much or somewhat?' 1 Approve very much, 2 Approve somewhat, 3 Disapprove somewhat, 4 Disapprove very much. *Economic power*. 2002: 'Which of the following do you think is more important in determining a country's overall power and influence in the world – a country's economic strength, or its military strength?' 1 Economic strength, 2 Military strength. 2003 and 2004: 'Please tell me whether you agree or disagree with each of the following. Do you agree/disagree strongly or somewhat: Economic power is becoming more important in world affairs than military power.' 1 Agree strongly, 2 Agree somewhat, 3 Disagree somewhat, 4 Disagree strongly. *Internationalism*: 'Do you think it will be best for the future of [own country] if we take an active part in world affairs or if we stay out of world affairs?' 1 Active part, 2 Stay out. *Gender*: 1 Male, 2 Female. *Age* (in years, in 2002 year of birth in two digits); *Education* (in four classes in 2002 and 2003, age left education in 2003). *Left–right continuum*: 7-point scale: 1 extreme left – 7 extreme right.

*** = p significant >.001.** = p significant >.01. * = p significant >.05

think that it is quite a minority view in France, Germany, Italy and the UK. There are consistent and stable differences across countries, with France always coming up first in terms of anti-Americanism and Germany and Italy struggling for the last place. But trends in anti-Americanism have moved in parallel lines over time and, also, have become closer. The data also shows that anti-Americanism is not a constant in these four countries, but rather an oscillating manifestation, related presumably to US foreign policy. Already this result may lead us to reappraise the visceral sources of anti-Americanism. If anti-Americanism is, among other things, a reasoned reaction to American foreign policy, its irrational nature has to be somehow toned down.

The importance of foreign policy as a factor in explaining anti-Americanism is found in the present crisis of transatlantic relationships. A reconstruction of the available survey data in the aftermath of the September 11 attacks show the deep reservoir of pro-American feelings in all European countries, France included. When, on 12 September 2001 the North Atlantic Council determined 'that this attack ... against the United States ... shall be regarded as an action covered by Article 5 of the Washington Treaty' (NATO press release, quoted in Sloan 2003: 186), it was truly expressing the feelings of the majority of the European public. And this is even more remarkable if one considers that these feelings also muted doubts and perplexities entertained by a majority of the European public in regard to the military strategy adopted by the first Bush administration to tackle the terrorist threat. The willingness to overcome these doubts in order to show support for the attacked ally was, in itself, a strong show of pro-American sentiments. One can anticipate the hollowness of this sentiment, ready to dissipate after a few days. In fact, pro-American sentiments wore out quite early. Signs of a more critical stance towards the United States appear already at the end of 2001.

However, this was not a reflex of underlying anti-Americanism, but rather a consequence of an increasing puzzlement and preoccupation with the direction the American foreign policy was taking. In this context, the 'axis of evil' speech confirmed and strengthened the worst apprehension held by the Europeans and the ensuing debate on Iraqi issues magnified these preoccupations. In this context, the fact the transatlantic crisis erupted over what to do about Saddam's regime was neither surprising nor unforeseeable. At the same time, it reveals that the causes of the transatlantic friction were at once simmering under the surface well before the crisis itself but also limited in their purport. The Iraqi crisis magnified preoccupations with the American unilateral mood which were already present in the Afghanistan operation, in which the NATO offer was substantially overlooked and sidetracked. The causes of the present drift, however, are also less dramatic and structural than many claim them to be. Looking at some determinants of the critical attitudes towards Iraq in the period 2002–2004, it is found that most of the difference is traced back to a sentiment of hostility towards Bush's first administration and the wisdom of its foreign policy. Anti-Americanism, once controlling for these factors, does not play a significant role in explaining opposition to the military operation in Iraq.

Having examined the nature and effects of anti-Americanism over more than 40 years and coming out of this examination with a minimalist view of the scope and importance of anti-Americanism as a source of resentment and hostility towards the US, one is still left, however, with some puzzling questions. If the picture here offered is an accurate one, then why are so many people, both in government and elsewhere, so ready to grab the anti-American banner to explain the causes of Atlantic tensions between Europeans and Americans? In other words, if anti-Americanism is a minority view and quite transient over time, why dedicate so much attention to it? Why be worried about something that is not really there?

One might say, these same reactions can explain the rapidity with which anti-American sentiments recede in the public mind. If elites were not ready to denounce it, it might last longer and take deeper root with wider ramifications. However, the analysis presented so far stresses that anti-Americanism is not rooted in firm beliefs about the US and its role. Anti-Americanism appears rather shaped, to a greater extent, by situational and contextual factors, mostly related to what the American government does – or the Europeans' perception of what it does – in foreign policy than by emotional or instinctual anti-American reflex. If this is the case, then, there is no reason to believe that, once the crisis is overcome and Euro–American relations go back to normal, anti-Americanism should not recede. In this connection, it might be the very reactivity of the anti-American sentiments that is appealing to elites searching for a quick fix for domestic and international problems, on both sides of the Atlantic. In other words, it is the implicit awareness of the shallow grasp of anti-American attitudes that make them so appealing to elites for use for political purposes. Anti-Americanism, as a political weapon, has here the twofold advantage of being quickly activated, but also of lasting only for a short period of time, so as not to constrain too much the very elites agitating it. One can speculate, however, whether this playing on anti-Americanism has any political cost for transatlantic relations. Over time, we have seen a widening of the margin of oscillations once each new transatlantic crisis erupts and this is particularly important in a period in which, with the end of the Cold War, Euro–American relationships are entering into new, uncharted lands.

Notes

1 I wish to thank Sergio Fabbrini and Philip Everts for their generous comments on the previous draft of this chapter, and Richard Eichenberg, for allowing me to use the data he collected. All data and documentation necessary to replicate the analyses described herein are available either through the Inter-University

Consortium for Political and Social Research at the University of Michigan or the ZA-Central Archive for Empirical Social Research, University of Cologne, Germany.

2 A quick search on LEXIS-NEXIS for references to anti-Americanism in the headlines of 'international news' produced 315 references in 2003. In 1998, there were only 22 references.

3 This is what Hollander (1995) has in mind in defining anti-Americanism as

> an attitude of distaste, aversion, or intense hostility the roots of which may be found in matters unrelated to the actual qualities or attributes of American society or the foreign policies of the United States. In short, as here used, anti-Americanism refers to a negative predisposition, a type of bias which is to a varying degree unfounded. I regard it as an attitude similar to its far more thoroughly explored counterparts, hostile predispositions such as racism, sexism, or anti-Semitism.
>
> (Hollander, 1995: lxxviii)

4 Without pretending to be exhaustive, I have based my analysis on the following texts: Craveri and Quagliarello (2004); Crockatt (2003); Fabbrini (2004; 2002); Kroes and van Rossem (1986); D'Attorre (1991); Defleur and Defleur (2003); Diner (1996); Elwood (1999); Haseler (1985); Hollander (1995); Kuisel (1993); Lacorne (1986); Pells (1997); Rubinstein and Smith (1985); Spiro (1998); Strauss (1978); Teodori (2002; 2003); Toinet (1988). I thank Linda Fratini for helping me in the bibliographic search and analysis of the material.

5 The United States Information Agency has been asking, with slight changes, the following question for more than 30 years: 'Please, use this card, to tell me your feelings about various countries. How about US?' The respondent had an option between the Eurobarometer series of the European Commission which has been asking, once in a while, a straighter version of this same question, worded as follows: 'Do you have a very good, fairly good, neither bad nor good, rather bad or very bad opinion of the United States?' Those who answered 'neither good nor bad' were probed: 'on balance would you say that your feelings towards the United States are more favourable or more unfavourable?'. This question has been asked in the Eurobarometer 22, 24, 27 and 28. Alternatively, in Eurobarometer 17, the question was 'What is your overall opinion of the US? Do you have a very favourable, somewhat favourable, somewhat unfavourable, or very unfavourable opinion?'. This wording was also used in the PEW Global Attitudes Survey in 2002.

6 In the period between October 1952 and April 1956 the intermediate option 'Fair' was used. Since November 1956, the option 'Neither good nor bad' has been used. In November 1956 and in May 1957 the two formats were offered two halves of the sample each, presumably to test for possible differences. Of the eight available comparisons (two for each of the four countries here examined) in France and Italy no difference is greater than 2–3 points per cent, in Germany in one case (May 1957) the difference is of 8 points per cent and in the UK is of 10 and 13 percentage points respectively for November 1956 and May 1957. In all the three cases in which the wording of the intermediate category makes a difference greater than 3 percentage points, the effect is in the same direction: to increase the number of

those who have a 'good opinion' when the 'neither good nor bad' category is offered in comparison to when the 'Fair' category is supplied. Apparently, the item 'Fair' seems to capture some of the positive feelings while 'neither good nor bad' seems more neutral. For my purposes, this source of difference is unproblematical, before I will use the net favour (favourable minus unfavourable).

7 An example of this question format is found in Eurobarometer 10/A: 'Here is a sort of scale. You will notice that the 10 boxes on this card range from the highest position for plus 5, for something you have a very favourable opinion of, all the way down to the lowest position of minus 5, for something you have very unfavourable opinion of. How far up or down the scale would you place [United States].' The standard feeling thermometer scale has been tried also by the Transatlantic Trend Survey (drawing upon the Chicago Council of Foreign Relations Survey for the United States) since 2002. The question is as follows: 'Next I'd like you to rate your feelings towards some countries, institutions and people, with one hundred meaning a very warm, favourable feeling, zero meaning a very cold, unfavourable feeling, and fifty meaning not particularly warm or cold. You can use any number from zero to one hundred. If you have no opinion or have never heard of that country or institution, please say so [The United States].'

8 Since 1970, Eurobarometer has been irregularly asking, in slightly different formats, a question about trust in the American people using slightly different wordings: 'I would like to ask you, now some questions about the trust you have in different people of the world. I will give you the names of different people; will you tell me if you have a lot of trust in them, some trust, not so much trust, or no trust at all. You can answer with the help of this card [the Americans]?' Or: 'Now I would like to ask you about how much you would trust people from different countries. For each country please say whether, in your opinion they are in general very trustworthy, fairly trustworthy, not particularly trustworthy, or not at all trustworthy? [Americans]'. This question has been asked in Eurobarometer 6, 14, 17 and 25. In Eurobarometer 33 the question was: 'Now I would like to ask you a question about how much trust you have in people from various countries. For each, please tell me whether you have a lot of trust in them, some trust, not very much trust or no trust at all? [Americans].'

9 An exact comparison between the 1958 and 2002 versions is complicated by the fact that in the 2002 PEW survey the intermediate, stand-by, category of 'Fair' was not offered. This inflates the number of those opposing and favouring somewhat the United States or the Americans.

10 The question was worded as follows: 'Now, I would like to ask about how much you would trust people from different countries. For each country please say whether in your opinion they are in general very trustworthy, fairly trustworthy, not particularly trustworthy or not at all trustworthy [Americans, specify Americans from the United States].'

11 The question was: 'What is your overall opinion of the United States? Do you have a very favourable, somewhat favourable, somewhat unfavourable or very unfavourable opinion?'

12 'In general, how much confidence do you have in the ability of the US to deal responsibly with world problems? A great deal, a fair amount, not very much or none at all?'

13 'All things considered, what do you think is better for [own country's] national interest: to coordinate our foreign policy closely with the United States or to conduct our foreign policy without giving special consideration to the interests of the US?'

14 'When the United States makes decisions which affect the security of [our country] how much do you think it takes [our country's] views into account: a great deal, a fair amount, a little, or not at all?'

15 'On balance, do you think that US policies and actions during the past year have done more to promote peace or more to increase the risk of war?'

16 'Recently, there has been some expression of anti-American feelings among West-Europeans. How would you describe your own feelings? Strongly anti-American, somewhat anti-American, somewhat pro-American or strongly pro-American?'

17 In the Eurobarometer 22 (October–November 1984) the feelings towards the United States and the anti-Americanism questions were posed again. The correlation among the two is, for the four countries pooled, −0.604, significant at the 0.001 level for a two-tailed test.

18 I first normalized the four series starting from the raw data in Figure 7.1 and then converting it into an index computed as 100 plus the percentage of those in favour of the US minus the percentage of those opposed to the US. I then standardized each score, using the mean average and standard deviation across the four series. These calculations were done for all the four series. As an example, in October 1954 the average percentage of those with a good opinion of the US (very good plus good) was 59 per cent, those with a bad or very bad opinion represented 10 per cent, the net favour was 59–10 = 49 + 100 = 149.

19 In Figure 7.2 the 2003 data overlooks this recovery, being a yearly average of different surveys (but something can be seen from the raw data in Figure 7.1). Positive feelings go from a net average feeling of 47 down to –7 in February 2003, to an all-time low of −31 in March 2003 (the start of the Iraq war) and then rising again and becoming positive by April 2003.

20 The data here discussed has been collected by Philip Everts and myself. I thank Phil Everts for allowing me to use this data. For a wider analysis of the consequences of 9/11 on attitudes towards the United States see Everts and Isernia (2002) available at: http://www.gips.unisi.it/circap/opimon-behavior

21 A comparison of this question with the previous one, asked by Gallup in the same period, points out that an explicit reference to Al Qaeda and its leader Osama bin Laden does not apparently move public opinion in either direction.

22 The question was worded as follows: 'In any case [COUNTRY] is to take or has already taken decisions about which policy should be applied now. Among the following measures which ones seem appropriate to you ...? ... to send [NATIONALITY] troops to fight with the US forces.'

23 In the United States, 48 per cent of the public answered that the US was 'taking into account the interests of its allies' and 41 per cent that the US was 'acting mainly in its own interests'.

24 The question read as follows 'There has been some discussion about whether the US should use its troops to invade Iraq and overthrow the government of Saddam Hussein. Which of the following positions is closest to yours: 'The US should invade Iraq even if they have to do it alone; the US should only invade Iraq with UN approval and the support of its allies; or the US should not invade Iraq?'

25 The question was worded as follows: 'Do you think the war in Iraq was worth the loss of life and the other costs of attacking Iraq, or not?'. Those who answered 'No' were coded 1, those who answered 'Don't know' 2, and those who answered 'Yes, it was worth the costs' 3.

26 For this, the second half of the sample the question was: 'Do you think the war in Iraq *to liberate the Iraqi people* was worth the loss of life and the other costs of attacking Iraq or not?' For both groups 1 was 'not worth' and 2 'worth the costs'.

27 The question in 2002 was: 'How do you rate the George W. Bush administration's handling of the following problems? Would you say the American administration's handling of [overall foreign policy] has been excellent, good, fair or poor?' 1 Excellent, 2 Good, 3 Fair, 4 Poor. In 2003 and 2004 the question was: 'Do you approve or disapprove of the way the President of the United States George Bush is handling international policies? Very much or somewhat?' 1 Approve very much, 2 Approve somewhat, 3 Disapprove somewhat, 4 Disapprove very much.

28 It was measured in terms of years spent in education in 2004 while using formal degrees obtained in four classes in 2002 and 2003.

References

Abravanel, M. and Hughes, B. (1973) 'The Relationship between Public Opinion and Governmental Foreign Policy: *A Cross-National Study*', in Patrick J. McGowan (ed.) *Sage International Yearbook of Foreign Policy Studies.* Vol. 1, Beverly Hills/London: Sage, pp. 107–34.

Asmus, R.D., Everts, P.P. and Isernia, P. (2004a) 'Power, War and Public Opinion', *Policy Review*, 123: February–March.

Asmus, R.D., Everts, P.P. and Isernia, P. (2004b) '*Across the Atlantic and the Political Aisle: The Double Divide in U.S.–European Relations.* Paper available at http://www.transatlantictrends.org

Craveri, P. and Quagliarello, G. (eds) (2004) *L'Antiamericanismo in Italia e in Europa nel Secondo Dopoguerra*, Soneria Mannelli: Rubbettino.

Crockatt, R. (2003) *America Embattled: 9/11, Anti-Americanism and the Global Order*, London: Routledge.

D'Attorre, P.P. (ed.) (1991) *Nemici per la pelle. Sogno Americano e Mito Sovietico nell'Italia Contemporanea*, Milano: Angeli.

Defleur, M.L. and Defleur, M.H. (2003) *Learning to Hate Americans: How U.S. Media Shape Negative Attitudes Among Teenagers in Twelve Countries*, Spokane, WA: Marquette Books.

Diner, D. (1996) *America in the Eyes of the Germans: An Essay on Anti-Americanism*, Princeton, NJ: Markus Wiener Publ.

Elwood, D.W. (1999) 'Anti-Americanism in Western Europe: A Comparative Perspective', *Occasional Paper European Seminar Series*, N.3, Johns Hopkins University, Bologna Center.

Everts, P. and Isernia, P. (2005) 'Poll – Trends: The War in Iraq.' *Public Opinion Quarterly*, 69 (2): 264–323.

Everts, P. and Isermia, P. (2002) 'Reactions to the 9/11 2001 Terrorist Attack in Countries Outside the U.S.', *CIRCAP Occasional Papers*, N. 10, University of Sienna.

Fabbrini, S. (2002) 'The Domestic Sources of European Anti-Americanism', *Government and Opposition*, 37 (1): 3–14.

Fabbrini, S. (2004) 'Layers of anti-Americanism: Americanization, American unilateralism and anti-Americanism in a European perspective', *European Journal of American Culture*, 23 (2): 79–94.

Haseler, S. (1985) *Varieties of Anti-Americanism: Reflex and Response*, Lanham, MD: Rowman & Littlefield.

Hollander, P. (1995) *Anti-Americanism: Irrational & Rational*, London: Transaction Publ.

Johnston, G. and Ray, L. (2004) *Balancing Act? Anti-Americanism and Support for a Common European Foreign and Security Policy*, Paper presented at the annual meeting of the Southern Political Science Association, New Orleans, 7–10 January 2004.

Kagan, R. (2003) *Paradise & Power. America and Europe in the New World Order*, London: Atlantic Books.

Kroes R. and van Rossem, M. (eds) (1986) *Anti-Americanism in Europe*, Amsterdam: Free University Press.

Kuisel, R. (1993) *Seducing the French. The Dilemma of Americanization*, Berkeley, CA: University of California Press.

Lacorne, D. *et al.* (1986) *L'Amérique dans les Têtes. Un Siécle de Fascination et d'Aversions*, Paris: Hachette.

Larson, E.V., Levin, N.D., Bak, S. and Savych, B. (2004) *Ambivalent Allies? A Study of South Korea Attitudes toward the U.S.*, Rand Corporation, TR-141-SRF.

Nye, J.S. jr (2004) *Soft Power. The Means of Success in World Politics*, New York: Public Affairs.

Pells, R. (1997) *Not Like Us. How Europeans have Loved, Hated, and Transformed American Culture since World War II*, New York: Basic Books.

Rubinstein, A.Z. and Smith, D.E. (eds) (1985) *Anti-Americanism in the Third World: Implications for U.S. Foreign Policy*, New York: Praeger Publishers.

Schattschneider, E.E. (1960) *The Semisovereign People. A Realist's View of Democracy in America*. New York: Holt, Rinehart and Winston.

Sloan, S.R. (2003) *NATO, The European Union, and the Atlantic Community*, Lanham, MD: Rowman & Littlefield.

Smith, S.K. and Wertman, D.A. (1992) *US–West European Relations during the Reagan Years*, New York: St. Martin's Press.

Spiro, H.J. (1998) 'Anti-Americanism in Western Europe', *Annals of the American Academy of Political and Social Science*, 497: 120–32.

Stimson, J.A. (1991) *Public Opinion in America: Moods, Cycles, and Swings*, Boulder, CO: Westview.

Strauss, D. (1978) *Menace in the West: The Rise of French Anti-Americanism in Modern Times*, Greenwood, CT: Greenwood Publishing Group.

Teodori, M. (2002) *Maledetti Americani. Destra, sinistra e cattolici: storia del pregiudizio antiamericano*, Milano: Mondadori.

Teodori, M. (2003) *Benedetti Americani. Dall'alleanza Atlantica alla guerra al terrorismo*, Milano: Mondadori.

Toinet, M.-F. (1988) 'French Pique and Piques Francaises', *Annals of the American Academy of Political and Social Science*, 497: 133–41.

Woodward, B. (2002) *Bush at War*, New York: Simon & Schuster.

Part III

Which future for American conservative nationalism?

8   America after the 2004 elections

Bold policies and political quicksand

Bruce E. Cain

Introduction

In the aftermath of his surprisingly 'decisive' re-election victory, there were many attempts to define President Bush's second term mandate. Focusing on the absolute number of votes George Bush received and the historically unusual gains by the President's party in both houses of Congress, his allies boldly pronounced that the President's victory vindicated his pre-emptive interventionist foreign policies and gave him the presumptive right to initiate new conservative domestic programmes remaking social security and cutting discretionary domestic spending. On the 'blue' side of the partisan divide, Democratic critics denied the existence of any foreign policy or domestic mandate, arguing that a swing of 70,000 votes in Ohio would have given the victory to the challenger, John Kerry, and that the electorate was more polarized than it had been since the 1960s.

Inevitably, this debate ended in a draw since there can be no consensus about mandates inferred from election results alone. The unanswered question was not whether President Bush was sufficiently encouraged by his victory to advocate for an aggressive policy agenda. The answer to that was obvious from the moment of his re-election: the size of electoral margins does not matter to a president with a visionary agenda of promoting conservative ideals. After all, his narrow 2000 Electoral College victory did not put President Bush on a cautious path four years earlier. Given the institutional division of power in the US system, the key consideration is not what the president wants to do, but what he will be able to achieve with Congress and key interest groups. Mandates in the US are conditional on the circumstances in which key system players find themselves after the election, not on the interpretive fluff that supporters and opponents spin out for public consumption.

In this chapter, I will argue for a theory of 'conditional mandate' that focuses on incentives and circumstances that dictate the behaviour of Congress and key interest groups after the election. The critical factors in this theory areas follows.

1   Will the conditions that got the President elected (i.e. a good enough economy and bare majority approval of the war) improve or worsen?
2   Will members of Congress in colour-discordant seats (Democrats in red seats won by Bush or Republicans in blue seats won by Kerry) feel pressured to conform to or rebel against the President's positions?
3   To whom are the election debts owed and what do these electoral 'creditors' want?

Under a best case scenario for the President, the economy continues to improve, the US is able to hand Iraq over to the Iraqis fairly quickly, Democrats in 'red' states and seats fold under electoral pressure, and the 'halo' effect of good circumstances allows the President to push a broader, more radical mandate than the one announced during the campaign. In the President's worst case scenario, his core interest groups push the President forward on policies that fall well outside median voter preferences at a time when economic conditions and the war in Iraq are deteriorating, causing defections from blue area Republicans.

In the sections that follow, I will first examine the faulty logic of the simple electoral mandate theory. Then I will outline my theory of the conditional mandate. Last, I will assess the President's likely policies under the conditional mandate theory.

Simple mandate theories

Intuitively, it seems incontestable that President Bush has put himself in a stronger position by moving from a purely Electoral College win (i.e. winning the Electoral College vote but losing the popular one) in one election to a combined Electoral College/popular vote victory in the next. Moreover, since the Republican margins increased, then surely the President is in a stronger position to carry out his agenda. But, will this translate into enough support for the bold domestic and foreign policy agenda the Bush administration has laid out in the past few years?

A simple electoral mandate theory might answer 'Yes'. Why? Because as the margins of victory increase, so does the level of cross-party support. Very large margins of victory – e.g. Reagan in 1984 or Clinton in 1996 – indicate a fair amount of bipartisan support. And more decisive victories should lead to more bipartisan support than less decisive ones. The losing party has to worry about how to win back their defecting partisans, which makes them more cooperative with the winning party than they might otherwise be. This was certainly the case in the 1980s for the Democrats. In both 1980 and 1984, the Democrats could see that the so-called Reagan Democrats were defecting from the party and resonating with President Reagan's call for a stronger national defence, smaller domestic programmes and socially conservative policies. The desire to win back the Reagan Democrats and to make in-roads into a potential Republican defecting bloc – working women – set in motion a number of changes in the party that led eventually to regaining the White House in 1992. It also made Congressional Democrats less likely to oppose Reagan on defence issues and the programmatic cuts he wanted.

In short, what caused the Democrats to change in the late 1980s and early 1990s was the need to compete for moderate voters and to hold onto vulnerable southern, rural and suburban Democratic legislative districts. Twenty years later, the white southern seats have realigned almost completely into the Republican ranks (Polsby 2004). The Reagan Democrats are gone. The Democratic party base is more loyal than it was in the 1980s. When Ronald Reagan defeated then incumbent President Jimmy Carter in 1980, only 67 per cent of self-identified Democrats voted for their own party's nominee. By contrast, 86 per cent of self-identified Republicans voted for Ronald Reagan. Even in the 1992 victory of Bill Clinton, only 77 per cent of Democrats supported their party's nominee. This was sufficient because dissatisfaction among Republicans with George Bush senior and Ross Perot's candidacy resulted in the lowest Republican Party loyalty since 1976: 73 per cent. Since 1996, Democratic loyalty rates have been consistently over 80 per cent, and in the last election 89 per cent voted for John Kerry and only 11 per cent of self-identified Democrats voted for the President, despite the advantage of a 'wartime' incumbent. Republican loyalty was very high in both 2000 and 2004: i.e. 91 per cent and 93 per cent respectively. In 2004, both parties claimed roughly equally sized partisan bases (37 per cent self-identified Democrats and 37 per cent self-identified Republicans) and comparable loyalty rates of about 90 per cent (see Table 8.1).

But the comparability of the Democratic base in terms of size and loyalty masks a deeper problem. The Republicans have had the ideological advantage since the 1980s as more Americans view themselves as conservatives than as liberals. By 2004, 34 per cent of the voters called themselves conservatives and only 21 per cent called themselves liberal (see Table 8.2). This ideology gap is even larger in some of the so-called purple or swing states such as Ohio, Florida and Pennsylvania. While almost half of voters call themselves moderate (46 per cent), it is clear that there has been a shift in the dominant ideology since the New Society programmes of the 1960s. The Clinton wing

Table 8.1 Partisan identification and presidential vote

		1976	1980	1984	1988	1992	1996	2000	2004
Republican PID	Dem.	9	9	7	8	10	13	8	6
	Rep.	90	86	92	91	73	80	91	93
	Other	–	4	–	–	17	6	1	–
Democratic PID	Dem.	77	67	74	82	77	84	86	89
	Rep.	22	26	25	17	10	10	11	11
	Other	–	6	–	–	13	5	2	–

of the Democratic party tried to address this problem by pursuing welfare reform, backing away from controversial changes in the health care system, and downplaying the most aggressive forms of affirmative action (i.e. the 'mend it but don't end it' approach). But this tactical shift to the right did not help to win back the House after 1994, despite a resounding Democratic presidential victory in 1996, and both Al Gore in 2000 and John Kerry in 2004 struggled with their ideological label. This was graphically illustrated in the 2004 election by the fact that the Bush camp used the liberal label to paint Kerry as an extremist to swing voters, whereas Kerry did not, and probably could not, use the conservative label in the same way in his television ads.

There is a greater awareness of this problem in Democratic circles now than in 2000. Bill Clinton's skill as a politician and the economic prosperity the country enjoyed when he was in office covered up the ideological gap. Some progressives believe that the problem is one of rhetoric: that the Republicans have found a way to argue for their ideological problems in values language, and that the Democrats need to adopt a similar tactic. Still others think that the party needs to rethink its basic principles and perhaps redefine liberalism much as Tony Blair has redefined Labour ideology in Britain. This task of party redefinition is complicated by the emergence of the second dimension of American politics: social issues.

The social dimension, as opposed to the economic left–right divide, actually encompasses three aspects. There is a racial component. The Democratic party introduced and supported most of the major civil rights legislation since the 1960s (Carmines and Stimson 1989). This alienated many Southern whites and drove them out of the Democratic party, contributing to the emergence of Republican domination in the South. The Democrats attempted to moderate their position on issues like affirmative action under Clinton, but the white–black divide between the parties is still strong. The second

Table 8.2 Ideology and presidential vote

		1976	1980	1984	1988	1992	1996	2000	2004
Conservative	Dem.	71	60	70	81	68	78	80	85
	Rep.	26	25	28	18	14	11	13	13
	Other	–	11	–	–	18	7	6	–
Moderate	Dem.	51	42	47	50	47	57	52	54
	Rep.	48	49	53	49	31	33	44	45
	Other	–	8	–	–	21	9	2	–
Liberal	Dem.	29	23	17	19	18	20	17	15
	Rep.	70	73	82	80	64	71	81	84
	Other	–	4	–	–	18	8	1	–

dimension is cultural. People in the rural areas of the country resent what they perceive to be a cultural and media domination by the coastal elites. Of the 16 per cent who live in rural areas, George Bush got 59 per cent of their vote in both 2000 and 2004 (see Table 8.3). Then, there is a religious component. The 41 per cent of the electorate who attend church regularly preferred the Republicans to the Democrats by 61 per cent to 39 per cent. As a minimum, the gay marriage issue helped Karl Rove to mobilize conservatives through the churches, and perhaps it did more (for example, Bush did better among Catholics than the Catholic candidate Kerry, and better than any Republican since Reagan).

The existence of a second dimension complicates the task of interpreting an electoral mandate. A party might be preferred on one dimension but not the other, but the final outcome might reflect the greater salience of one of these dimensions. It was striking that on most of the pre-election polls, John Kerry and the Democrats were preferred to George Bush and the Republicans on many domestic issues, but lost the election nonetheless. It is plausible to argue that George Bush was preferred on terrorism and some social issues, but not on taxes, social security and the environment. Does a victory based on one dimension create a mandate on the other? It would seem logically not, but how can anyone know for sure, and in the absence of certainty, the winner can claim the benefit of the doubt.

So the first problem with the simple electoral mandate theory is that because there is more than one policy dimension, a victory does not necessarily imply electoral agreement on both (Polsby and Wildavsky 2004). This presents a problem to the losing party as they try to fix what caused them to lose. Does the Democratic party have to moderate on all issues or only the social ones? Does the majority party make a mistake if it assumes that it won because the voters preferred them on both dimensions, causing them to overreach in areas where their support is actually weak?

The simple theory of an electoral mandate also fails to link the reasons for one party's victory with the economic and military conditions that made success possible. A mandate based primarily on good economic conditions or 'rally round the flag' patriotism is conditional on the circumstances of that

Table 8.3 Suburban and rural voters

		1980	1984	1988	1992	1996	2000	2004
Suburban	Dem.	35	38	42	41	47	47	47
	Rep.	55	61	57	39	42	49	52
	Other	9	–	–	21	8	3	–
Rural	Dem.	39	32	44	39	44	37	40
	Rep.	55	67	55	40	46	59	59
	Other	5	–	–	20	10	2	–

economy or war. If conditions are good, then the President will have power in the Neustadt sense of the power to persuade (Neustadt 1990). If not, things can unravel quickly, causing his coalition to fall apart and the opposition to gain strength. This I call the conditional mandate.

Conditional mandate theory

A conditional mandate theory asks three specific questions. First, what role did conditions play in getting the President elected and will they improve or worsen (i.e. the electoral question). Second, will members of Congress in colour-discordant seats (i.e. the Congress question) line up for or against the President? And third, to whom are the electoral debts owed and what do the creditors want (i.e. the interest group question)?

Conditions and retrospective judgment

Most American elections are won or lost on economic conditions. Swings in the public's so-called retrospective judgment often determine the fate of presidential and congressional incumbents (Kramer 1971: Tufte 1978; Nordhaus 1975). Lost in the post-election focus on the Iraq war and the 11 state gay marriage referendums was the key statistic that, by historical standards, the economy was good enough to get the incumbent President re-elected. The models that political scientists and economists used to forecast the election before the Fall campaign all predicted a Bush victory by single digit margins (Campbell 2004; 2005). This despite the fact that these models varied in terms of the aggregate economic indicators, subjective economic perception variables and specifications they used. Based on economic performance alone, President Bush should have won, as he eventually did.

However, economic predictions sometimes fail when wars or national crises intervene. This was, for instance, the case in 1968 when the economic models predicted a Democratic victory but dissatisfaction with the war on Vietnam gave the election instead to the Republican presidential candidate, Richard Nixon. Sometimes wars work to the advantage of incumbents. That was certainly the case with the Afghanistan war prior to the 2002 Congressional elections. The President skilfully used the victory in Afghanistan along with the homeland security issue to win back control of the US Senate for the Republicans. On the other hand, a war that does not go well can erode the President's support, which is what happened in 2004.

By January 2004, support for the war in Iraq had fallen dramatically as it became clear that the initial military victory had not been complete, and as the costs, monetary and human, of staying in Iraq mounted. Opposition to the war coalesced initially behind the Dean candidacy, but by the time of the Iowa caucuses, John Kerry and others voiced their criticisms of the conduct of the Iraq war. Approval of the President's handling of the war and his overall job ratings dropped, and what seemed like an electoral strength became an electoral liability. As the casualties and expenses mounted, and the evidence of weapons of mass destruction failed to materialize, public support for the war began to drop, especially among Democrats and independents.

While the Iraq situation was worsening, this did not translate automatically into support for the Democratic candidate. The reason for this was partly John Kerry's own indecisiveness on the issue. His highly qualified opposition to the war and the fact that he famously voted for the resolution supporting the President's decision to invade Iraq before he voted against it were problems that he never completely surmounted during the 2004 Fall campaign. Add in as well the attack ads from the swift boat veterans questioning whether John Kerry deserved his Vietnam war medals and his less-than-inspiring oratorical style, and it is clear that Kerry the candidate did not help the Democrats.

But even if John Kerry had been a stronger, more decisive candidate, the Democratic party would have had trouble riding the rising wave of opposition to the Iraq war into the White House. While the party was fairly unified in its criticism of the decision to go into Iraq, it was divided as to how to get out of Iraq. Some of the more 'progressive' left preferred immediate withdrawal, arguing that our presence only worsened the crisis and that we could help things more by departing. But the more internationalist wing of the party felt that, however wrong the decision to intervene in Iraq, it would have been irresponsible to leave before the country was fully stabilized and rebuilt. Any Democratic candidate would have had trouble bridging this divide among party activists and voters.

In the end, elections are about comparisons. A good issue for an opposition party is one in which there are clear and favourable contrasts between it and the governing party. With respect to the question of what to do about Iraq, the contrast between the Democratic and Republican positions was neither clear nor favourable. What worked for them was the general retrospective perception that the decision to go into Iraq was mistaken and, more generally, that the Bush doctrine was flawed. When John Kerry finally focused on those themes in the first debate, he was at least able to rally an increasingly demoralized Democratic base, and make the election close. But not having a different solution to the problem of what to do in Iraq now that the US was there undercut the rationale for changing the leadership mid-war. In the key purple, or swing, states the President was marginally preferred to his Democratic opponent on handling the war in Iraq because there was no real choice being offered about what to do with the Iraq situation, and because the President seemed a more decisive leader who was more likely to carry the war through to a successful conclusion.

So if the President's victory was heavily influenced by economic and wartime conditions that were just good enough to win, what does this imply for his mandate? I would argue that, like his electoral fortunes, his chances of governing successfully depend upon the conditions that got him elected. The fact that voters were never really given a choice over different economic or foreign policies means that the willingness to follow the President is more determined by how well things are going than a commitment to his positions. A retrospective election gives rise to a retrospectively determined administration (Key 1966; Fiorina 1989). With much uncertainty about the means of getting a better economy (e.g. did the tax cuts really help to restart the economy?) and succeeding in Iraq (is the President's plan to transition out of Iraq working?), voters rely on what they observe to be the outcomes of policies. Setbacks lead to drops in the President's approval ratings and successes (e.g. the Iraqi elections) lead to upturns. Since the administration cannot fully control the circumstances that determine outcomes, its fate is at least partly exogenously determined.

This is not altogether a bad thing for a president. If the economic and war conditions stay stable or improve, it might create a broader mandate (i.e. one based on implicit confidence in him) than he would have otherwise had he been elected on specific policies. So in this sense, the fact that the President in his 2005 State of the Union address claimed a mandate to reform social security and tax reform even though neither issue was debated seriously during the campaign makes perfect sense. The people knew that he was a bold President willing to take risks to pursue a conservative agenda. While the details of his policy agenda were not fully disclosed, his general themes and leadership style were, and thus his re-election was at least implicitly a vote of confidence in his judgment. As long as things appear to be turning out well with respect to the economy and the Iraq war, then confidence in his leadership expressed in opinion polls gives him the mandate to ask for more.

But presidential mandates based on the goodness or badness of observed conditions can dissolve if events conspire against the president. If economic conditions worsen, and the planned exit strategy seems to fail (especially the ability to train Iraqi troops to deal with the insurgency), confidence in the President will drop, and the agenda could easily stall. As compared to the simple electoral mandate, the retrospective or conditional mandate is an evolving entity that can shift in either direction depending upon circumstantial fate. When things are good, policies that voters have not thoroughly considered or understand might get passed because they have confidence in the president, and his legislative members will stand behind him. But if conditions worsen, an agenda that they might have accepted in good times might not get passed in bad times. A government that lives by a conditional mandate can die by one as well.

Colour-discordant members

Related to the theme of conditions and confidence in presidential leadership is the critical role of members in colour-discordant seats: Democratic or Republican senators and congressmen in states and districts that were carried or nearly carried by the other party in the 2004 presidential race. They are the weathervanes of presidential power. If conditions are good and support for the president is high, then Democrats representing red areas/states will feel the pressure. Conversely, deteriorating conditions will shift the pressure to blue areas/states Republicans (e.g. New England Republicans).

This pressure comes in various forms. First, there is the possibility of a primary or general election challenge. Conservatives have in recent years used the threat of a primary challenge to enforce party discipline: incumbent Senator Arlen Specter's difficult 2004 primary in Pennsylvania is the most obvious example of conservative challenges against wavering party moderates. Moveon.org and other liberal groups are now discussing a similar strategy against Democrats who support the President's social security reforms. So one type of error a colour-discordant representative can make is not being loyal enough to the party, and drawing a primary challenge. But the second type of error is being too loyal to your party's position at a time when conditions turn sour, resulting perhaps in a well funded general election challenge.

In addition to the pressure of negotiating between these two types of strategic miscalculations, there is the pressure of dealing with the White House. A key element of the Bush strategy is to campaign for issues between elections in colour-discordant states and areas. With the tax cuts in the first administration and now social security reform in the second, the President has taken to the road to campaign for his issues in the red state Democratic districts. This tactic shines the spotlight on a representative's issue position, thereby depriving him or her of being able to hide behind a cloak of voter ignorance. His opposition is 'outed' by the President for all who might bring pressure upon him or her to see. Of course, the effectiveness of this tactic for the President is itself dependent upon good conditions and favourable retrospective presidential assessments.

But can representatives in swing or competitive areas be forced into adopting a conservative agenda? In theory, competitive seats are more moderate, and should therefore have more reservations about clearly liberal or conservative policies. This is related to a question recently posed by Morris Fiorina's recent work on the discrepancy between elite and mass polarization (Fiorina 2004). There has always been strong evidence that activists in America are more polarized than the electorate as a whole. However, Professor Fiorina has empirically demonstrated that the perception of increasingly polarization in the US is more an elite than a mass phenomenon. Public opinion, even on polarizing social issues like abortion, has been relatively stable and unimodal (i.e. most people take a moderate position of abortion rights with restrictions not absolute pro- or anti-abortion positions). And yet perceptions of the parties indicate that elected representatives are farther apart, or more polarized. How can the elected officials move out of synchronization with public opinion?

This issue has not been as well explored by American political science as it should, so in the absence of systematic evidence one can only speculate. To some extent, the discordant polarization of Congress may be related to the decline of the seniority norm under the Republicans and the insertion of party loyalty as the key determinant of promotion, much as in the British parliament. Seniority thrived in the era of Southern Democrats because it helped to keep the disparate coalition of Southern conservatives and urban liberals together by sharing power on some other basis than ideological agreement. With the realignment of the South, the functional basis of seniority was undercut, and loyalty and ideological agreement emerged as the dominant rule. This has worked well for the Republicans during the Bush presidency, making it possible for them to maintain over 90 per cent loyalty on key issues throughout (i.e. 90 per cent of the Republican members voting with a majority of their caucus on key votes).

A second suspect, which has been getting increasing attention in the US, is the artificially and naturally caused spatial separation of Democratic and Republican voters that creates the blue and red maps. The natural component of this is demographically based. People in the US move around a lot, especially for work-related reasons. As they move, they are attracted to communities with individuals who have views, consumer habits and, implicitly at least, political views like themselves. This creates politically homogeneous areas of Democratic and Republican strength. On top of this, there is a redistricting process that in most states gives the job of drawing new district lines to state-elected officials (Butler and Cain 1992). As divided government has become more common, the number of bipartisan gerrymanderers has increased. Democratic and Republican elected officials make complementary trades with one another: Democrats giving Republicans their Republican areas, and vice versa, Republicans trading away their Democratic voters. The upshot is that both Democratic and Republican seats get safer. So even though Fiorina's point about public opinion in general may be true, redistricting adds more homogeneity on top of the natural social sorting process in America. The upshot is fewer truly competitive areas, and fewer moderate members. This has led some groups to put redistricting changes at the head of their reform priorities.

A third suspect is money and interest group support. The proliferation of interest groups, not only as lobbyists but as election funders, has added to the ideological pressure on the system. As elections continue to become more professionalized and expensive, parties and their candidates have greater financial needs than ever. The funding groups – now organized as PACs and nonprofits – have learned to use their money to extract promises and enforce agreements from elected officials. Since most members do not have competitive seats, they can trade off heightened interest group pressure against a lower risk of electoral rejection. The situation is more difficult for those in marginal or colour-discordant seats. They need the money, but the price of non-moderation is higher for them than for the rest of their party caucus. This, as was stated previously, makes them the weathervanes for presidential power and the pivotal votes on key issues.

To return to an earlier point, even more than the margin of Bush's victory, the level of a party's representation in the House and Senate determines the kind of mandate the President can claim. Given the majorities in the House and Senate in 2005, votes needing simple majorities will not formally require the President to have Democratic support. So bills such as denying undocumented immigrants the right to obtain driving licences can pass without much Presidential intervention. On the other end of the spectrum, the Senate confirmation of Supreme Court appointment runs up against the supermajority rules of the US Senate. The President's mandate has to extend to Democrats to avoid a filibuster. So the colour-discordant areas become critical.

Some policies will fall between the two extremes: for instance, social security reform. In theory, it requires only a majority vote, and that the President only has to carry his own party. But confidence, or lack thereof, in the President's leadership brings the colour-discordant representatives to the foreground. Since social security reform was not highlighted in the previous election and representatives have no way of knowing what the public reaction will be to the President's plan, Republicans have initially been cautious about, and in some cases resistant to, the so-called privatization provision (which would allow younger workers to divert part of their payroll tax into a private investment account). Since this issue has been used against Republican candidates in the past, they would prefer to have some Democrat support for the plan to give them political cover in the next election. So, immediately after announcing his social security plan in his 2005 State of the Union speech, the President took to the road, visiting red state and district Democratic seats to put pressure on them to support his plan openly. So while, formally, the President does not need Democratic support, politically he would like it as a way of calming some of the wavering members of his own party.

Credits and debts

The last aspect of a conditional mandate theory is the role that election creditors play in determining the President's agenda. A President's election coalition consists of many different groups, some of them outside the party, that have pledged support and resources. In return, they have expectations that their policies will get a fair hearing at a minimum, and hopefully be passed and implemented. Some of them, especially corporations and trade unions, are mandated by law to deliver election resources through political action committees (PACs) and by individual donations. Other groups, often more issue-based, such as Moveon.org or the NRA, can operate in several non-profit forms that allow them to collect money with less restriction but limit how they can spend their money. The proliferation of PACs, 527s and 501c organizations has been spurred by the recent campaign finance reform bill, which in essence banned the collection of soft money (money which was given to the parties for so-called party-building activities and was not regulated by the strict limits of federal campaign finance laws). This gave outside groups the incentive to form non-profit organizations to raise money to spend on the presidential campaign. Ironically, the Democratic party, which pushed the hardest for the McCain-Feingold Campaign Finance reform, raced ahead of the Republicans in 2004 in terms of taking advantage of this loophole in the law. By the end of the campaign, the gap had lessened considerably.

This growth of independent groups trying to affect the election has proliferated the policy expectations which the President and members face. In a simple electoral mandate theory, the President responds to the voters who put him in office. But in the complex new world in which interest groups play a more independent and salient role, their post-election expectations matter. The members of the President's winning coalition are not equally weighted. Minimum winning coalition theory teaches us that the group that makes the difference in victory can claim greater rewards than others who joined the coalition earlier. In this sense, the debts owed to the conservative Christian churches could be important in determining the President's agenda.

Despite Professor Fiorina's evidence that most Americans prefer a moderate position on abortion and survey data during the 2004 election which suggests that most Americans do not favour a constitutional ban on gay marriage, it is likely that the Bush administration will have to attempt certain moves in these directions to pay off their debts. A simple electoral mandate theory would not lead to a gay marriage amendment or to strongly pro-life Supreme court appointees. A conditional mandate theory recognizes that polarized position-taking maintains and rewards the base.

As the base of the Republican party has changed, their assumptions about what it takes to turn out their voters have also shifted. Before the Southern realignment and the defection of the Reagan Democrats, the Republicans did not have to worry as much as the Democrats about electoral turnout. Since their normal supporters were better educated and more economically upscale, they could be counted on to turn out to vote on their own. But as the party's social conservatism came to attract lower SES voters into their party, the Republicans inherited the same turnout problems that the Democrats had been wrestling with for decades. The 2000 election was a wake-up call to the Republicans in this regard since the polls had predicted a comfortable Bush victory but the returns did not follow script. Karl Rove, Bush's key political advisor, was determined to avoid a similar gap in 2004; hence, the strategy of organizing conservative voters through their churches and running gay marriage initiatives in 11 states. There is considerable academic controversy over whether those tactics made the difference in the election, but an important and indisputable point is that there was no gap between the polls and Republican turnout this time. Church-goers, and evangelicals especially, turned out at the same high rate as the rest of the electorate.

The Rovian strategy of playing to the conservative base flew in the face of conventional campaign wisdom which for years had dictated that the parties should move to the middle to compete for the swing voter. Karl Rove concluded that the number of truly uncommitted voters was going to be lower in 2004, and that more votes could be had by getting higher turnout from conservative voters: if their turnout could be upped by 10 per cent, it would matter more than fighting for undecided voters in the middle.

But what are the implications of this new electoral strategy for the President. Since he did not campaign as a moderate and the party's platform was not geared to the swing voter, the President could rightly conclude that even if voters are overwhelmingly moderate, they chose a conservative candidate. Playing to the base as a candidate leads to rewarding the base as an office-holder. Still, whether the base gets what it wants may partly be linked to the status of conditions. A booming economy and successful Iraqi transition will put pressure on colour-discordant Democrats, forcing them to pick and choose the spots for their opposition to the President's policies and appointments.

The fact that the President did not take public money in the primary, and that business groups spent large sums of money independently, will create another important debt for the President: namely to the business community. Tort reform, Clear Skies (which will loosen air resource regulations), tax reform and making the tax cuts permanent were not highly salient issues in the election. Nonetheless, the President has indicated that he will push forward on these measures. This cannot be explained by a simple electoral mandate theory. But clearly business backed the President heavily, and he cannot ignore their expectations. As years of research on the effects of money suggest, it is hard to pinpoint the exact causal effect that money has on elected officials in America. There is a correlation between the sources of money elected officials receive and their policy positions. However, it is hard to statistically separate the fact that money flows to support allies from the possible effects that money may have had in converting elected officials into allies. Given President Bush's and Vice-President Chaney's backgrounds in business, it is implausible to argue that campaign contributions created their pro-business agenda. But in the exchange economy of politics, those who help you get into office are owed some support from you when you get into office.

Lame ducks and mandates

Having outlined a conditional mandate theory, it is worth asking whether mandates in the second term are different from those in the first. There are reasons to think that they might be. A president in the first term is aiming for re-election for a second term. Legislators in his own party will cooperate in order to keep the incumbent in power. So, for instance, the Republicans supported the President's prescription drug bill even though many of the fiscal conservatives had grave reservations about expanding expensive government programmes at a time of high deficits. Fiscal conservatives wanted to 'shrink the beast' and approved the successive rounds of tax cuts in order to keep the surplus of the Clinton years from being spent by the Congress. When the surpluses turned to deficits, their unease with new spending programmes increased. Nonetheless, the President was able to prevail on the prescription drug bill because the party anticipated a close election, and this bill was seen as helpful to his re-election prospects. In a second term, the incentive to cooperate to help the President get re-elected is removed.

Another problem for the second term mandate is the so-called lame duck perception. At some point, attention shifts to those who might hold the office in the future and away from those who currently hold the office. Moreover, able people in the cabinet and administration start to depart for lucrative or powerful positions in the private sector, weakening the administration's authority. The degradation of power, according to conventional wisdom, accelerates in the second half of the second term. Accordingly, President Bush has front-loaded his agenda, moving on several policy fronts very ambitiously.

The effect of term limitation combined with the institutional separation of power in the American system adds to the conditional nature of the President's mandate. If, like his ally Tony Blair, George Bush could run for yet another term, he would face less time pressure. But by putting so much before the Congress, he raises the threshold of confidence that his party and colour-discordant Democrats have to have in him to support his policy agenda. That in turn accentuates the importance of the economy and Iraq. And unlike the British Prime Minister, the President could lose one or both of his Congressional majorities in 2006. In the British system, the executive and the legislature submit themselves to elections at the same time. In the American system, Congress will have mid-term election in 2006 so the consequence of bold choice will be felt by them immediately. So, given the President does not have to worry about re-election and the Congress does very soon after the President's re-election, there are potential divergent perspectives at work. The President, looking to his legacy, will likely be more risk-acceptant. The legislature, hoping to get re-elected, will probably be more risk-averse. This adds further to the obstacles in the way of realizing a bold second term conservative agenda.

Conclusion

To summarize the argument, the boldness of President Bush's second term agenda has little to do with the size of his electoral margin or the issues that the campaign was fought over. His ability to realize his aims will depend in good measure upon conditions in the economy and Iraq. The public confidence he gains from good conditions might enable him to carry out a policy agenda that far exceeds what was discussed and promised during the 2004 campaign. Conditions will also determine how members in colour-discordant seats react. Professor Fiorina's observation that mass politics and elite politics are incongruent could become even more true if all the right conditions emerge for the President. The unusual Republican strategy of targeting the conservative base and the heavy dependence on private money created strong conservative forces on this second term President. Weak conditions and declining confidence could frustrate these conservative forces. But strong conditions and rising confidence could pave the way for a radical policy agenda.

As many of the other chapters in this book discuss, there is much concern in Europe and elsewhere about the future direction of US foreign policy. Will it continue on the path of unilateral policy, or will it conform more to the wishes of the international community? Judging from the appointments to the second administration (for instance, the elevation of Condoleezza Rice to Secretary of State), the President intends no doctrinal change and has rewarded those who have most loyally supported the so-called Bush doctrine. But even if there is no likely change in doctrine, will there be a change in practice?

I would argue that this is possible for several reasons. First, the Bush administration has reacted very differently to the nuclear proliferation dangers in Iran and North Korea than it did with Iraq. It has shown more patience, more willingness to employ diplomatic strategies and more collaboration with allies and neighbouring nations. It is hard to tell at this point whether this is because the President has been chastened by the unexpected difficulty of the Iraq intervention, or whether the prospect that North Korea at least has nuclear weapons already, is making an invasion look very costly. Second, public support for the President on Iraq is still relatively weak despite a slight and temporary rise after the Iraq elections of 31 January 2005. The cost in lives and money continues to weigh heavily on the minds of American voters. Third, the Bush administration has outlined for itself an extremely ambitious domestic agenda, taking on such potentially difficult issues as social security and tort reform. Add to that the prospect of at least one, and probably more, Supreme Court appointments, and it is quite possible that the energy expended in fighting fires on the domestic front will alter the course of and distract the President from his international policies.

More than at any time in recent memory, domestic and foreign policy are linked in two senses. First, there is a strong fiscal connection. The tax cuts combined with the Iraq war and prescription drug bill passed in the first Bush administration have contributed to a growing national debt. The President's determination to stay the course in Iraq will mean billions more in additional appropriations. At the same time, his social security proposal would cost trillions in the short run before any benefits of privatization kick in. Second, there is a connection between the public's confidence in the President's boldness in both realms. Few Americans knew much about Iraq before the invasion, and relied heavily on the President's judgment. The President's call for bold domestic policies asks the public to trust him once again. The reservoir of trust depends upon the outcomes of past decisions, especially the war in Iraq or domestic programmes such as the prescription drug bill and the tax cuts that have driven up the deficit. Members of his party in Congress who want to keep their majorities in the House and Senate will make their own political calculations about the potential risks and benefits of the President's policies.

In short, victory in a presidential election does not ensure smooth sailing for a second term American president with a bold agenda. The willingness of voters to trust a leader on foreign policy in the wake of an attack does not last forever and does not automatically carry over to domestic policy. Retrospective judgment forms the basis for prospective trust. Mandates are given conditionally in the US.

References

Butler, D. and Cain, B.E. (1992) *Congressional Elections*, New York: Macmillan.

Campbell, J.E. (2004) 'Introduction: The 2004 Presidential Election Forecasts', *PS: Political Science and Politics*, 37, October: 733–35.

Campbell, J.E. (2005) 'Introduction – Assessments of the 2004 Presidential Vote Forecasts', *PS: Political Science and Politics*, January: 23–25.

Carmines, E.G. and Stimson, J.A. (1989) *Issue Evolution: Race and the Transformation of American Politics*, Princeton, NJ: Princeton University Press.

Fiorina, M. (1989) *Retrospective Voting in American National Elections*, New Haven, CT: Yale University Press.

Fiorina, M. (2004) *Culture War? The Myth of a Polarized America*, New York: Pearson Longman.

Key, V.O. (1966) *The Responsible Electorate*, New York: Vintage.

Kramer, G. (1971) 'Short Term Fluctuations in US Voting Behavior', *American Political Science Review*, 65: 131–43.

Neustadt, R.E. (1990), 3rd edn, *Presidential Power and the Modern Presidents. The Politics of Leadership from Roosevelt to Reagan*, New York: The Free Press.

Nordhaus, W. (1975) 'The Political Business Cycle', *Review of Economic Studies*, 42 (1): 169–90.

Polsby, N.W. (2004) *How Congress Evolves: Social Bases of Institutional Change*, New York: Oxford University Press.

Polsby, N.W. and Wildavsky, A. (2004) 11th edn, *Presidential Elections*, New York: Rowman and Littlefield.

Tufte, E. (1978) *Political Control of the Economy*, Princeton, NJ: Princeton University Press.

9 The economic constraints on American unilateral foreign policy

Roberto Tamborini

Introduction

Substantial agreement exists that the Bush administration has announced, and is undertaking, a major shift in the foreign policy of the United States (or US) aimed at the unilateral exercise of global power according to an extensive definition of 'national interest' and 'national security', inclusive of the establishment of the 'world democratic order' by means of armed force. This new strategy is considered to be inspired by the so-called 'neoconservative' doctrine, which stresses the right and power of the US to lead the politics of the free world, with no permanent commitments towards, and constraints by, multilateral organizations. What has an economist to say about this new foreign policy stance of the US?

It is well known to economists, as well as to political scientists of almost all persuasions, that economic and political choices are intimately related. Generally speaking, the influence of the economy on the political sphere can be traced back to two main factors: *motivations* whether 'need' or 'greed' that induce political choices, and *constraints* that set limits on political choices (Gilpin 2003). While much debate focuses on the former factor e.g. control over oil production and other vested interests of major Bush supporters in this chapter attention will be drawn to the role of the economy as a constraint on political choices.

If one considers whether the new US foreign policy stance has been tested against its long-run economic feasibility, not only does one realize that remarkably scant attention seems to have been paid to this dimension, but one is also led to suspect that little pressure is felt to focus on it.[1] Indeed, the extent of economic resources and the extent of power are often interrelated, and each may be instrumental to expanding the other. Thus, a politician may use his/her power to relax economic constraints on his/her set of feasible choices; and if political power is considerable, the politician (and his/her supporters) may be tempted to believe that economic constraints are negligible. History, however, as argued by Paul Kennedy (1988) and many others, suggests that this belief is groundless even for international 'superpowers'.

This chapter is organized in the following way. First, a few basic insights into the domestic as well as international economic implications of foreign political choices are discussed. The key message is that the feasibility of these choices can be ranked according to their consistency with the long-run sustainability of the ensuing economic implications. Second, these basic principles will be seen in action examining two major historical antecedents when a single country ruled the political–economic world system of capitalist countries, Great Britain from 1870 to 1915 and the US from 1945 to 1973. The purpose of these historical comparisons is to highlight patterns of world political–economic governance which should not and cannot be mechanically applied to the present situation of the US, but can offer better guidance in gauging the long-run feasibility of the neoconservative strategy than mere (unreliable) projections of the costs of wars. Third, this assessment exercise will be utilized to draw attention to the present world debtor position and international financial phase of the US economy. This position is at odds with succesful antecedents and appears highly problematic for the neoconservative programme for two reasons: one is that considerations of international financial stability leave too little room for the large fiscal deficits and external borrowing required by the programme; the other is that high external debt is hardly consistent with the 'free-hand', unconditioned exercise of political will invoked by the neoconservatives. Finally, a few concluding remarks will be advanced.

Some economics of international politics

It is well known that a country's international political status does not come as a 'free lunch' or by pure political will. It is the long-run outcome of a complex mixture of historical pre-conditions and political and economic choices. Both private and public economic choices concur to determine a country's feasible international political stance. For instance, the geographical extent of a country's political influence is often dictated by the extent of its 'national interests', which in turn depends on the expansion of international trade and finance developed by the private sector. The endeavour to protect national interests is generally accompanied and enforced by the development of the foreign affairs apparatus (diplomacy and army), and this in turn implies a consistent path of public expenditure both domestically and abroad.

A paradigmatic example of modern analysis of the economic implications of international political status is provided by Kindleberger (1976; 1981), who examined the role of the US in the post-World War II international order and proposed that it should be defined as one of *international leadership*. Kindleberger pointed out that sheer will, political power or even command over material and strategic resources are not enough in themselves for a country to become an international leader. The difference lies in the presence of *international responsibility* among the government's objectives. In other words, an international leader must be aware of the external consequences of its actions, must be able to include its partners' benefit among its own targets, and to this effect it must be ready to restrict its set of feasible choices according to its international commitments. This general principle is shared by a variety of other analyses of international power, not only concerning leadership but also hegemony (Kehoane 1980) or even imperialism (Arrighi 1978).

The case that Kindleberger took from the economist's tool box is the so-called provision of public goods. Defence is the textbook example of a public good, and it was indeed the key issue in international politics during the 1960s and 1970s. Defence is a public good because everyone benefits from it, but no one in isolation has enough resources or incentives to pay for it, once account is taken of the fact that if any single individual or coalition of individuals pays for defence then it is not possible to exclude from the benefits those who have not contributed. Hence, no one will ever pay for defence on a voluntary basis. When the coalition of individuals that we call 'the state' exists, the solution to the provision of public goods is compulsory contribution enforced by law and legal sanction – i.e. taxation. In the post-war Western international coalition of states, in the absence of a super-state authority, the solution was a type of informal semi-voluntary exchange. The leader of the coalition would bear the (bulk of the) costs of defence and reap the benefits of leadership. The members of the coalition would enjoy defence with limited loss of sovereignty and minimal waste of resources. Total security supply would be maximized, total defence expenditure would be minimized. If, drawing on Arrighi's taxonomy (1978), we move from the informal to formal exercise of international power, such as modern colonialism or imperialism, we find that participation in the exchange is, of course, no longer voluntary, and the loss of sovereignty and economic resources by subject countries is substantial. Nonetheless, the mother country still faces a number of costly international commitments towards subject countries as well as other countries. Inwardness and pure domestic self-interest are not compatible with the pursuit of high international status. This is a recurrent theme in the culture of international powers, from Rome to Great Britain to the United States (Kennedy 1988).

The fact that the exercise of international power imposes an international constraint on the leader's or emperor's domestic choices is made clear by another economic textbook story. *Insofar as resources are limited*, any government is confronted by the alternative between producing 'butter or guns'. If more guns are produced to meet international commitments, less butter is left for home taxpayers. Note that the problem of the 'costs of the empire' is wider and deeper than the so-called 'war finance', though this may be predominant in some circumstances. Likewise, direct public expenditure abroad or the burden of military expenditure may be relevant, but they should not be our exclusive concern. As will become clear later, the key factor in this respect lies in the interaction between the budgetary choices of governments, on the one hand, and the long-run saving and investment choices of the private sector, on the other, according to the basic open-economy financial account:

external lending (+) or borrowing (–) = net private saving
(saving investment) + public budget

Since external lending amounts to capital outflows whereas external borrowing amounts to capital inflows, the external financial position of the country is also connected with its international accounts:

current account (goods + services + incomes)
+ net capital flows = balance of payments

Note that the international impact of the government budget can be viewed in financial as well as real terms. If, say, a government seeks to provide more guns *and* more butter, it may run into budget deficits. In financial terms, fiscal deficits matter because they determine the borrowing requirement of the public sector; if this exceeds the saving–investment balance of the private sector, the difference should result in net lending or borrowing with the rest of the world. In real terms, fiscal deficits add to the domestic absorption of resources of the private sector (consumption and investment): if total domestic absorption exceeds gross domestic product, additional resources should come from the rest of the world, imports should exceed exports and a trade deficit develops. Typically, a country running large fiscal deficits tends to develop current account deficits too ('twin deficits') and to borrow from abroad.

The balance of payments (or BOP) acts as a constraint because persistent negative (positive) unbalances would require either reserves losses (gains) by the central bank or depreciation (appreciation) of the exchange rate. Therefore, since no country can go on losing reserves or depreciating the exchange rate indefinitely, the capital and the current account should match *over the medium run*. However, indefinite borrowing is also precluded, hence both the current account and the capital account should evolve around a balanced path *over the long run*. Consequently, *an international political stance is feasible as long as it is associated with a sustainable international economic position of the country*. Although full external balance (zero borrowing and lending, zero current account) is hardly observable in practice, it acts as a 'gravity centre' around which actual country positions revolve, and, more importantly, it represents the benchmark against which they can be measured and assessed. The unsustainability of creditor–debtor positions can materialize more or less smoothly depending on the growth speed of foreign debt, the country-risk assessment, the level of world interest rates and exchange-rate expectations.

On the other hand, it is widely believed that political and economic resources are also complementary: roughly speaking, the hard laws of the economy do not apply to international powers. There is more than a grain of truth in this view; history, however, suggests that financial techniques supported by international power may relax and postpone economic constraints but cannot eliminate them in the long run (Ardant 1976; Kindleberger 1984;

Kennedy 1988; Gilpin 2003). The institutional set-up in which power is to be exerted is also a key element in this respect. Contemporary powers that recognize and subscribe to the principles of democracy and free markets not only meet higher constitutional limits to the government's discretionary power in the economic sphere, but even in the apparently unregulated international arena they are exposed to the 'constituency of markets' too (e.g. by allowing free capital movements). As we shall see in the subsequent parts of this chapter, although markets are sensitive to the international status of a country and can misallocate resources by far more than economists would like to admit, the law of political power cannot repeal the law of the market forever; this eventually imposes, sometimes painfully, a reconciliation between domestic economic choices and international political aspirations.

Patterns of world political–economic governance

The best way to grasp the implications of the general ideas put forward in the previous section, and to introduce examination of the present situation of the US, is to provide brief sketches of two major historical cases of the economic success and crisis of international powers: Great Britain and the Empire in the second half of the nineteenth century, the US and its world leadership in the 30 years after World War II.

Great Britain and the Empire, 1850–1914

The British empire in the second half of the nineteenth century is generally regarded as a paradigm of the economic sustainability of international political ambitions. Great Britain entered her golden age as a leader in industry and trade, and as a world creditor country. In 1850, Britain held 25 per cent i.e. the largest share of both world manufactured products and world trade. From 1860 to 1890, London invested some 1.3 billion pounds abroad, at a pace of 65 million a year. Between 1890 and 1914, foreign investment surged to 2.7 billion pounds, averaging 108 million each year. On the eve of World War I the British capital invested abroad amounted to about 4 billion pounds accounting for 45 per cent of total foreign investment by major industrialized countries (Hobsbawm 1968: ch. 7).[2]

A key institutional aspect of Britain's relations with other independent countries was participation in the international monetary system known as 'gold standard'. Formally, this was a system with gold as exclusive means of international payment, and currencies quoted in terms of gold, which resulted in mutually fixed exchange rates. The common wisdom in the international community was that gold reserves were critical, and that the BOP constraint was binding since persistent payments imbalances would give rise to unsustainable gold transfers from deficit to surplus countries. From this viewpoint, the most striking feature was the composition and evolution of Britain's international accounts. From 1850 to 1900, the British economy lost its supremacy in industry and trade, halved its share of world manufactured goods and took a path of growing deficits in merchandise trade barely corrected by large remittances from transport services. How could a heavily capital-exporting country with a worsening trade account survive the BOP constraint? *The key to success was foreign incomes.* In an 'average year', interests and dividends from abroad were by themselves larger than the deficit in goods and services. Thus, the current account (the sum of goods, services and incomes) was consistently positive and more than sufficient to pay for foreign investments. Hence, Britain was able to manage her BOP and maintain her commitment to gold as long as her economy was broadly consistent with a *mature creditor*, or international rentier, position. In parallel, Britain's *mature debtor* countries were able to service their debts thanks to their sales of goods to the mother country.

Since the British BOP was tendentially positive, a stabilizing role was also increasingly played by short-term capital movements in paper sterlings from and to London. Overall, world gold reserves, and the British ones in particular, were unable to keep pace with the growth rate of world trade. As a number of studies have pointed out, the gold standard was in fact turned into a sterling standard, with the British currency being largely used in international transactions and reserves instead of gold (Triffin 1969; Williams 1968; De Cecco 1975). And as a rentier, Britain offered absolute security to those who came even from the Moon to deposit in London. Thus, a few basis points of increase in interest rates sufficed to attract enough short-term capitals to rebalance overall payments.

In a long-run perspective, however, the decline of Britain in international trade and her persistent trade deficits were fatal for the British world order. Its economic erosion was due to a number of deep-lying causes, prominent among which were obsolescence of technology, unfavourable specialization *vis-à-vis* emerging competitors in the free Western world, and import-dependent consumption habits. However, political–economic macro-factors should also be considered. Hobson's analysis of the British Empire (1902) provided one of the earliest and clearest accounts of the costs of the empire, first, by dispelling the naive idea that empires are always built in the interest of the nation as a whole, and, second, by pointing out how the growing absorption of public expenditure by the foreign affairs apparatus, *vis-à-vis* a declining GDP capacity, set the British economy on an unsustainable path. According to Hobson's data, from 1870 to 1900 public expenditure rose from 61.7 to 128.7 million pounds, with the military share escalating from 31.9 to 53.5 per cent, i.e. three and a half times in nominal terms and more than four times in real terms.[3] The increasing costs of international power put the public budget under pressure, eventually forcing Victorian governments to abandon the cornerstones of the liberist tradition by introducing a heavier income taxation system and by resorting to borrowing. Debt financing of the military apparatus rose from almost nil in 1870 to about 50 million pounds before World War I (Hobsbawm 1968: ch. 12). Thus, in modern economic textbooks' terms, the persistent British trade deficits were due to excess domestic real absorption in a vicious circle of upper-class consumption and investment trends sustained by foreign incomes, and of growing excess public expenditure necessary to support the global power that made high consumption, investment and foreign incomes possible.[4]

It is remarkable that this system maintained a high degree of stability, given that its pivot was a chronically dependent country as to real resources. This situation, in fact, raises the question of sustainability: how long can a country live above its means? One stability factor was, as pointed out above, that Britain was not a debtor but a rentier: the flow of world rent necessary to sustain excess domestic real absorption was, to a great extent, guaranteed. Another factor was the Empire, a two-edged sword by itself. The term 'vicious circle' can be used to denote the role of military expenditure in the excess absorption mechanism; yet contemporaries would probably view it as a virtuous circle. Indeed, as the case of India shows, the Empire also offered a large area of administered and protected trade whereby the mother country was able to secure outlets for her goods and to shelter herself against the threats of free trade with emerging Western competitors.

As suggested initially, political power may relax economic constraints or hide them from view. Nonetheless, they eventually become compelling. As is often the case, the alarm bell was rung by a sudden financial crisis. In the summer of 1914, on the eve of war, the sophisticated network of short-term capitals mastered by the London bankers broke down when, for the first time, London was unable to serve a massive withdrawal of liquid funds in sterling and gold by foreign depositors. Technically, the crisis was overcome in a few days, but with hindsight we can say that it marked 'the end of an era' (De Cecco 1975: Ch. 7). Not only was the pre-war monetary order mortally wounded, but the unsustainability of Great Britain's international political–economic stance became manifest. And after the war, as Keynes emphatically warned in his pamphlets (1931), the obdurate attempts by British governments to restore the vestiges of the past world order played a major role in destabilizing both the international system and their own country.

The leadership of the United States after World War II, 1950–1973

One of the most famous interpretations of the inter-war political, economic and financial instability which culminated in the 1929 crash and then in the World War is Kindleberger's major book (1973), the keystone of which is the idea that the collapse of the British world order left a vacuum of political–economic leadership, with no country able to assume the pivotal role that would guarantee an orderly, growth-inducive, network of debtor–creditor positions as well as ensuring the supply of international public goods.

The leading country that presided over the reconstruction of a sustainable world scenario after World War II was the US. During the 1950s the US took an international economic stance similar to that of Great Britain examined in the previous paragraph but with some crucial differences. In the aftermath of World War II, like Britain in post-Napoleonic Europe, the US enjoyed a substantial industrial advantage over the rest of the world in terms of fixed capital, infrastructures, production capacity and financial resources. Absent a formal empire, the role of leader of the victorious Allied Army was quite naturally extended and confirmed in the new confrontation against the Communist bloc: economic supremacy went hand in hand with political leadership. Again, the new mix of leadership-*cum*-partnership on the Western front was sealed by a 'monetary pact' quite similar to the gold-sterling system centred in London one century before: the gold-dollar system of pegged exchange rates devised at Bretton Woods in 1944.

As can be seen from Figure 9.1, in the 1950s the gold-dollar system, too, was pinpointed by the dominant country as a world creditor, with net capital outflows averaging 500 million dollars per year *vis-à-vis* trade surpluses of 3.6 and incomes (interests and dividends) of 1.4 billion dollars. This was the typical, healthy pattern of a *young creditor-country*. However, a major problem was hidden in the US international accounts, namely unilateral transfers abroad due to private and public non-market payments and obligations. These transfers amounted to 5 billion dollars per year, two-thirds of which were government payments. These figures are highly indicative of the US's growing international military and non-military commitments.[5] Since transfers are recorded in the current account, the balance of trade, incomes and transfers was almost nil, leaving capital outflows uncovered and hence the BOP with an average *deficit* of 500 million dollars each year. In other words, the US economy, as a consequence of domestic excess capacity, was transferring real and financial resources abroad to the benefit of the reconstruction and development of foreign partners, but the compound effect of foreign investments with military and non-military government commitments was too large relative to net export capacity.

The first half of the 1960s, marked by the escalation of the Vietnam war, saw an increase in US net export capacity, lower transfers, better current accounts, but also larger and larger foreign investments which outweighed the improvements in the current account, and deteriorated the fundamental imbalance of US payments dramatically (−1.4 billion dollars per year in 1960–64). This was a signal that the US role as world provider of goods, capitals and defence was unsustainable. The survival of the Bretton Woods system in spite of the pivot's increasing weakness was a variation on the theme of the economic benefits of international power that we have already met in the gold-sterling system. The US was able to practise 'benign neglect' towards her payments imbalances thanks to the special status of the dollar as world means of payment and reserve. No foreign recipient of dollars would put the Federal Reserve under pressure to convert dollars back into other currencies or gold. This was one of the benefits of leadership that compensated the leader for the costs of providing defence for all, and at the same time it

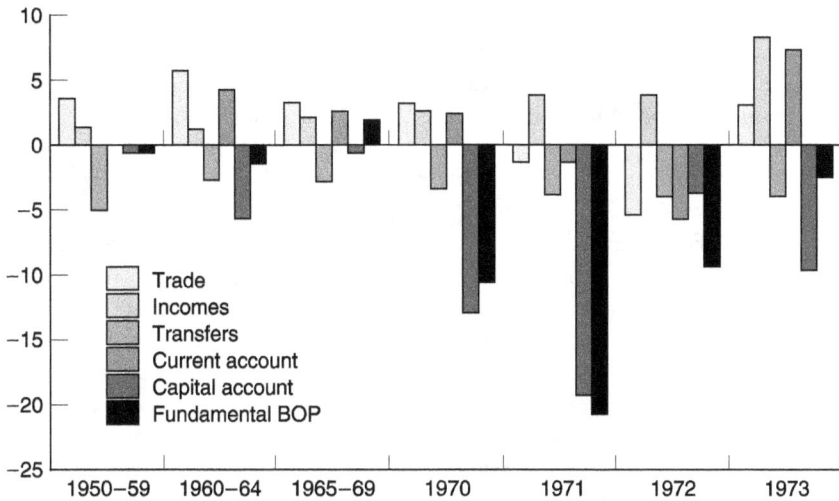

Figure 9.1 The United States' international payments, 1950–73 (billions of dollars)

allowed the exchange-rate system to survive. In fact, as Argy (1984) stresses, in the 1950s the world overflow of dollars was probably demand-driven as the fast growth of international trade generated demand for means of payments in excess of gold supply, and dollar shortage was one of the troubles of the time. However, this was no longer the case in the 1960s. Robert Triffin (1960) predicted ten years in advance the collapse of the international monetary system brought about by the unsustainable growth of paper dollars in the world relative to the US gold stock.[6]

Either a cut in foreign investments and unilateral transfers or a cut in domestic absorption to further improve foreign trade became necessary in the second half of the 1960s. With unilateral transfers being quite rigid, these corrections recovered the BOP but drove the economy into the sharp recession of 1968–69.[7] Thus, at the end of the 1960s markets and governments realized the inconsistency between the international political order based on the US leadership and what are now called the underlying economic fundamentals. Speculative attacks against the dollar were triggered during 1970–71 with massive capital outflows that self-fulfilled the belief that the US BOP was bound to founder. The official breakdown of the Bretton Woods Agreements occurred in August 1971 with a subsequent official devaluation of the dollar by 7.9 per cent. In 1972 the US economy recovered, yet in February 1973 a further 10 per cent devaluation was necessary, which in fact brought the trade account back to surplus and reduced the BOP deficit. In November, however, the first oil crisis broke out and definitively disrupted the post-war political–economic order.

Overall, in spite of similarities in favourable factors (supremacy in industry and trade, world creditor position, gold-based fixed-exchange-rate monetary pact) and in unfavourable ones (growing external–internal conflicting targets and long-run unsustainability of the BOP constraint) the US leadership model proved to be weaker and shorter-lived than the British imperial system. As a matter of fact, the latter was undermined by the slow erosion of the British world rent, but never were there substantial world payments imbalances. By contrast, the US proved unable, or unwilling, to correct the structural imbalance in her international payments, and blatantly resorted to inflating dollar circulation regardless of the monetary pact. To return to Kindleberger's definition of international leadership, we may conclude that the US broke the rule that a leader must be ready to give priority to international commitments over domestic concerns. Indeed, the end of the coalition pact on which the post-war political–economic order rested was declared as early as 1968 by Charles De Gaulle and his central banker Jacques Rueff, when they announced that the privileges enjoyed by the US thanks to the international role of the dollar were extravagant and no longer acceptable.

Global power and global finance: the 'Star Wars' programme

The US retreated from international commitments and organized world governance after the events described in the previous section. Not surprisingly, neoconservatives are extremely critical of the lack of a grand view and of the piecemeal approach in foreign affairs of the 1970s, for which they indict Richard Nixon and Henry Kissinger, let alone subsequent administrations. This criticism seems unaware of the collapse of the economic conditions underlying the US leadership, and of the advent of conditions unfavourable to any other possible design of global governance. It was only with the 'Star Wars' programme under the Reagan administration that the US sought to return to global exercise of power; yet both the US and the world economy were dramatically different than in the Bretton Woods era. The interesting question raised by the Reagan parable is whether the world political–economic leader can also be a debtor. The lesson may be relevant to G.W. Bush as well.

President Reagan took office in 1981 and his economic programme was based on dismantling market protections and limitations, on the one hand, and on strong fiscal expansion through low taxes and high strategic expenditure, on the other. High strategic (military and non-military) expenditure also reflected an international political choice to restore the US to its role as world leader in the final attack against the Communist bloc. The rationale of the 'Star Wars' programme was essentially to raise the cost of mutual deterrence so enormously as to shatter the USSR economy. In our metaphor, the 'butter *versus* guns' alternative would have strangled the USSR, whereas the US economy would have enjoyed 'more butter and more guns'. Was this design accomplished? Who actually paid for the 'Star Wars' programme? The answers to these questions provide a clear exemplification of the principles put forward so far.

First of all, the Reagan fiscal programme produced a sequence of large deficits escalating from 2.1 per cent of GDP in 1981 to 5.2 in 1985 to return to 2.8 in 1988 (see Table 9.1 and Figure 9.2). In the eight years of the two Reagan administrations (1981–1988), defence expenditure rose constantly from 157 billion dollars in 1981 to 290 billion dollars in 1988, and it reached the historical peace-time peak of 6.2 per cent of GDP in 1986. As explained in the first section of this chapter, the international consequences of the government budget policy can be viewed in real as well as financial terms. Owing to the addition of fiscal deficits to domestic real absorption, the US experienced the so-called 'twin deficits' phenomenon – that is, trade deficits *vis-à-vis* government deficits – as can be seen in Figure 9.2. In financial terms, the public sector's borrowing requirement rose from 3.1 of GDP in 1981 to 9.3 in 1986. In spite of a sustained net lending capacity of the private sector (excess of private saving over private investment), the consequence was an increasing external borrowing requirement which peaked at 5 per cent of GDP in 1986.

Thus, the most striking feature of the first attempt to return to global power after the crisis of the 1970s, in the new context of global finance and floating exchange rates, was that *the US had to take a typical world debtor position*. The US had net foreign assets for more than 10 per cent of GDP in 1980, which were reduced to almost nil in 1988, and then turned into net liabilities towards the rest of the world from 1989 onwards (see Figure 9.3).

As stressed by Kindleberger (1984, chaps 12, 16), it is a recurrent faulty idea that the best financial policy to pay for wars is debt, on the illusion that it dispenses with the need to raise taxes. Debt is only a means to shift higher taxes, or lower non-military expenditures, to the future: '[recourse to] debt is irrelevant to the question as to whether the country [can], or [cannot] pay for the war', and to this effect 'one has to take into account repercussions throughout the system (Kindleberger 1984: 172). The system, for a global player, is the world. Credit-worthiness may be largely supported by international status but it cannot be so indefinitely. A world debtor has to pay higher interest rates and/or appreciate its currency in order to induce foreign lenders to accommodate increasing shares of its liabilities in their portfolios. From 1981 to 1985 the US recorded the most dramatic peace-time increase in nominal and real interest rates. In the same period, the dollar appreciated by 51.2 per cent in real terms *vis-à-vis* the US trading partners' currencies (see Figure 9.2). The other side of the coin was that high interest rates worsened the income account, while the strong dollar worsened the trade account, thereby widening the external borrowing requirement in a vicious circle. As to lenders, the world expansionary effect of US trade deficits was outweighed by the contractionary effect of financial resources absorption and high interest rates. The overall negative impact of the new US international stance was

Table 9.1 Reagan and G.W. Bush administrations – selected indicators

	Defence % total exp.	Defence % GDP	Budget % GDP	GDP growth	Inflation	Long int. rate	REER[a]	Curr. acc. % GDP	NFA[b] % GDP
Reagan									
Previous admin.[c]	23.1	4.4	-2.2	3.4	7.9	8.6	101.7	-1.1	16.2
1981	23.2	5.1	-2.5	2.5	5.1	12.9	107.9	-0.5	11.5
1982	24.8	5.7	-4.5	-2.1	5.7	12.2	125.5	-0.7	7.3
1983	26.0	6.0	-5.7	4.3	6.0	10.8	132.9	-1.6	7.4
1984	26.7	5.8	-5.0	7.3	5.8	12.0	142.1	-2.8	3.4
1985	26.7	6.1	-5.2	3.8	6.1	10.8	148.8	-2.9	2.3
1986	27.6	6.2	-4.7	3.4	6.2	8.1	126.5	-3.1	2.3
1987	28.1	6.0	-3.5	3.4	6.0	8.7	113.9	-3.2	1.1
1988	27.3	5.7	-2.8	4.2	5.7	9.0	107.5	-2.3	0.2
G.W. Bush									
Previous admin.[c]	16.4	3.1	1.2	4.2	1.7	5.8	117.0	-2.9	-12.8
2001	16.4	3.0	-0.4	0.3	2.4	5.3	129.9	-3.9	-23.1
2002	17.3	3.4	-3.8	2.5	1.1	5.2	126.4	-4.6	-25.1
2003	17.6	3.5	-4.6	2.9	1.9	4.8	121.3	-5.7	-28.5
2004	18.0	3.8	-4.7	4.6	1.8	4.5	116.7	-6.2	-32.6

Source: *Economic Report of the President*, Washington DC, 2004; IMF, *International Financial Statistics*, CD-Rom.
Notes:
a Real effective exchange rate (1995 = 100).
b Net foreign assets.
c Four-year average.

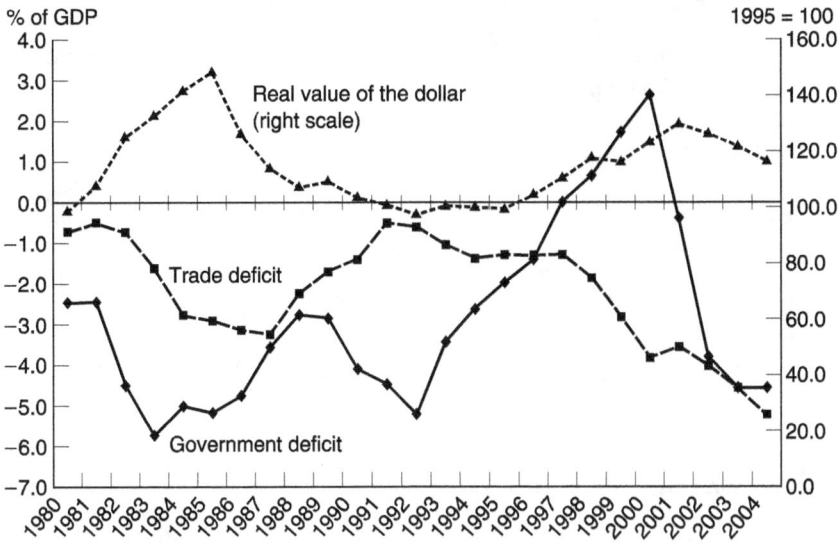

Figure 9.2 The United States' 'twin deficits' and the real value of the dollar, 1980–2004

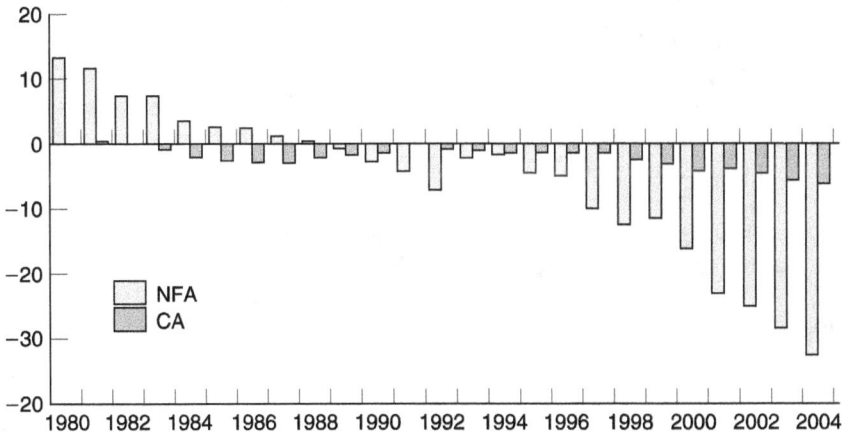

Figure 9.3 The United States' current account (CA) and net foreign assets (NFA) (% of GDP), 1980–2004

felt both in Europe, which experienced a twin spike in interest rates and unemployment (Fitoussi and Phelps 1988), and in the developing countries, which were no longer able to meet their external dollar-denominated debt services (Strange 1998).[8]

The blatant financial unsustainability of the 'Star Wars' programme on the one hand, and its negative effects on the partner economies on the other, disrupted the US's new international stance in a handful of years. In June and October 1985 two meetings of the major industrialized countries 'talked the dollar down', thereby putting an end to the world lending-to-America frenzy and, at the same time, to the tale that America could do by herself. The legacy of Reagan's global war finance experiment was the devastating third-world debt crisis of 1982–85 and, as a final *coup de theatre*, the Wall Street crash of October 1987.

Global war finance and unilateralism

The numerous analogies between Reagan's and G.W. Bush's global war finance programmes are evident. Both have taken place in a context of weak domestic economy, fiscal expansionary policies and large reliance on external debt. While aware of the pitfalls of historical analogies as guidance to future developments, it is nonetheless worth examining in greater detail the initial conditions of the two programmes. This task is helped by Table 9.1, which summarizes a few selected economic indicators of the two administrations *vis-à-vis* the previous administration.

To begin with, let us point out possibly *more favourable* conditions. First and foremost, George W. Bush inherited healthier public finances than Reagan: the overall budget was in surplus in 2000, public debt was diminishing, and defence expenditure was relatively low, in relation both to total expenditure and to GDP. These conditions allowed greater room for manoeuvre than that available to the Reagan administration. The impact of Bush's military programme seems at the moment to be less dramatic than Reagan's: even in 2004, after one year of the Iraq war, defence expenditure is estimated to have reached 18 per cent of total expenditure and 3.8 per cent of GDP,[9] well below the peaks of 28 per cent and 6 per cent, respectively, in 1986–87. The overall budget deficit is expected to be between 4.5 and 5 per cent in 2004–05, whereas it reached 5.7 per cent in 1983.[10]

Second, whereas the top priority assigned to fighting inflation in the early 1980s led to tight monetary policy and high interest rates, the Federal Reserve has so far been able to run a 'friendly' monetary policy by keeping interest rates low and domestic activity brisk thanks to non-inflationary conditions both domestically and worldwide.

Third, the world debtor 'locomotive' position of the US is, at the moment, consistent with partners' (especially Japan, China and Europe) willingness to enjoy the complementary position of world (mostly US) creditors mainly because they need high exports of capitals and goods for domestic structural reasons.

Let us now turn to a list of *less favourable* conditions than those faced by the Reagan administration. These essentially affect the US borrowing capacity, and hence the long-term sustainability of the neoconservative programme.

First of all, G.W. Bush inherited an international financial position of the country that was much harder than that inherited by Reagan (see Figure 9.3). In 1980 the US had net claims towards the rest of world of 378.7 billion dollars; at the end of the 1990s the US was one of the world's largest debtors, with net liabilities amounting to 1588.7 billion dollars, 16.3 per cent of GDP. With back-paddling government deficits, massive external borrowing was nonetheless necessary to sustain the new economy investment bubble.[11] High expected returns on stocks and capital inflows pushed the dollar along a robust appreciation path. In parallel, the trade account, after the recovery of the late 1980s, pointed again towards larger and larger deficits, reaching the post-war record of 375 billion dollars (3.8 per cent of GDP) in 2000. Large interest payments owed to foreign investors have added to trade imbalances to produce the concomitant current-account negative record of 421.3 billion dollars (4.3 per cent of GDP). In the first G.W. Bush administration, these tendencies have worsened further, with the government budget again taking the lead of financial imbalances. Thus, the neoconservative programme not only hinges on a *replica* of Reagan's idea of global war finance, but it also presumes that the replicant can be a massive world debtor with yawning current-account deficits.

Second, international financial markets and policy-makers have already set in motion the adjustment process of the US external position required by a *mature debtor*. As after 1985, the 'must' of world markets and policy-makers is now the so-called soft landing of the dollar. If, on the one hand, the Federal Reserve keeps interest rates low, on the other hand capital inflows are slowing down, and the dollar is depreciating, with the effect of correcting the current-account imbalances. At the same time, the domestic absorption of real as well as financial resources should be reduced, which requires less consumption, more saving and balanced fiscal budgets. Thus, the US economy is now being driven through the same phase that *followed* the Reagan era in the late 1980s and early 1990s: that is, the adjustment process that had to be managed by George H.W. Bush (see Figure 9.2). Viewed in this perspective of financial phases, George W. Bush's policy is, literally, anachronistic.

It is problematic that the mature-debtor phase of the US economy can be inverted as any attempt to move in that direction would be fraught with danger to international stability. Along the soft-landing path, little room is left for persistent fiscal deficits as these would result in a sharp increase in interest rates or, alternatively, massive monetization of federal deficits by the Fed. The first alternative is precluded by three considerations:

1   high interest rates would create recessionary conditions and would defeat the effect of tax cuts which are the hallmark of Bush's programme;

2   they would produce a fall in stock prices, which on the one hand would amplify recessionary conditions while on the other might trigger capital flights and attacks against the dollar;

3   they would also reduce the value of US T-bonds in world portfolios, and massive foreign sales of T-bonds would soon make financial and monetary policy in Washington unmanageable.

The alternative to high interest rates represented by monetization of fiscal deficits encounters no less serious obstacles.

a   This policy is nowadays strictly inhibited by central banking doctrines. Although the Fed has a tradition of pragmatism and flexibility, this policy would represent a U-turn in its strategy and reputation, setting the clock back to the 1960s and 1970s, when, as explained previously, US monetary policy was seen as one of the causes of the collapse of the world monetary system.

b   Consequently, fast growing money supply dictated by fiscal deficits would hardly be consistent with the soft-landing strategy. Financial markets might read monetization as signalling that fiscal policy is unsustainable and react by selling T-bonds and speculating against the dollar.

Finally, since politics has not completely disappeared from the stage of world finance, it should also be borne in mind that a substantial share of the US T-bonds circulating in the world is bought and held by institutional investors in Japan, China and 'old Europe', that is to say countries which are quite moderately favourable to, or openly against, Bush's foreign policy. Thus, in spite of the neoconservative ostentation of unilateralism, the new US international political stance should to some extent rely upon the financial interests of its opponents.

Conclusion

Current analyses of the neoconservative turn in US foreign policy tend to neglect its economic requirements and consequences. This is probably due to their long-run and uncertain nature, which stretches far beyond the accounting of the Afghan and Iraq campaigns. The assessment of these economic implications presented in this chapter has focused on the long-run sustainability of international political choices as determined by the ensuing international economic pattern of the country. The success of candidates to world governance in a frame of free market relations does not only depend on the extent of their political will or power. The fiscal counterpart of governments' foreign policy interacts with the private sector's saving and investment choices, co-determining the evolution of external trade and of external borrowing or lending. Thus, a country's international political stance is feasible as long as it is consistent with a sustainable international economic pattern.

The historical experiences of world governance of pre-World War I Britain and post-World War II America showed that financial sustainability of borrowing or lending positions was indeed a crucial factor in the long run, and that they remained sustainable as long as:

1　both countries were world creditors,
2　their international commitments were contained within not too large fiscal imbalances, and
3　their international economic positions were beneficial to their partners as well.

Although international power may relax or push these economic constraints into the far future, they turn out to be binding in the long run.

America was still world creditor when President Reagan launched his global war finance venture, which, however, transformed the Americans into world debtors. The instrinsic fragility of that (comparatively) short-lived experience lay in the violation of all three previous successful conditions. President George W. Bush's fiscal counterpart of his foreign policy looks very similar to Reagan's, with a mix of more and less favourable conditions. At present, it is hard to foresee which side will prevail, and whether complementarity between world power and economic conditions will shield the US from the hardships of market discipline reserved for 'ordinary' countries. It is fair to conclude, however, that today's US unilateralism in the political arena has weak roots in the economic ground.

Notes

1　The resignation of Paul O'Neill from the Treasury, which seems motivated by most of the concerns raised in this paper, has apparently had no substantial impact on the political–economic line of the first Bush administration.
2　Hobsbawm (1968), like many others, argues that Britain's international economic relations mostly developed independently of political power. If one looks at the geographical composition of foreign investment one indeed finds that up to 1870 territories under direct British control accounted for less than 35 per cent of total investment, the remainder being concentrated in Southern Europe, North America and Latin America. Yet data on new issuances in London in the subsequent three decades show that the concentration of foreign investment in controlled territories increased sharply, so that by the end of the century its geographical composition between dependent and independent countries was almost balanced (De Cecco 1975: 53; Hobsbawm 1968: Table 36).
3　Hobsbawm (1968: Table 43) reports similar figures. It should be noted that the last quarter of the nineteenth century saw a *decline* of prices in all major industrial countries. In Great Britain the general price index fell by about 25 per cent.

4 For a more detailed and analytical treatment of this process see Tamborini (1992).
5 Military expenditures abroad averaged at 2.1 billion dollars per year with a five-fold increase in the decade (see Argy 1984: Table 3.1).
6 The mounting threat to the convertibility commitment is highlighted by two figures: in 1959 short-term liabilities amounted to 19.4 billion dollars and were 1:1 with gold reserves, in 1971 they amounted to 67.8 billions, more than 6 times the value of gold reserves.
7 The incidence and importance of unilateral transfers in US international payments revived research on a 'minor' point of BOP theory, the so-called 'transfer problem' concerning whether BOP adjustment mechanisms exist such that a country can honour unilateral transfers: see e.g. Machlup (1963; 1969), Johnson (1956; 1975; 1976), Kindleberger (1968).
8 Remember that, by contrast, in the post-war period US international *lending* and trade deficits, albeit structurally unbalanced, played a crucial role in recovering and sustaining world economic activity in a context of monetary stability, to the general benefit of partners.
9 In 1991–92, after the first Iraq war, defence reached 21.8 per cent of total expenditure and 4.8 per cent of GDP.
10 The administration itself has announced a target for the defence budget of 451 billion dollars in 2007, with total expenditure amounting to 2144 billion dollars from 2002 to 2007. Assuming a 5 per cent yearly increase in nominal GDP, the US would end up with defence expenditure absorbing about 5 per cent of GDP in 2007, a figure in line with its order of magnitude in the 1980s. Overall, one may expect that the fiscal impact of the Bush programme will eventually be comparable with that of Reagan's.
11 The US financial and international accounts in the second half of the 1990s displayed a pattern similar to that of the 1980s (see Figure 9.2) except that the driving force was not government deficits but the longest private investment and consumption cycles in post-war history. The private saving–investment balance has been shrinking since 1995 and has turned to negative since 1998.

References

Ardant, G. (1976) *Histoire financiere de l'antiquité a nos jours*, Paris: PUF.
Argy, V. (1984) *The Postwar International Money Crisis. An Analysis*, London: Allen & Unwin.
Arrighi, G. (1978) *Geometria dell'imperialismo*, Milano: Feltrinelli.
De Cecco, M. (1975) *Money and Empire: The International Gold Standard 1890–1914*, Oxford: Blackwell.
Fitoussi, J.P. and Phelps, E.S. (1988) *The Slump in Europe*, Oxford: Blackwell.
Gilpin, R. (2003) 'The Nature of Political Economy', in Goddard C.P., Gormin P., Dash K.C. (eds), *International Political Economy*, London: Palgrave.
Hobsbawm, E.J. (1968) *Industry and Empire*, London: Weidenfeld & Nicolson.
Hobson, J. (1902) *Imperialism. A Study*, 2nd edn, London: Allen & Unwin, 1938.
Johnson, H.G. (1956) 'The Transfer Problem and Exchange Rates Stability', in *International Trade and Economic Growth*, London: 1958.
Johnson, H.G. (1975) 'The Classical Transfer Problem: An Alternative Formulation', *Economica*, 65: 710–31.

Johnson, H.G. (1976) 'Notes on the Classical Transfer Problem', *The Manchester School*, 44: 538–63.

Kennedy, P. (1988), *The Rise and Fall of the Great Powers: Economic Change and Military Conflict from 1500 to 2000*, London: Unwin Hymann.

Keohane, R. (1980) 'The Theory of Hegemonic Stability and Changes in International Economic Regimes, 1967–1977', in Goddard C.P., Gormin P., Dash K.C. (eds), *International Political Economy*, London: Palgrave.

Keynes, J.M. (1931) *Essays in Persuasion*, London: Macmillan.

Kindleberger, C.P. (1968) *International Economics* 4th edn, Homewood, IL: R.D. Irwin.

Kindleberger, C.P. (1973) *The World in Depression 1929–1939*, London: Allen & Unwin.

Kindleberger, C.P. (1976) 'Systems of International Economic Organization', in Calleo P. (ed.), *Money and the Coming World Order*, New York: Harpers & Row.

Kindleberger, C.P. (1981) 'Dominance and Leadership in the International Economy. Exploitation, Public Goods and Free Rides', in The International Economic Order. Essays on Financial Crisis and International Public Goods, New York: Basic Books,1988.

Kindleberger, C.P. (1984) *A Financial History of Western Europe*, London: Allen & Unwin.

Machlup, F. (1963) 'The Transfer Problem Revisited', in *International Monetary Economics*, London: Macmillan, 1965.

Machlup, F. (1969) 'Il "transfer gap" degli Stati Uniti', *Moneta e Credito*, 22: 137–51.

Strange, S. (1998) *Mad Money*, Manchester: Manchester University Press.

Tamborini, R. (1992) *Il trasferimento mondiale delle risorse. Un approccio finanziario ai pagamenti internazionali*, Firenze: La Nuova Italia.

Triffin, R. (1960) *Gold and the Dollar Crisis*: New Haven, CT: Yale University Press.

Triffin, R. (1969) *Our International Monetary System*, New York: Random House.

Williams, D. (1968) 'The Evolution of the Sterling System', in Whitlesley C.R., Wilson J.S.G. (eds) *Essays in Money and Banking in Honour of R.S. Sayers*, Oxford: Clarendon Press.

10 The cultural resistance to American political values

A global perspective

Scott M. Thomas

We are destined to be a barrier against the returns of ignorance and barbarism. Old Europe will have to lean on our shoulders, and hobble along by our side.

Thomas Jefferson to John Adams, 1 August 1816

Our security is not merely founded in spheres of influence or some balance of power; the security of our world is found in advancing the rights of mankind.

President George W. Bush

It is true that the Arab and Islamic peoples are primarily responsible for their conditions and their negativity. But the West, led by the US, has also consolidated such conditions, seeing as it does that their perpetuation is in its strategic interest.

'Who Hates Who?', Al-Ahram Weekly On-Line Edition (Cairo),
7–13 September 2004

A European statesman stated the issue very well recently with these words. 'We are grateful to America for saving us from communism. But our gratitude does not prevent us from fear that we might become an American colony. That danger lies in the situation of America's power and Europe's weakness.' The statesman, when reminded of the strain of genuine idealism in American life, replied: 'The idealism does indeed prevent America from a gross abuse of its power. But it might well accentuate the danger Europeans confront. For American power in the service of American idealism could create a situation in which we would be too impotent to correct you when you are wrong and you would be too idealistic to correct yourself.'

Reinhold Niebuhr, The Irony of American History, 1952, pp.132–33

Introduction

There seems to be a paradox regarding the way the United States (or US) engages with the rest of the world.[1] Various surveys show that American patterns of religious belief and practice are closer to those found in the developing world compared to those in Western Europe (Pew Research Center 2003a). Many sociologists of religion, increasingly influenced by rational choice theory, contrast the American free-market or competitive model of religious freedom with its separation of church and state, to the monopolistic or European model of state churches, which has contributed to the vibrancy of American religious life, and to the secularism and decline of religion in most Western European countries (Wilcox and Jelen 2002). Many Europeans seem to feel quite pleased and satisfied with their path of enlightened secularism and humanitarianism – Robert Kagan's (2003) notion of Europe as a Kantian paradise.

However, given the global resurgence of religion, this is clearly at odds with the way most people in the world interpret and live out their moral and social lives. Europe increasingly looks like an exceptional case when it comes to matters of religion and secularization. Many Europeans, if the truth is told, find this very hard to believe, since they have always understood, going back to Marx, Weber and Durkheim, that European society is the model of the future. What we now call modernization theory (the idea that modernization and secularization go together, so what happened to religion in Europe will occur in societies in the rest of the world) is simply not happening and is unlikely to occur any time soon (Davie 2002).

Given this contrast, it can be argued that the religiosity of American civil society and the vitality of American religion ought to provide what Joseph Nye has call untapped soft power resources for US foreign policy, and for the spread of American political values in the world. Soft power is usually described as the power of desirable or attractive ideas or culture. In contrast to the hard power of mainly military might or economic influence, ideas and culture can become a form of power when they become part of the attitudinal capabilities that make up the intangible elements of power for actors in international relations. They are able to influence the popular beliefs, perceptions and attitudes of particular constituencies (Nye 1990).

Thus, on the face of it, this religious vitality and commonality ought to provide the basis for the US to have stronger links with the developing world, including the Islamic world, than with the more secular EU or the older states of Western Europe. However, the US seems to find itself on the defensive, and its foreign policy opposed by more people than ever before in recent memory. How is this paradox to be explained and what can be done about it?

Explaining the cultural resistance to American political values

The simplest explanation is to say that there is no paradox at all. Any kind of strong religious belief promotes the kind of blinkers, blind spots and intolerance that can lead to political disagreements or violent conflict. The mixing of culture, religion and politics is almost always a combustible combination and, far from providing a new basis for America's soft power resources, under the presidency of George W. Bush religion and politics seem to be providing the basis for new wars of religion and clashes of civilization (Northcott and Hassell 2004).

There are a number of problems with this explanation. The first is that it simply adopts the political mythology of liberalism, which is the myth of the modern secular state as our saviour from the horrors of modern wars of religion or clashes between civilizations (Cavanaugh 2002). The only problem with this myth is that it is historically untrue, but like many myths, it stays with us because its totemic power tells something we want to believe about ourselves as modern men and women (Cavanaugh 1995).

The second problem is that it confuses the way the religious right in the United States mix religion and politics together with the way Evangelicals mix together religion and politics. American Evangelicals, at least those connected to the religious right, are increasingly estranged from Evangelicals in the rest of the world, including those in other Western industrialized countries. Few Americans seem to realize that the churches in other industrialized countries were not nearly as divided over the war in Iraq, for example, as they were in the US. Most Evangelical leaders in Britain, Australia and New Zealand, for example, were opposed to the war (Sine 2004). Globally, most Evangelicals hold what in the US would pass as more liberal or Democratic views on many social policy issues, such as social welfare, employment and international development (abortion and homosexuality are more complicated).

The third problem with this explanation is that it moves too swiftly from the ideas of the religious right to US foreign policy without any examination of the process of foreign policy-making. Whatever the personal religious views of President Bush or even the foreign policy positions of the religious right,[2] most of those Americans who consider themselves to be religious do not rely only on their clerics, priests or ministers of religion for their views on foreign affairs (Pew Research Center 2003b). It is broadly accepted that, unlike the area of personal morality – abortion or homosexuality – formulating foreign policy is an arena of public life which requires expertise and technical competence (Amstutz 2001). However, religious groups can influence the frame (nationalist or internationalist) within which foreign policy is elaborated.

The devil is always in any case in the details. The real issue is the *type* of religion that has influenced US foreign policy. More recently it has been the more muscular and militant forms of American Evangelicalism that have influenced what Walter Russell Mead has called the more militarist or Jacksonian tradition of US foreign policy, rather that the liberal Protestantism or Christian realism (they are not the same thing) that has influenced the Wilsonian tradition of American foreign policy (Mead 2001). The surveys show, for example, that those people who considered themselves to be born again or evangelical Christians were more likely to support the war in Iraq than other types of Christians or the rest of the general population.

What needs to be examined, as Tom Sine argues, are the consequences for US foreign policy of the takeover of leadership of American Evangelicalism by the religious right in the 1980s – represented by Jerry Falwell, Tim LaHaye, Pat Robertson and James Dobson (Sine 2004).

Josef Joffe has rightly pointed out that the US is unlike any other hegemonic power in history. Previous hegemons sought to conquer the world; but the US after the Second World War built a whole array of international institutions – the United Nations (or UN), NATO, General Agreement on Trade and Tariffs (or GATT), etc. (Joffe 2001). What he does not point out is that it was Reinhold Niebuhr and an influential coalition of 'Christian realists' and 'Christian liberals' who became what Heather Warren has called the theologians of a new world order. They, perhaps, more than any other group, helped to change America's political culture so that it was willing to accept the responsibilities of hegemonic leadership after the Second World War. They not only backed the Marshall Plan, but also actively supported the creation of the United Nations – almost as a religious obligation – and the construction of the international institutions we now call the Bretton Woods system (Warren 1997).

This relationship between ecumenical Protestantism and a guiding moral quest for stability during the turbulent post-war era is all the more striking today. There is a relative absence in the religious right or among many American Evangelicals (as it has already been pointed out, they are not the same thing) of any similar substantive theology of world order supporting an active engagement of the US in foreign affairs.[3] What we seem to have now has degenerated into a kind of '"democratic globalism", a kind of muscular Wilsonianism – minus international institutions – that seeks to use US military supremacy to support security interests and democracy simultaneously' (Fukuyama 2004: 57–58).

The second explanation for the paradox between America religiosity and global hostility, which is perhaps the most obvious one, and is popular among many scholars of international relations, is to say that whatever cultural or religious sentiments or similarity there may be between the US and many developing countries, the structural dynamics of international relations located at the level of analysis of the international system are what explain the cultural opposition to American political values. It is often argued, for example, that the cultural and political opposition to the US is a natural and structural response by states to the end of the Cold War, and the fact that the US is now the only superpower.

There is an absence of a balance of power in world politics, until the further rise of the European Union (or EU), China, India and Russia as great powers. The calls by the Chinese, Russians, or Europeans, from this perspective, for multipolarity or for the Security Council and the UN to be the final arbiter of international security, as was envisioned by the UN Charter, is realism masquerading as idealism. It is an attempt by these emerging great powers to restrain the power of the US, and its unipolar domination of international relations (Rodman 2000). In fact, one way of interpreting the purpose of European integration – political as well as economic, was from the beginning, even during the Cold War, about creating a European power to balance US hegemony (Layne 2003).

What many of these explanations miss is the impact of culture and religion on conceptions of polarity and international order. Many commentators, not least of whom is Charles Krauthammer, have pointed out the degree to which our unipolar era has no equivalent in history, even going back to the Roman Empire (Krauthammer 2002/2003). This comparison, as Niall Ferguson and others have pointed out, understates the degree of US hegemony, not only because of its military and economic power (Ferguson 2003). However, the Roman Empire coexisted with rather than conquered the great civilizations of India and China, and Parthia (roughly the area today of Iran and Iraq) was never subdued (Bell 1999).

The US, despite its military, economic, political and cultural hegemony, is faced with the problem of taking cultural and religious pluralism seriously in world politics in ways that never confronted the Roman Empire or the British Empire. This is the fundamental source of the cultural resistance to American political values around the world in our post-Cold War and postmodern era. Americanization is not the same as modernization, and cultures and societies throughout the world are now seeking economic prosperity, but without losing their soul (Thomas 2005). My focus will be primarily on the Islamic world, although my analytical framework can be used to understand the European resistance to the American values as well.

Irony, wisdom, tragedy and progress: beyond a problem-solving approach to foreign policy

'What is missing in recent American commentary is not so much an appreciation of history – there has been too much of that, with "Munich" invoked at every turn. What is lacking is a sense of the tragic' (Judt 2003: 31). Why is a sense of irony and tragedy so crucial for understanding international politics today?

Ever since Thomas Kuhn's analysis of the structure of scientific revolutions was applied to the social sciences, the study of international relations has been dominated by the inter-paradigm debate between the main images, paradigms or traditions of thought in international relations. Kuhn defined a paradigm as a particular way of looking at the world that was shared by a group of committed participants, and established a set of concepts that define a field of debate or inquiry in the social sciences. Paradigms were unprecedented enough to attract a group of adherents away from other competing paradigms, yet open-ended enough with problems for adherents to solve. Kuhn called normal science this routine problem-solving approach adopted by the adherents of a particular paradigm. This problem-solving approach in international relations, for example, might involve the balance of power between the superpowers, deterrence in the nuclear age, alliance formation and cohesion, or how to promote international cooperation in the absence of a hegemon or a single power to maintain international order.

Almost a generation before Kuhn was beginning to influence the social sciences, Martin Wight, one of the founders of what is now called the English School of international relations, opposed this problem-solving approach to the substantive issues in international relations. This was the tendency to see foreign policy as simply a succession of 'problems' or – to use the UN's language – 'questions' to be solved along the road towards greater democracy, world peace and economic prosperity.

> [I]t has been usual in modern times to see public affairs as a succession of 'questions' or 'problems' (from the venerable Eastern Question down to the Palestine Question, one of its contemporary progeny, the question of sovereignty, the problem of Veto, the exports problem, and so on) with the implication that they have answers and solutions, being incidents in the broad if irregular trend of progress.
>
> (Wight n.d.: 35–36)

Wight was concerned about the temptation among scholars and the public to embrace the idea of social and political improvement in international relations, and to mistake what Christopher Lasch in our time has called this promised land of progress for the true and only heaven (Lasch 1991). There is, Wight says, a great temptation, to think we have learned our lesson from the collapse of the League of Nations, to consider the UN an improvement on the League, and to think that with enough vigilance it will work out, and the world will live happily ever after with justice and peace for all. 'I am convinced', he says, 'these are dangerous fallacies.'[4]

Wight did not say this as a realist, political reactionary or conservative opposed to social change or improvement – he opposed British imperialism from his youth – nor was he a realist who believed that only power and not morality dominated international affairs. Wight arrived at these conclusions because he had a different substantive understanding of international relations than those scholars of the foreign policy establishment committed to a positivist epistemology and a doctrine of progress in international relations (Thomas 2001).

A positivist epistemology accepts that knowledge is, or can be, cumulative – even in international relations. Wight doubted that the events, passions and personalities that inevitably constituted the knowledge of international relations was cumulative in this way. He doubted that international relations could be studied as a form of problem-solving – as a succession of problems to be solved, which in the end will lead to a more just and peaceful world. This problem-solving approach is the conventional wisdom of the foreign policy establishment.

In our day, Bernard Lewis has warned against this problem-solving approach to the international politics of the Middle East, as if the resolution of today's main problems – Iran, Iraq, the Palestinians, etc. – can bring peace to the region. Europeans often talk as if the main obstacle to peace in the Middle East is Israel or the Bush administration.

But why is there this hostility [toward the West] in the first place? If we turn from the general to the specific, there is no lack of individual policies and actions, pursued and taken by individual Western governments, which have aroused the passionate anger of Middle East and other Islamic peoples. Yet, all too often, when these policies are abandoned and the problems resolved, there is only a local and temporary alleviation. The French have left Algeria, the British have left Egypt, the Western oil companies have left their oil wells, the westernizing Shah has left Iran – (and, I add, quite possibly, if the Americans leave Iraq as they have left Saudi Arabia) yet the generalized resentment of the fundamentalists and other extremists against the West and its friends remains and grows and is not appeased (Lewis 1990: 47–60).

It can be argued that looking at the Arab world, the Islamic world, or the international politics of the Middle East as a succession of problems to be solved, doesn't go deep enough to get at the foundations of the wounds, the political disagreements, or the fundamental differences between the Islamic and the Western worlds. We need to do what Fouad Ajami admonishes us to do:

> It is easy to judge but hard to understand the ghosts with which people and societies battle, the wounds and memories that drive them to do what they do. Even if we disagree with people's choices of allegiance, we must understand the reasons for their choice, the odds they fight against, the range of alternatives open to them.
>
> (Ajami 1981: 198)

We need to take the hopes and aspirations as well as the rage, anger, self-pity, fears and wounds of other people or civilizations seriously, and, like the prophet Jeremiah, recognize that they can not be healed lightly – by a problem-solving approach to foreign policy.[5]

Wight believed the tendency to see international politics as a succession of problems to be solved was based on certain underlying and unquestioned assumptions about history and progress which have dominated the study of international relations. In so far as these assumptions comprise the common wisdom of the day, this is why most scholars, journalists, politicians and members of the public adopt a problem-solving approach to international relations.

Wight believed that moral idealism was as an essential part of statecraft, but he rejected the idea that any permanent moral and legal international order could be constructed in international relations. The reason, following in some respects the analysis of Reinhold Niebuhr, his contemporary in the US, appears to be his recognition of irony and tragedy in political life. Irony for

Wight is a category of practical experience, and so politicians, diplomats and journalists are often more aware of it, or can detect it more often than, in Wight's day, the liberal idealists and Wilsonians, with their general concepts and schemes for improving international politics; and, in our time, the neo-conservatives, who under the influence of Leo Strauss seek to democratize the whole of the Islamic world (Schlesinger 2004; Norton 2004). Wight's ironic vision of international life is one deeply influenced by reading the speeches, statements and memoirs of great politicians and diplomats.

Tragedy or *peripeteia* is a 'surprising turn of events', or as in Aristotle's *Poetics*, it is 'the reversal of fortune'.[6] Wight says:

> [T]his is the word Aristotle uses for the reversal of situation that pro-
> vides the hinge of tragic drama. It is the train of action intended to
> bring about a certain end, but results in something different. The situ-
> ation swings around and recoils against the agent who is attempting to
> deal with it.
>
> (Wight n.d.: 40)

Wight could almost have had in mind the crisis unfolding in Iraq and Afghanistan, or what experts in national security call blow-back in international affairs.

Wight calls *peripeteia* 'irony in action', and he says, 'it is the warping of political intention by the historical context, is the regular, repeated, one is tempted to say fundamental experience of international politics' (*ibid.*). Now, most of us do not really want to really believe any of this at all. Wight says, 'We are accustomed to recognise the ironies and *peripeties* of politics in any particular case, when they illustrate the backwardness of the Germans or the Russians, the imbecility of the Foreign Office', and he adds in his day, the perversity of Dulles, Salazar and Nkrumah. We could no doubt all compile our own list of culprits today – Bush, Cheney, Rice, Rumsfeld, Armitage and Wolfowitz, etc.

Wight says the judgments we make in this regard are self-satisfying, and

> so confirm our special political dislikes. After all, they provide half
> the ammunition of political debate in a free society. But we are reluctant
> to recognise them [i.e. the ironies and *peripeties* of politics] in general.
> They affront our belief in the rational control of our affairs and our con-
> sciousness of moral rectitude. ... Academic students of politics, being
> usually wedded to schemes of political improvement, tend to neglect the
> phenomenology of political experience.
>
> (Wight n.d.: 43)

Perhaps, students of politics today, however, are less wedded to schemes of political improvement than they are to the cynicism, scepticism and relativism of our postmodern era.

The concept of irony 'recognises that the reversals and incongruities of life are a part of common experience. The sense of irony, at its simplest, is aroused by the recognition that in politics intentions are seldom fulfilled, and consequences elude reckoning' (*ibid.*: 44). For Wight the irony and the tragedy of international politics come from the direct experience of international life.

Wight's call for a recognition of irony in international politics contrasts with the assumptions about cumulative knowledge in the social sciences as part of a positivist epistemology. This methodological approach to the theory of international relations would seem to indicate 'that irony is an illusion engendered by simply not knowing enough about the matter at hand. But more detailed knowledge of a part is often bought at a price of a less clear apprehension of the whole' (*ibid.*: 46).

Mimetic rivalry and the structure of international society

One of the main problems with the way the opposition to American political values is interpreted is to adopt a problem-solving approach to foreign policy, and to see this opposition as simply a result of particular policies. What if the cultural resistance to American political values is based on more than specific policy positions? In order to understand why this might be the case we have to understand better the relationship between culture, religion and social institutions in world politics.

One of the most significant approaches in our time to the study of culture and social institutions has been developed by the French philosopher, anthropologist and literary theorist Rene Girard, who was the Andre B. Hammond Professor of French Language, Literature and Civilization at Stanford University (Williams 1996). For the past 30 years his ideas on culture and religion have been widely influential in the humanities and in anthropology, comparative literature, theology, religious studies and the sociology of religion. Unfortunately, Girard's ideas are not as widely known as they ought to be in political science and international relations.[7]

Girard's mimetic theory of culture and religion helps us to see why adopting a problem-solving approach to foreign policy is not going to help resolve the cultural opposition to American political values in world politics. It also shows why structural explanations of international relations located at the level of analysis of the international system may be insufficient to explain the cultural opposition to American political values.

What is Girard's theory of mimetic rivalry? A full analysis of Girardian theory can be found elsewhere.[8] Here only some of those elements that may be useful to analysing the cultural opposition to American political values will be examined. According to Girard, the key to understanding the roots of rivalry and violence between individuals and social groups is to be found in a basic insight from anthropology: the way human beings learn. He argues that the way in which human beings learn is why they are prone to the kind of rivalry that can lead to collective violence.

Fundamentally, Girard has observed, through his study of human behaviour in literature and anthropology, human beings are social beings, and the way they learn is by imitating other people in society. Girard does not only mean that people copy a style or pattern in the actions, speech, appearance or mannerisms of others, but more importantly, what human beings copy or imitate is connected to *acquisitive desire*. It is because of the strong connection between desire and imitation that he uses the word, *mimesis*, the Greek word for imitation, which includes the idea of borrowed desire. In other words, as social creatures, human beings are also mimetic, i.e. they are the kind of creatures that acquisitively imitate other people.

Thus, from a Girardian perspective, the desires of human beings do not aim at a definite good or object (contrary to economic notions of scarcity), but what is desired is socially constructed. How desire is socially constructed occurs through what Girard has called the triangular structure of desire. Triangular desire is made up of three parts: the self, the Other as mediator or model of desire, and the object that the self or subject desires because the person knows, imagines or suspects that the model or mediator desires it as well. Therefore, the goods or objects people desire, and their ideas about what to desire, are based on the ideas and desires they learn from others (Girard 1996).

The concept of mimetic desire is also an inevitable part of the rough and tumble of politics. 'Politics', says Mark Shields, one of the leading syndicated columnists in the United States, 'is a very imitative art, probably almost as imitative as political journalism.' 'The thing about it', he says, 'is you can always tell if somebody is doing well by whether his opponents imitate him' in their ideas, concepts and strategy.[9] In a similar way, the states that make up international society learn what it means to be influential or to be a great power by imitating other great powers. In other words, Girard's theory of mimetic desire provides an underlying cultural explanation for why great power rivalry takes place in an anarchical international society.

Mimetic desire can, and usually has in history, take on competitive and destructive forms. There can be negative mimetic desire, in which rivalry and competition lead to violence or anti-social behaviour with the imitation of negative models. Mimetic desire can be seen more ominously in Israel and Palestine where young people learn how to be suicide bombers – as one dark cartoon on the internet put it, of a young boy in Gaza holding hands with and looking admiringly at an older suicide bomber, 'I want to be like you when I blow up'. And it may even be seen in the competitive and destructive behaviour of some of the people involved in the anti-globalization movement.

Girard argues that the whole process of mimetic desire in culture and society is prone to violence and conflict. Why is this the case? If the models for what human beings desire – the ideas and the objects of desire, are based on the desires and ideas they have learned from others, then the rivalry and competition with other human beings for the same objects of desire has the potential to cause violence and conflict.

At the state and society or the individual levels of analysis a Girardian perspective emphasizes that mimetic desire, as a social mechanism, is an inevitable part of the way identity is socially constructed. However, he argues that liberal modernity has exaggerated the extent of individual autonomy in the social construction of identity. The notion of agency or autonomy, the idea that identity is freely chosen, so dear to the conceptions of liberal modernity or liberal individualism which underlay the social construction of identity, is premised on what Girard calls the myth or illusion of spontaneous desire. It is the illusion that individuals choose the objects of their own desire. Liberal modernity, with its abstract conception of the self, 'overplays the role of the will in the construction of persons' (Williams 2000: 107). Social constructivists are right to point out that people do not have ready-made identities, they are socially constructed. They are wrong, however, or Girard would say they are misled by the liberal assumptions of what he calls 'the reigning ideology of the age', regarding the autonomy of desire in the way identity is constructed.

Girard says this because the triangular structure of desire is important for understanding the social construction of identity. The assumptions of liberal modernity shift desire from the object to the subject, i.e. to the individual, but this ignores the triangular structure of desire – a point we will come back to when we examine religious terrorism. Girardians, by pointing to the imitative nature of desire, emphasize that individuals or social groups learn what to desire through others as a model or mediator of what to desire.

The United States as the mimetic model of modernity

We can now see more clearly the origin of the cultural opposition to American political values. It has already been pointed out that the social construction of identity involves forces of attraction and repulsion that are part of the triangular structure of desire. It is possible to argue that some of the analysis of religious militancy and fundamentalism is based on what Girard would call the illusion of spontaneous desire.

Girardian theory suggests that resentment arising from the triangular structure of desire is one of the underlying sources of cultural resistance to American political values. Girard, in the immediate aftermath of the September 11 attacks argued, 'what is occurring today is a mimetic rivalry on a planetary scale', but something more is required as a part of this explanation.[10] There are non-ethnic origins of nationalism in Asia or the Middle East, in which anti-Western nationalism is an expression of a deeper sense of humiliation by the secular West.

What took place on 11 September 2001 was an Islamic phenomenon as well as a terrorist phenomenon. It is widely regarded that the nature of the object – Islam, the object inspiring such passion or militancy – is not sufficient to account for such desire, and so analysis shifts from the object – Islam – onto the subject – the Islamic militant – and so the person's agency, liberty or psychology are what is examined. We, in the West, ask questions such as, 'Why do men rebel?' or 'Why do Muslims rebel?' (Hafez 2003). What is lacking is a critical evaluation of the assumptions about modernity behind why these questions are framed in this way.

What needs to be examined as part of the triangular structure of desire is how the US is the model or mediator of Islamic desire, and so the source of Islamic militancy, or the cultural opposition to American political values more generally. Sheik Yusuf al-Qaradawi offers a good example of the way the triangular structure of desire influences the social construction of identity in the Arab world. Sheik al-Qaradawi is arguably Sunni Islam's most influential cleric, with an immensely popular television programme on al-Jazeera, broadcast throughout the Islamic world.

The mimetic model for his religious mission is provided by the US, the most modern country in the world, and the tele-evangelists that are part of American culture. The country is 'acting like a god on earth' he says, and yet, as Fouad Ajami (2003) argues, even as he 'rails against the United States' in his sermons, and is repelled by the US, he and his followers embrace 'its protection, its gossip, and its hipness'. The mimetic model for the al-Jazeera reporter in the 'flak jacket, irreverent and cool against the Kabul or Baghdad background, borrows a form' – a mimetic model – 'perfected in the country [the United States] whose sins and follies that reporter has come to chronicle'.

Hisham Sharabi, a noted Palestinian nationalist who studied at the American University of Beirut in the 1940s, provides an older example of triangular structure of desire. Sharabi recalls from his student days:

> Our leaders and teachers hated the West but loved it at the same time; the West was the source of everything they despised and the source of their misery and contempt. It was thus that they implanted in us an inferiority complex toward the West combined with a deification of it.
>
> (Ajami 1998: 61–62)

The US as mimetic model mediates reality about life-settings to the object, in this case the Islamic world. The US, as the world's mimetic model of modernity – and only superpower – is inevitably in this kind of mimetic relationship towards the Islamic world; indeed, as it is towards the entire world. According to Girard this is what mimetic desire is, a form of borrowed desire, in this case the fast-paced, hip culture of the US, which bears the mimetic model of modernity, democracy and globalization, and so those who want it, and who are attracted to it, also rail against it, and are repelled by it at the same time.

The mimetic rage against the US 'is oddly derived from that very same attraction', a process that can also be seen in modern Saudi Arabia, the source of so many of the hijackers, and the key members of al Qaeda. The US helped to invent modern Saudi Arabia, and the mimetic model of the country can be seen in Saudi suburbs, in its urban sprawl, shopping malls and in the education of its elite at American universities. It should not be surprising that this is also a place where anti-Americanism is fierce. 'A culture [like that of the United States] that casts so long a shadow is fated to be emulated and resented at the same time' (Ajami 2003: 61–62).

Understanding the nature of the mimetic relationship between the US and the Arab world is crucial for foreign policy. This mimetic relationship, in addition to the examples given already, is also borne out more generally in the results of public opinion surveys found in the UNDP's *Arab Human Development Report*. When the question is asked, would respondents like to emigrate to the United States, the overwhelming result is positive in nearly every Arab country, and yet similar surveys by the Pew Research Center for the People & the Press shows a steep decline in positive feelings toward the United States.

What is identified here as the mimetic rivalry between the US and the Arab world appears to many observers as a tragic discrepancy, and is often explained by simply adopting a problem-solving approach to US foreign policy. Fukuyama, for example, argues that contrary to what might be the case regarding al Qaeda and other radical Islamic groups, who hate the US for what it is, the data show that most moderate Muslims are simply expressing a familiar set of grievances about US foreign policy: the lack of concern for Chechens, Kashmiris, Palestinians and other Muslim minorities, US support for Muslim dictators, and now their opposition to the occupation of Iraq (Fukuyama 2004). Zbigniew Brezezinski (2003/2004), who was President Jimmy Carter's advisor on national security during the time of the Iranian Revolution, also argues that the Muslim world's opposition to the US is based on specific grievances rather than a generalized religious bias. These examples could be multiplied, but they still do not explain why US foreign policy has not changed in response to these grievances since they have been known about and commented on for a very long time (Anonymous 2004).

What if these grievances continue to exist because they are only the most recent examples of the underlying mimetic rivalry between the West and the Islamic world? Islamic civilization, like other non-Western civilizations, has had to respond to the conquering West. The wounds to the Islamic world's self-esteem, which itself had once been a conquering civilization – let us not forget – have stimulated Islamist reformist or revivalist movements for generations. However, the way the US is resented and emulated – picked up in these public opinion surveys – is because the US is now the Islamic world's mimetic model of modernity. What appears to be a discrepancy found in the responses in the surveys is really the result of the underlying triangular structure of cultural desire in world politics.

Cultural opposition to American political values is not the same thing as opposition expressed through violence or terrorism. The triangular structure of desire does not fully explain the rise or the legitimacy of religious violence in the Arab world or the Islamic world.

Something more was required, and that something is a particular form of Islamic resentment, and terrorism as a form of behaviour that had to be desired and learned through the mimetic models of Islamic militancy. Religious violence has sources quite apart from, or in addition to, the political dynamics of collective violence. Large-scale religious change in world politics or shifts in the popularity and distribution of the main world religions are not the result of individual conversion or the spread of global missions. They are the result of shifts in the power of the religions or civilizations in which they are embedded.

The primary issue between the US and the Islamic world is the shift in world power since the sixteenth century. At its root is cultural and religious resentment, which cannot be resolved by greater economic development or modernization. What is resented in the Arab, Ottoman or Islamic world is their inferiority, and the gradual fall of Islam, and the object of desire – the rise of the West (really the US, which is the model of modernity) (Watt 1988). Western modernity, as a form of borrowed desire, has been prevalent in the Islamic world for over two centuries. Muslims have wrestled with the question of what ideas and institutions they could borrow from the West and still remain Arabs or Muslims (Hourani 1970). The struggle in the Islamic world has always been for authenticity as well as development (Lee 1997).

The point of departure was the modernizing mythology of the West. The modern Islamic revival, like the rise of modern Evangelicalism, begins with a rejection of this modernizing mythology as the only point of departure, and is a turn towards a revitalization of the religious tradition. These projects of religious renewal do not necessarily lead to violence or terrorism, but that they sometimes have done so is because of what Girard has called the sacrificial crisis in world politics (Thomas 2005: ch. 5).

Conclusion

Machiavelli said that it is better for a ruler to be feared than loved, but the underlying mimetic rivalry in world politics suggests that the choices in foreign policy, at least for hegemonic powers, if not always for great powers, are not that starkly drawn. Hegemonic powers will *inevitably* be admired and resented at the same time. It is, to some extent, up to hegemonic powers to determine what it is that is most admired and what is so fiercely resented. However, the US, as state – a state whose global reach has been facilitated by what we have come to call globalization – is pluralistic as well as democratic, and so it offers to the world in complex ways its cultural, military or economic power. It is for this reason that the opinion surveys show that while many people around the world may resent aspects of US foreign policy, they continue to have a positive view of the people of the US.

If mimetic rivalry is an inherent part of the underlying dynamics of world politics it cannot be mitigated, but its results at times may be defused through cooperative arrangements or US support for what are often called global public goods. Does the US define its national interests in ways that many states could support, such as strong international institutions or the rule of international law, or does it define the national interest in narrower terms, which some constituencies think is only good for the US? This kind of support for global public goods will not resolve all of the main problems of US foreign policy. The US also will have to recognize that there are multiple ways of being modern, becoming developed, in our global and post-modern era, and foreign policy, public diplomacy and foreign aid policy will increasingly have to take seriously the degree of cultural and religious pluralism that characterizes international politics today.

Notes

1 I wish to thank Sergio Fabbrini for his very helpful comments and editorial work.
2 See, 'Faith, God & the Oval Office', *Time*, 21 June 2004.
3 Mark Noll, Professor of History at Wheaton College, the premier Evangelical college in the United States, has lamented, 'We remain inordinately susceptible to enervating apocalyptic speculation, and we produce and consume oceans of bathetic End Times literature while sponsoring only a trickle of serious geo-political analysis' Noll (2004).
4 Letter from Martin Wight to J.H. Oldham, 27 September 1946 (LSE Archive).
5 'They have healed the wound of my people lightly, saying, "Peace, peace," when there is no peace' (Jeremiah 6:14; 8:11).
6 *Oxford Companion to Classical Literature* (Oxford: Oxford University Press, 1989), p. 450.
7 See the webpage for the Colloquium on Violence and Religion (COV&R) set up in 1990 by the University of Innsbruk, Austria <theol.uibk.ac.at/cover/index.html>.
8 The best basic introduction is Kirwan (2004).
9 See, '[Mark] Shields and [David] Brooks', The Newshour with Jim Lehrer, transcript, Online Newshour, 5 September 2003.
10 Rene Girard, 'What is Occurring Today is a Mimetic Rivalry on a Planetary Scale', An Interview by Henri Tincq, *Le Monde*, 6 November 2001, translated for COV&R by Jim Williams at <theol.uibk.ac.at/cover/index.html>.

References

Ajami, F. (1981) *The Arab Predicament: Arab Political Thought and Practice Since 1967*, Cambridge: Cambridge University Press.

Ajami, F. (1998) *The Dream Palace of the Arabs: A Generation's Odyssey*, New York: Random Books.

Ajami, F. (2003) 'The Falseness of Anti-Americanism', *Foreign Policy*, September: 52–61.

Amstutz, M.R. (2001) 'Faith-Based NGOs and U.S. Foreign Policy', in E. Abrams (ed.), *The Influence of Faith: Religious Groups & U.S. Foreign Policy*, Oxford: Rowman & Littlefield, pp. 175–202.

Anonymous (2004) *Imperial Hubris: Why the West is Losing the War on Terror*, Washington DC: Brassey's Inc.

Bell, C. (1999) 'American Ascendancy: And the Pretense of Concert', *The National Interest*, 57, Fall: 55–63.

Brezezinski, Z. (2003/2004) 'Hegemonic Quicksand', *The National Interest*, 74, Winter: 5–16.

Cavanaugh, W.T. (1995) 'A Fire Strong Enough to Consume the House: The Wars of Religion and the Rise of the State', *Modern Theology*, 11 (4): 397–420.

Cavanaugh, W.T. (2002) 'The Myth of the State as Savior', in W. T. Cavanaugh, *Theopolitical Imagination: Discovering the Liturgy as a Political Act in an Age of Global Consumerism*, London and New York: Continuum, pp. 9–52.

Davie, G. (2002) *Europe: The Exceptional Case: Parameters of Faith in the Modern World*, London: Darton, Longman and Todd.

Ferguson, N. (2003) 'Hegemony or Empire', *Foreign Affairs*, 82 (5) September/ October: 154–61.

Fukuyama, F. (2004) 'The Neoconservative Moment', *The National Interest*, 76, Summer: 57–68.

Girard, R. (1996) 'Triangular Desire', in J.G. Williams (ed.) *The Girard Reader Reader*, New York: Crossroad/Herder, pp. 33–44.

Hafez, M.M. (2003) *Why Muslims Rebel: Repression and Resistance in the Islamic World*, Boulder, CO: Lynne Reinner.

Hourani, A. (1970) *Arabic Liberal Thought in the Modern Age, 1798–1939*, Oxford: Oxford University Press.

Joffe, J. (2001) 'Whose Afraid of Mr. Big?', *The National Interest*, Summer: 43–52.

Judt, T. (2003) 'America and the World', *The New York Review of Books*, 10 April 2003: 28–31.

Kagan, R. (2003) *Of Paradise and Power: America and Europe in the New World Order*, New York: Alfred A. Knopf.

Kirwan, M. (2004) *Discovering Girard*, London: Darton, Longman and Todd.

Krauthammer, C. (2002/2003) 'The Unipolar Moment Revisited', *The National Interest*, Winter: 5–20.

Lasch, C. (1991) *The True and Only Heaven: Progress and Its Critics*, New York: W.W. Norton.

Layne, C. (2003) 'America as Hegemon', *The National Interest*, 72, Summer: 17–30.

Lee, R.D. (1997) *Overcoming Tradition and Modernity: The Search for Islamic Authenticity*, Boulder: Westview.

Lewis, B. (1990) 'The Roots of Muslim Rage', *Atlantic Monthly*, September: 47–60.

Mead, W.R. (2001) *Special Providence: American Foreign Policy and How it Changed the World*, New York: Alfred A. Knopf.

Niebuhr, R. (1952) *The Irony of American History*, New York: Scribners.

Noll, M. (2004) 'The Evangelical Mind Today', *First Things*, 146, October: 34–39.

Northcott M. and Hassell, T. (2004) *'An Angel Directs the Storm': Apocalyptic Religion and American Empire*, London: I.B. Tauris.

Norton, A. (2004) *Leo Strauss and the Politics of American Empire*, New Haven, CT: Yale University Press.

Nye, J. (1990) 'Soft Power', *Foreign Policy*, 80, Fall: 160–64.

Pew Research Center for the People & the Press (2003a) 'America's Image Further Erodes, Europeans Want Weaker Ties', Washington DC, 18 March 2003.

Pew Research Center for the People & the Press and The Pew Forum on Religion & Public Life (2003b) 'Different Faiths, Different Messages: Americans Hearing About Iraq from the Pulpit, But Religious Faith Not Defining Opinions', Washington DC, 19 March 2003.

Rodman, P. (2000) 'The World's Resentment', *The National Interest*, 60, Summer: 33–41.

Schlesinger, A. Jr. (2004) The Making of a Mess', *The New York Review of Books*, 23 September 2004: 40–43.

Sine, T. (2004) 'Divided by a Common Faith', *Sojourners Magazine*, October: 29–31.

Thomas, S.M. (2001) 'Faith, History, and Maritin Wight: The Role of Religion in the Historical Sociology of the English School of International Relations', *International Affairs*, 77 (4): 905–29.

Thomas, S.M. (2005) *The Global Resurgence of Religion and the Transformation of International Relations: The Struggle for the Soul of the Twenty-first Century*, New York and London: PalgraveMacmillan.

Warren, H.A. (1997) *Theologians of a New World Order: Reinhold Niebuhr and the Christian Realists, 1920–1948*, Oxford: Oxford University Press.

Watt, W.M. (1988) *Islamic Fundamentalism and Modernity*, London: Routledge.

Wight, M. (n.d.) 'Fortune's Banter: Fortune and Irony in Politics', unpublished MSS, LSE Archive, p. 35.

Wilcox C. and Jelen, T.G. (2002) 'Religion and Politics in an Open Market: Religious Mobilization in the United States', in T.G. Jelen and C. Wilcox (eds) *Religion and Politics in Comparative Perspective*, Cambridge: Cambridge University Press, pp. 314–24.

Williams, J.G. (ed.) (1996) *The Girard Reader*, New York: Crossroad.

Williams, R. (2000) *Lost Icons: Reflections on Cultural Bereavement*, Edinburgh: T & T Clark.

Conclusion

America contested or rejected?

11 Contested but indispensable

The missing point of European discontent

Mark F. Gilbert

Introduction

The preceding chapters of this book have developed what amounts to a three-stage argument. First, they have maintained that the United States (US) has turned its back on liberal internationalism in favour of a narrow form of nationalism. The belief that the conviction of national supremacy is now driving US policy informs almost all the essays in the first half of the book.

Sergio Fabbrini traces the origins of this conviction of national supremacy to a crucial shift in the balance of power of domestic politics in the US. For complex sociological reasons, the fundamentalist values of the Southern states have become dominant in national politics and Texas, not cosmopolitan Massachusetts or New York, is now the 'epicentre of national politics'. But the values of small-town and rural America, with their deep-rooted nationalism and blind faith in the American way, have inevitably come into conflict with what Fabbrini calls the 'post-nationalist multilateral vision' espoused by 'Old Europe'.

Continuing the theme, Mario Del Pero's essay sees neoconservatism as 'the last remake of US exceptionalist nationalism'. Neoconservatives in effect hark back in their writings on foreign affairs to the US tradition of 'missionary idealism' – they want, in short, to approximate the rest of the world to the US city on the hill, by force if necessary. After 9/11, the neoconservative 'persuasion' triumphed because it seemed to offer a better *psychological* response to the immense challenge of global terrorism than any kind of diplomatic realism, which could only fatalistically suggest that terrorism could be contained but not defeated. But, Del Pero insists, the implementation of neoconservative doctrine can only exacerbate tensions between the United States and the rest of the world and, indeed, will likely 'normalize' them.

Richard Crockatt, by contrast, arrives at an almost identical conclusion from an analysis of the America's role in the global system. For Crockatt, the US is at once the driving force of globalization and the only nation big, strong and stubborn enough to demand an exemption from globalization's rules. The US is a Westphalian state in a post-Westphalian world: a state that insists on its sovereign rights even as it benefits from the economic and cultural processes of greater interdependence. As Crockatt says, the encounter between America and the world is thus 'ripe for conflict and dissension'.

If a supremacist national ideology is the problem, what is the solution? Running through the chapters of this book is a strong preference for what Douglas T. Stuart calls 'engagement'. The US should realize that it cannot make the world in its own image but needs a 'transformative' foreign policy based around a 'collaborative network of liberal nations'. The Bush administration should take Harry Truman, not any more messianic figure, as its model and work with its allies to strengthen ties and forge sophisticated common solutions to the gigantic problems posed by the post-Cold War world. Even Scott Thomas, whose chapter is in some ways the most pessimistic of any in this book, arguing as it does that the US by virtue of the fact that it is the 'mimetic model of modernity' is bound to generate permanent cultural rivalry and conflict, believes that engagement offers a way out. Thomas argues strongly that although mimetic rivalry cannot be 'mitigated', it can be 'defused' through strong internationalist institutions and US support for 'global public goods'.

If our contributors are right, anti-Americanism becomes more comprehensible. The chapters in this book that deal with the phenomenon of anti-Americanism in fact underline the extent to which anti-Americanism has become a fact of European political life. Carlo Ruzza and Emanuela Bozzini show that the anti-war movement has proved able to mobilize a far wider section of public opinion against the second Gulf war by the simple expedient of accentuating anti-Americanism in its public discourse and by contrasting American policy with a somewhat idealized perception of the goals and objectives of European integration. Yet according to Pierangelo Isernia, although anti-Americanism evokes a quick response from European public opinion, it recedes equally quickly when American government policy is more in harmony with European preferences. Isernia makes the interesting comment that anti-Americanism is thus a useful tool for unscrupulous politicians seeking a quick fix for domestic and international problems.

Rob Kroes' highly personal reflection upon US foreign policy articulates and encapsulates the unease that even passionately pro-American intellectuals have experienced when faced with the first George W. Bush administration's aggressively unilateralist foreign policy. For Kroes, as for many European intellectuals, Donald Rumsfeld personifies a US whose values he rejects. The US, he says, is today characterized by a 'rampant patriotic conformism' which the 'Orwellian 1984 quality' of the Republican party's electoral strategy has cynically alimented. Kroes suggests that European integration, especially if the European Union can be enlarged to include Turkey and succeeds in building a functioning multinational and multicultural democratic order, offers the world a much more enticing 'neo-Wilsonian promise' than the Bush administration's policy of exporting democracy at gunpoint.

This brief summary of the preceding chapters is inevitably a simplified account of this book's core arguments. Broadly speaking, the authors seem to agree that the current crisis in relations between the US and the rest of the West, which is evidenced in the anti-Americanism of European public and elite opinion, is ultimately attributable to a nationalistic turn on the part of American policy-makers and a concurrent rejection by the US government of more sophisticated approaches to the vast problems that have emerged in world politics since September 2001. Short of a radical change of heart by the Bush administration, or a reversal in the broad social and economic trends that have made the US a much more militant nation, it seems clear that the relationship between the US and the rest of the world is likely to remain a fraught one.

Less desire than duty

There is a great deal of truth in the picture presented in this book. Yet one might add some shades of grey. One striking feature of the essays presented here is that while the contributors to this book take neoconservatism's prescriptive recommendations seriously (because the authors unanimously think these prescriptions are gravely mistaken and hence are aggravating the acute dilemmas of the current international situation), they do not engage with the neoconservative *diagnosis* of the nature of world politics in anything like the same detail. This diagnosis is the starting point for the crusading spirit informing the first George W. Bush administration's foreign policy and for the ideology of national supremacy permeating US foreign policy pronouncements.

Briefly, the chief thinkers connected with the Bush administration, or at any rate influencing the climate of thought in which the current administration's foreign policy is being made, tend to concur in believing that world politics takes place in an essentially *insidious* environment. This has been true since the birth of the neoconservative movement, which as Mario Del Pero ably points out, occurred in the early and mid-1970s as a backlash to the cultural permissiveness of the 1960s and to the 'present danger' that the strategy of détente practised by the Johnson, Nixon, Ford and Carter administrations was thought to represent for American national security (Podhoretz 1980; Erhman 1995, ch. 4 *passim*).

The leading neoconservative writers' chief criticism with détente was that by recognizing the Soviet Union as an equal partner in the international system, rather than spending more on arms and rolling back Soviet-inspired actions in the Third World, the US was displaying a weakness that could only increase, not diminish, the risk of a nuclear conflict between the two Cold War camps since the Soviet Union would take advantage of any weakness on the part of the US to strengthen its overall position. For the early neoconservatives, the world was a Hobbesian environment in which the weak went to the wall. The US, according to the neoconservatives, therefore occupied a unique responsibility or duty in world politics. The US alone could, to recall J.F. Kennedy's famous words, pay the price and shoulder the burden of keeping the world free. It therefore had a moral obligation to do so. During the early Reagan years, the US proved its willingness to put such prescriptions into practice by greatly increasing defence spending and by matching bellicose Soviet actions and rhetoric with charged rhetoric and decisive actions of its own. Although Reagan's own détente with Gorbachev was watched with great scepticism by the neoconservative right, there is a sense in which the end of the Cold War proved something of a vindication for the neoconservatives' beliefs.

The end of the Cold War, however, left leading neoconservative writers almost bereft. Surely the international environment could not now be safe? In fact, almost at once, leading neoconservatives began urging the US foreign policy establishment not to drop their guard, to keep defence spending high and to maintain a vigilant watch out for new enemies. An extreme example of this tendency was provided by the influential neoconservative columnist Charles Krauthammer in a widely cited contribution to *Foreign Affairs*:

> International stability is never a given. It is never the norm. When achieved, it is the product of self-conscious action by the great powers, and most particularly of the greatest power, which now and for the fore-seeable future is the United States. If America wants stability, it will have to create it. Communism is indeed finished; the last of the messianic creeds that have haunted this century is quite dead. But there will constantly be new threats disturbing our peace.
>
> (Krauthammer 1990–1991: 29).

The main danger that Krauthammer (who was writing just before Desert Storm) could spot lurking on the horizon, however, was a somewhat shadowy entity that he called the 'Weapon State'. Krauthammer defined the 'Weapon State' as a Third World state with 'an obsessive drive to high-tech military development as the only way to leapfrog history and to ... challenge a Western-imposed order' (Krauthammer 1990–1991: 31).

Unfortunately, the only country in the world that met Krauthammer's definition precisely was Iraq, although North Korea and Libya and a number of other 'maturer' states – he specified Argentina, Iran, Pakistan and South Africa – were candidates for this role. On the basis of these rather skimpy findings, Krauthammer asserted that:

> the proliferation of weapons of mass destruction and their means of delivery will constitute the greatest single threat to world security for the rest of our lives. That is what makes a new international order not an imperial dream nor a Wilsonian fantasy but a matter of simple prudence.
>
> (Krauthammer 1990–1991: 32)

For good measure, he added that the spread of weapons of mass destruction was only the most obvious danger facing the US. Other threats to 'the peace of the 21st century' were 'as invisible today as was, say, Nazism in 1920'. Krauthammer argued, however, that only a 'hopeless utopian' could believe that such threats would not materialize. The end of the Cold War, he implied, was a lull before the onset of new challenges that it would be the US's duty to the world to meet.

During the two Clinton administrations, other neoconservatives voiced similar concerns. William Kristol and Robert Kagan evoked a new 'present danger' in an influential (and extremely sophisticated) *National Interest* article of that title in 2000. Their essay bewailed 'drift and evasion' in American defence policy and charged the outgoing Clinton administration with the neglect of American security – though even they had to admit that 'the international scene seems fairly benign to most observers' (Kagan and Kristol, 2000: 7). Nevertheless, Kagan and Kristol argued for sustained extra defence spending of between $60 billion and $100 billion per year over and above the relatively measly $280 billion being spent by Bill Clinton in 2000. While they, too, were alarmed about the threat posed by rogue states with advanced weaponry, their principal concern was to ensure that the US military had enough resources to preserve American hegemony, which they regarded as the principal source of the relatively benevolent post-Cold War world. Peace had not broken out by chance since 1991, Kagan and Kristol insisted. Rather, it was being actively maintained by American power. America could not, therefore, in the interests of global security, afford to cut back on the Pentagon (*ibid.*: 11–12).

September 11 gave a huge fillip to arguments of this kind since the world was suddenly revealed (to the Bush administration as much as to anybody else) to be the wildly irrational, dangerous place that neoconservatives had always claimed it was. September 11 validated the neoconservatives' Manichean diagnosis of the nature of world politics and hence gave credibility to their prescription, since followed to the letter by the Bush administration, that the US should pursue the 'robust brand of internationalism' historically associated with Theodore Roosevelt (Kagan and Kristol, 2000: 23). It is this 'robust brand of internationalism' that has been broadly identified in this book as a surge in American nationalism and has been defined as 'triumphalist fundamentalism' by a first-rate (and usually pro-American) commentator on transatlantic questions (Garton Ash 2004: 238). Neoconservatives believe, apparently sincerely, that the US must fulfil its hegemonic duty, whatever the cost, if international anarchy is to be averted. It is the latest 'implacable challenge', to use George F. Kennan's historic and hugely influential phrase, that the US is called upon to overcome (Kennan 1951: 106).

The point of this excursus into the neoconservatives' peculiarly pessimistic world view is that the way in which we interpret the foreign policy of the first George W. Bush administration depends upon our prior understanding of the nature of the global system itself. If we believe that the world is no longer Hobbesian in character, but is gradually evolving post-national institutions of real durability and efficacy, then our perception of current US policy cannot be anything other than critical (and we are also bound to associate assertive US policy actions with nationalism). If, however, we share the neoconservatives' assumption of the fundamental insidiousness of international politics then the policies of European countries like France and Germany are bound to appear as an opportunistic attempt to undermine the US's *self-sacrificing* role as the preserver of world order. Unless it is understood that the current US leadership – not without reason, for the US is spending vast sums in blood and treasure – sees itself as a global benefactor, it will be difficult to undertake any policy of transatlantic engagement. There is a need, in short, for European policy-makers to exert themselves and make an effort to empathize with the US leadership's concerns, even if they ultimately come to the conclusion that the policies prompted by those concerns are mistaken.

To this extent, the problem of the rift in transatlantic relations is at least as much European as American. A well-known neoconservative is not wholly wrong to write that 'It is European leaders not American ones, who are loosening transatlantic ties' (Frum 2005). Since the invasion of Iraq in particular, much European elite opinion has been abysmal in quality and in certain cases repugnant morally. What is one to make of a Jean Baudrillard, who could write, less than two months after the destruction of the World Trade Center, that the terrorist attacks were a symbolic act of resistance to globalization that had brought 'immense joy' to all those onlookers who had 'dreamed' of some such act for years (Baudrillard, 2002: 8–9)? Or a Harold Pinter who could maintain that today 'America is the most dangerous power the world has ever known'; a country that 'knows only one language – bombs and death'; a country that has 'effectively declared war on the world' (Pinter 2002: 66). This is not to say, of course, that the open dislike of the first George W. Bush administration's policies displayed by a number of leading European politicians, notably Jacques Chirac, evinces the same visceral anti-Americanism. But these statesmen, too, might have reflected more deeply on the US's role in the world and its continued importance for Europe's defence. Given that EU states have steadfastly given a low priority to increasing their defence spending or improving their technical capacity to make war and to conduct large-scale intelligence operations, US assistance in the struggle against Arab terrorism is simply indispensable. Kagan is not wholly wrong to object that the US is 'stuck in history', dealing with 'the Saddams and ayatollahs, the Kim Jong Ils and Jang Zemins' and 'leaving most of the benefits to others' (Kagan 2003: 77). European criticisms of US policy, sensible as they may be, would sound much better if the countries making them were ready, singularly or collectively, to take on more responsibility for their own defence.

Back to the 1970s

The US is indispensable to Europe in another way. Its role as international consumer of the first resort is providing outlets for European exports and offering Europe, especially the more sluggish, big European countries such as

Germany, Italy and France, an opportunity for growth that internal demand has not been able to generate. Since the mid-1990s, the American consumer has thrown caution to the wind and has begun accumulating very large levels of consumer debt; since 2000, the American government, which during the Clinton years was a model of fiscal probity, has jumped on the bandwagon too. When George W. Bush first took office in 2001, the Congressional Budget Office was predicting, on then trends, that the US would enjoy trillions of dollars in surpluses over the coming decade. In 1999, the government surplus was 2.4 per cent of the US's huge GDP, 'one of the highest among big rich countries' (*The Economist*, 8 November 2003: 8). After four years of substantial tax cuts and increased government expenditure on both domestic and military programmes, the US is facing the prospect of 'a flood of red ink' (*ibid.*). The federal deficit in 2004 was over 4 per cent of GDP. This economic fact has major implications for the rest of the world. Were the US consumer and the US government to begin saving at European levels, the result would be a global economic crunch of drastic proportions. On the other hand, if the US carries on spending at current levels, the effects on the world economy may be equally dire. The US's high spending is fuelling a colossal and growing trade deficit ($618 billion, or 5.5 per cent of GDP, in 2004) that sooner or later seems bound to lead to growing protectionist sentiment in Congress.

Roberto Tamborini's chapter on the economic weaknesses of American hegemony argues cogently that the neoconservative programme followed by the first George W. Bush administration is attempting to reproduce Ronald Reagan's policy of priming the pump with hugely increased defence expenditure despite the fact that the US is now 'a massive world debtor with yawning current account deficits'. He is distinctly sceptical, however, that this policy can be sustained without international financial stability being unbalanced or without the US putting itself in the hands of its creditors, many of whom are far from sympathetic to the goals of US foreign policy. America's current economic reliance upon substantial inflows of foreign money is, to say the least, a paradoxical position for a nation that boasts of its untrammelled power, and it suggests that the US's geopolitical supremacy is a good deal shakier than first appearances might suggest. It is also true that any analysis of the political economy of the US brings home with a vengeance the extent of interdependence between the European economy and that of the US. George W. Bush's foreign policy may be excoriated in Europe, but his economic policy is keeping Europe in highly paid industrial jobs.

If one is searching for historical parallels for the current relationship between Europe and the US, one cannot do better than go back to the late 1960s and early 1970s. Back then, the US was fighting a costly overseas conflict that was deeply unpopular in Europe. Vietnam was not the only cause of those protests, but 'American imperialism' was one of the chief targets of the movement. Certainly, President Nixon was condemned in far more vivid terms even than the 'toxic Texan'. Even the intellectual debates were similar. A book like Claude Julien's *L'Empire Américain* (1968), with its scathing analytical critique of the 'most original and powerful empire history has ever seen' would fit right into the website literature studied in this volume by Carlo Ruzza and Emanuela Bozzini (Julien 1969: 51). Julien, the long-time editor of the influential French publication, *Le Monde Diplomatique*, portrayed the US as a vast and ever-expanding colossus, possessed of a proud, national-istic ideology that was obliged to intervene in each and every dispute every-where around the world. The 'empire is everywhere' and so everything interested it, involved it and threatened it. 'No place on earth', Julien some-what portentously stated, 'can escape from the influence of the American economy, the dollar, American diplomacy or American rockets' (*ibid.*: 228). In Julien's work, as in the work of so many writers today, the US was depicted as a conscious personality insensible to the interests and desires of other, weaker nations.

Nevertheless, at the time many European politicians were determined that they *would* create a political and economic space that could act independently of the American hegemony in world politics. Charles de Gaulle spent most of his two mandates as president of France waging a diplomatic war against the US. After the US denied de Gaulle a veto over its use of nuclear weapons in 1959, de Gaulle tried very hard to turn the nascent European Economic Community (EEC) into a political organization, directed by France, with a foreign policy independent from that of the US. When Belgium and the Netherlands foiled de Gaulle's scheme (the so-called 'Fouchet Plan') in April 1962, by refusing to countenance any European defence structure outside of NATO, de Gaulle took his revenge by vetoing Britain's entry into the EEC, obstructing any growth in the power of the EEC's supranational institutions and gradually removing France from the command structure of NATO. The alliance itself, which had been headquartered in Paris, shifted to Brussels in 1966 (Newhouse 1970).

By the beginning of the 1970s, the desire for greater autonomy from the US was not restricted to the nationalist French right. Especially after Nixon's overtly protectionist abandonment of gold convertibility in August 1971, which provoked immediate turmoil on the world currency markets and led to a five-year slump in the value of the dollar that left the rest of the industrial-ized world holding large assets denominated in a steadily depreciating cur-rency, relations chilled between almost all the principal Western European countries and the US. Nixon and Kissinger also gave an impression of high-handedness to the nations of the European Community, who at Paris in October 1972 announced their intention to create a European Union by 1980 and who asserted that the 'construction of Europe' will allow it to 'establish its position in world affairs as a distinct entity determined to promote a better inter-national equilibrium' (cited Gilbert 2003: 126). The Nixon White House seemed determined to improve its relations with Moscow at the expense of its European allies. In response, the EC took a blatantly independent line from the US during the major international crisis provoked by the Arab–Israeli conflict in October 1973. European countries almost unanimously denied their air space to US aircraft flying to Israel and on 6 November 1973 EC foreign ministers declared that Israel should give back the territory it had held since the 1967 'Six-Day War' and should respect the rights of the Palestinians. The EC, albeit faced with an oil embargo by the Gulf states, had chosen to play hardball with the US.

The consequence was a diplomatic disaster. Kissinger grimly stated that 'European unity must not be at the expense of the Atlantic Community' (Goldesborough 1974: 539). The US, from President Nixon down, by threatening troop withdrawals from Europe, browbeat the Europeans into accepting an American plan for a consumers' cartel to counteract OPEC, the oil producers' cartel, and in June 1974 won from the Europeans the right to be consulted and informed in advance of any future European foreign policy initiative. As Diane Kunz has written, 'Nixon understood that in the Cold War period the combined American security umbrella and economic predominance gave the country unprecedented leverage over its allies. Western Europe and Japan needed the United States more than it needed them' (Kunz 1997: 204).

Conclusion

The difference between the early 1970s and 2000s, of course, is that Europe is no longer threatened by the Soviet Union. The Cold War is over and Europe is freer than it was for over 40 years to pursue its own independent course. But it would be a mistake to think that the fact that Europe has less need of US military support means that it has no need of the US at all, still less that it should 'pursue a half-baked dream of being a rival superpower to the United States' (Garton Ash 2004: 249). As this brief chapter has argued, the US and Europe are intimately intertwined, above all economically. A rupture in transatlantic relations would be a disaster for everybody. This book has illustrated that the new nationalist turn in American politics unquestionably represents a provoking challenge for the rest of the world, and for Europe in particular. Without wishing to dispute this analysis, this chapter has also suggested that the challenge of American nationalism should nevertheless be met with reasoned criticism, not abrupt condemnation. Engagement with the US requires others to understand the US worldview and to have a realistic assessment of their own power. As in the 1970s, the US remains indispensable for Europe. This indispensability of America seems to me the missing point of European discontent.

References

Baudrillard, J. (2002) *Lo spirito del terrorismo*, Milan: Raffaelo Cortina Editore.
Economist, The (2003) 'A flood of red ink', 8 November: 24–26.
Erhman, J. (1995) *The Rise of Neoconservatism: Intellectuals and Foreign Affairs 1945–1994*, New Haven, CT: Yale University Press.

Frum, D. (2005) 'The End of the Transatlantic Affair,' *Financial Times*, 31 January 2005: 15.

Garton Ash, T. (2004) *Free World: Why a Crisis of the West Reveals the Opportunity of our Time*, London: Penguin/Allen Lane.

Gilbert, M. (2003) *Surpassing Realism: The Politics of European Integration since 1945*, Lanham, MD: Rowman and Littlefield.

Goldsborough, J.O. (1974) 'France, the European Crisis and the Alliance', *Foreign Affairs*, 52 (3): 538–55.

Julien, C. (1968) *L'Empire Americain*, Paris: Grasset.

Kagan, R. (2003) *Of Paradise and Power: America and Europe in the New World Order*, New York: Knopf.

Kagan, R. and Kristol, W. (2000) *Present Dangers: Crisis and Opportunity in American Foreign and Defense Policy*, San Francisco, CA: Encounter Books.

Kennan, G. (1951) *American Diplomacy 1900–1950*, New York: New American Library.

Krauthammer, C. (1990–1991) 'The Unipolar Moment', *Foreign Affairs*, 70 (1): 18–32.

Kunz, D. (1997) *Butter and Guns: America's Cold War Diplomacy*, New York: The Free Press.

Newhouse, J. (1970) *De Gaulle and the Anglo Saxons*, New York: Viking.

Pinter, H. (2002) in *Granta*, 77: 66–69.

Podhoretz, N. (1980) *The Present Danger*, New York: Simon & Schuster.

Index

For Product Safety Concerns and Information please contact our EU
representative GPSR@taylorandfrancis.com
Taylor & Francis Verlag GmbH, Kaufingerstraße 24, 80331 München, Germany